Slavery
Throughout History
Biographies

Slavery
Throughout History
Biographies

Theodore L. Sylvester
Peggy Saari, Contributing Editor

AN IMPRINT OF THE GALE GROUP

DETROIT · SAN FRANCISCO · LONDON
BOSTON · WOODBRIDGE, CT

Slavery Throughout History: Biographies

Theodore L. Sylvester

Peggy Saari, *Contributing Editor*

Staff

Allison McNeill and Sonia Benson, *U•X•L Senior Editors*
Carol DeKane Nagel, *U•X•L Managing Editor*
Thomas L. Romig, *U•X•L Publisher*

Rita Wimberley, *Senior Buyer*
Evi Seoud, *Production Manager*
Mary Beth Trimper, *Production Director*

Kim Smilay, *Permissions Specialist, Pictures*
Martha Schiebold, *Cover Art Director*
Pamela A.E. Galbreath, *Page Art Director*
Cynthia Baldwin, *Product Design Manager*

Pamela Reed, *Imaging Coordinator*
Barbara J. Yarrow, *Graphic Services Supervisor*

Marco DiVita, Graphix Group, *Typesetting*

Cover images: Harriet Tubman (Corbis-Bettmann); Moses on Mt. Sinai (Archive Photos, Inc.); Korean comfort women demonstration (AP/Wide World Photos)

Library of Congress Cataloging-in-Publication Data

Sylvester, Theodore L.
  Slavery throughout history. Biographies / Theodore L. Sylvester.
    p. cm.
  Includes bibliographical references and index.
  Summary: Profiles thirty people affected by or involved in the institution of slavery throughout the world, from ancient times to the twentieth century.
  ISBN 0-7876-3177-9
  1. Slavery–History–Juvenile literature. 2. Slaves–Biography–Juvenile literature. [1. Slaves. 2. Slavery–History] I. Title.

HT861 .S942 1999
306.3'62'0922–dc21
[B]   99-049784

Printed in the United States of America

10 9 8 7 6 5 4 3

Contents

Reader's Guide vii

Timeline ix

Words to Know xxi

Biographies

Afonso I 1
Richard Allen 9
John Brown 17
Joseph Cinque 25
Levi Coffin 33
Ellen and William Craft 41
Frederick Douglass 49
Olaudah Equiano 57
William Lloyd Garrison 65
Sarah and Angelina Grimké 73
Hammurabi 81
Sally Hemings 87
Harriet Ann Jacobs 95
Haksun Kim 103

Harriet Beecher Stowe.
(Corbis-Bettmann. Reproduced by permission.)

Abraham Lincoln 111
Edmund Morel 121
Moses 129
Solomon Northrup 137
Saint Patrick 145
Mary Prince 151
Sacagawea 159
Aleksandr Solzhenitsyn 167
Spartacus 175
Harriet Beecher Stowe 181
Tippu Tib 189
Toussaint L'Ouverture 197
Sojourner Truth 205
Harriet Tubman 213
Nat Turner 221
Denmark Vesey 229

Index . . . . **xxxv**

Reader's Guide

Slavery Throughout History: Biographies presents the life stories of thirty men and women who made an impact on the institution of slavery or were profoundly affected by it. The many noteworthy individuals who were influenced by the institution of slavery could not all be profiled in a single-volume work. Stories were selected to give readers a wide perspective on the impact of slavery across the world from ancient times to the twentieth century. *Slavery Throughout History: Biographies* includes readily recognizable figures such as Frederick Douglass, Abraham Lincoln, Moses, Spartacus, Harriet Tubman, and Sojourner Truth, as well as lesser known individuals such as Haksun Kim, a Korean "comfort woman" who was sold in to sexual slavery for the Japanese army during World War II, and Mary Prince, the first African British female ex-slave to have her life story published. Still other individuals, such as Saint Patrick, the patron saint of Ireland, and Sacagawea, the Native American guide who accompanied explorers Lewis and Clark in the exploration of the American West, may be well known to readers, but their lives as slaves may not be as well known.

Other Features

Slavery Throughout History: Biographies begins with a timeline of events and achievements in the lives of the profilees, and a "Words to Know" section. The volume has more than 50 black-and-white photographs. Entries contain sidebars of related, interesting information and/or short biographies of people who are in some way connected with the main biographee. Sources for further reading or research are cited at the end of each entry. The volume concludes with a subject index so students can easily find the people, places, and events discussed throughout *Slavery Throughout History: Biographies*.

Acknowledgements

The author dedicates this book to Laurie Jo Wechter, and wishes to acknowledge and thank Maxine A. Biwer and Laurie J. Wechter for their editorial assistance and support on this project.

Comments and Suggestions

We welcome your comments on *Slavery Throughout History: Biographies,* as well as your suggestions for persons to be featured in future editions. Please write, Editors, *Slavery Throughout History: Biographies,* U•X•L, 27500 Drake Rd., Farmington Hills, MI 48331-3535; call toll-free: 1-800-877-4253; fax to 248-414-5043; or send e-mail via http://www.galegroup.com.

Timeline

1780 B.C.E. **Hammurabi** becomes the sixth ruler of Babylon and unites all of the kingdoms of Mesopotamia. He develops the Code of Hammurabi, a written list of about 300 laws that regulate many aspects of Babylonian life, including slavery.

1570 B.C.E. The Egyptians enslave all foreigners living in Egypt, including thousands of Hebrews, who are forced to work in the fields making bricks for the construction of new cities and temples.

c. 1300 B.C.E. Hebrew leader **Moses** delivers the Hebrew people (also called the Israelites) out of slavery from Egypt. According to the Bible, Moses is directed by God to lead the Hebrews out of slavery.

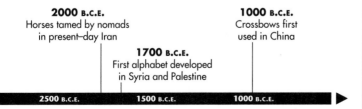

2000 B.C.E.
Horses tamed by nomads
in present–day Iran

1700 B.C.E.
First alphabet developed
in Syria and Palestine

1000 B.C.E.
Crossbows first
used in China

2500 B.C.E.   1500 B.C.E.   1000 B.C.E.

Moses.

73 B.C.E. Roman gladiator/slave **Spartacus** leads a breakout of about seventy gladiators from their training school. The rebels build a vast army of runaway slaves and hold off the Roman army for two years.

c. 401 When just sixteen years old, **St. Patrick** is captured by pirates and sold as a slave in Ireland. He works as a shepherd near present–day Ballymena in County Antrim, Northern Ireland. Six years later, a dream urges Patrick to escape, which he does, ending up in France.

1506 **Afonso I**, the Christian king of Kongo, takes the throne. During his reign (1506–43), his attempts to develop the first Europeanized kingdom in Africa are unsuccessful against the Portuguese fight to maintain the slave trade.

1619 Jamestown, Virginia, is the first English colony to receive Africans. Twenty blacks arrive on a small Dutch warship as indentured servants.

1641 Massachusetts is the first colony to recognize the legal institution of slavery.

1688 Pennsylvania's influential population of Quakers voice their religious opposition to slavery.

1761 **Olaudah Equiano** is captured along with his sister by African tribesmen and sold in to slavery. He is transported to the Caribbean island of Barbados, but when none of the planters in Barbados purchase Equiano, he is taken to the American colony of Virginia and there worked briefly on a tobacco plantation.

1780s The Underground Railroad begins to take shape when Quakers in a number of towns in Pennsylvania and New Jersey begin assisting slaves in their escape. By 1819, towns in Ohio and North Carolina act as way stations and shelters for fugitive slaves. Historians estimate that in

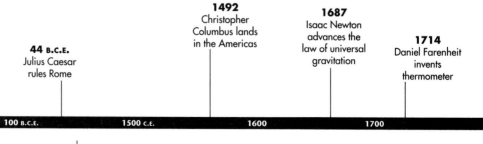

1492 Christopher Columbus lands in the Americas

1687 Isaac Newton advances the law of universal gravitation

1714 Daniel Farenheit invents thermometer

44 B.C.E. Julius Caesar rules Rome

100 B.C.E.   1500 C.E.   1600   1700

the fifty years before the Civil War, at least 3,200 "conductors" helped about 75,000 slaves escape to freedom.

1789 **Olaudah Equiano** publishes *The Interesting Narrative of the Life of Olaudah Equiano,* in which he expresses his antislavery views. The book increases his status as an abolitionist spokesman and is ranked with such great slave narratives as the *Narrative of the Life of Frederick Douglass* (1845) and others that were written around the time of the American Civil War (1861–65).

1790–1808 **Sally Hemings,** a slave, gives birth to seven children while residing at Monticello, the Virginia plantation of Thomas Jefferson, the third president of the United States (1801–1809). Many historians believe that Jefferson was the likely father of all seven children.

1791 A rebellion begins in Haiti, led by a slave named **Toussaint L'Ouverture,** that results in the abolition of slavery on the island in 1794 and ultimately to Haiti's independence from France in 1803.

1794 **Richard Allen** founds the first independent church for blacks in America, the Bethel African Methodist Episcopal Church (Bethel AME).

1800 **Sacagawea,** a Shoshone, and her band are attacked and captured by Hidatsa warriors. Soon thereafter, she is sold to (or won in a gambling match by) a French-Canadian trader, Toussaint Charbonneau, who lived among the Hidatsa. They eventually marry.

1804 Meriwether Lewis (1774–1809) and William Clark (1770–1838) are assigned to lead an expedition to explore the territory between the Mississippi and Columbia rivers and attempt to find a water route to the Pacific Ocean. Realizing they need someone to help communicate with the Shoshone in order to obtain supplies and

Thomas Jefferson. *(Library of Congress)*

Sacagawea. *(Corbis-Bettmann)*

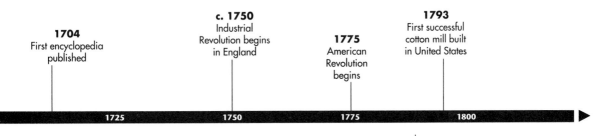

1704
First encyclopedia published

c. 1750
Industrial Revolution begins in England

1775
American Revolution begins

1793
First successful cotton mill built in United States

1725   1750   1775   1800

maintain friendly relations, they hire Charbonneau and his wife, **Sacagawea,** as interpreters.

1807 The U.S. federal government officially abolishes the African slave trade. The law is poorly enforced.

1808 The British Parliament outlaws the slave trade. Unlike the Americans, the British pass laws that contain harsh penalties for violators and rewards for those who catch them.

1816 Representatives from black Methodist congregations come together for a convention at **Richard Allen's** Bethel AME church in Philadelphia. Together they withdraw from the white-dominated mother church and form the nation's first independent black church, the African Methodist Episcopal (AME) Church.

1820–1821 In a series of acts known as the Missouri Compromise, Congress admits Missouri as a slave state and Maine as a free state. It prohibits slavery in all other territory north of Missouri's southern boundary (the 36th parallel). Missouri is allowed to keep a law in its state constitution that forbids free blacks from settling there.

1822 **Denmark Vesey,** a freed slave and carpenter, prepares slaves around Charleston, South Carolina, for a major uprising after whites close down the African Methodist church he helped establish. The planned attack, said by one of the witnesses to involve as many as 9,000 slaves, never takes place; information about it reaches the authorities and the leaders are hanged.

1826 **Levi Coffin's** Newport, Indiana home becomes one of the most important way-stations on the Underground Railroad. It will shelter over 100 fugitive slaves a year for the next twenty years and earn Coffin the title of "President of the Underground Railroad."

Richard Allen.

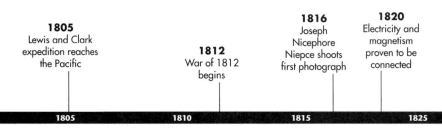

1805
Lewis and Clark expedition reaches the Pacific

1812
War of 1812 begins

1816
Joseph Nicephore Niepce shoots first photograph

1820
Electricity and magnetism proven to be connected

1805   1810   1815   1825

1826 **Sojourner Truth** escapes from slavery and begins her career as an abolitionist, women's rights advocate, and preacher.

1830 **Richard Allen** organizes the first Free People of Color Congress in Philadelphia. At that gathering, black delegates from six states begin what comes to be known as the National Negro Convention Movement. Every year until the Civil War, blacks convene in different cities "to devise ways and means of bettering our condition."

1831 **William Lloyd Garrison** begins publishing the abolitionist newspaper *The Liberator.*

1831 **Nat Turner**, a slave and preacher, leads a slave revolt in Southampton, Virginia. The rebels go from plantation to plantation killing whites and recruiting more slaves. Retaliation against all blacks in the area is severe.

1831 **Mary Prince**, a West Indian slave of African descent, publishes her autobiography, *The History of Mary Prince, A West Indian Slave, Related by Herself,* the first narrative in England by a British female slave —complete with tales of murder, torture, sexual abuse, and the general mistreatment of slaves in the British colonies.

1833 Abolitionist **William Lloyd Garrison** helps establish the American Antislavery Society (AAS). Only three black people are among the sixty-two signers of the society's Declaration of Sentiments.

1835 The right for blacks, slave or free, to assemble in groups for any purposes without a white person present is denied throughout the Deep South.

1836 **Angelina Grimké's** 36-page antislavery pamphlet *Appeal to the Christian Women of the South* is published and she

Sojourner Truth. *(Archive Photos, Inc.)*

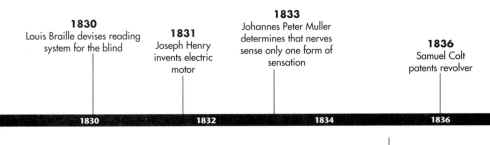

1830
Louis Braille devises reading system for the blind

1831
Joseph Henry invents electric motor

1833
Johannes Peter Muller determines that nerves sense only one form of sensation

1836
Samuel Colt patents revolver

1830   1832   1834   1836

becomes the first female speaker for the American Anti-Slavery Society.

1838 **Joseph Cinque** leads a slave revolt aboard the ship *Amistad,* is captured, put on trial with the other rebels, and found guilty of mutiny. In 1841, with former president John Quincy Adams acting as counsel and arguing before the U.S. Supreme Court, Cinque and the other Africans are found not guilty and allowed to return to Africa as free people.

1838 **Sarah Grimké** authors the first written statement in America on woman's rights to equality, *Letters on the Equality of the Sexes,* in which she argues that slaves and women hold very similar positions in American society.

1841 **Solomon Northrup,** a free black living in the North is kidnapped and sold into slavery in the deep South where he serves as a slave on a plantation for twelve years, eventually gaining his freedom and publishing his autobiography, *Twelve Years a Slave,* in 1853.

1845 The autobiography of **Frederick Douglass,** *Narrative ... of an American Slave,* becomes an international best-seller.

1847 **Frederick Douglass** begins publishing his abolitionist and reform-minded newspaper, the *North Star.*

1848 **William and Ellen Craft** make their daring escape from slavery in the deep South—Ellen disguised as a male Southern slaveowner who is traveling north with her "slave," William.

1849 **Harriet Tubman** escapes from slavery and in the next eleven years helps over 300 slaves escape from slavery in the U.S. South to freedom in Canada.

1850 In the Compromise of 1850, Congress admits California as a free state, leaves the status of territories to be decided

Frederick Douglass. *(Library of Congress)*

1837
English queen Victoria begins long reign

1840
Prepaid postage stamp introduced in England

1846
Smithsonian Institution founded

1848
Karl Marx and Friedrich Engels publish *Communist Manifesto*

1838   1840   1845   1850

later, outlaws the slave trade in the District of Columbia, and strengthens the fugitive slave laws of 1787 and 1793.

1852 *Uncle Tom's Cabin,* an antislavery novel by **Harriet Beecher Stowe,** sells 300,000 copies in its first year and convinces many readers that slavery must end.

1854 The Kansas-Nebraska Act of 1854 organizes Kansas and Nebraska as territories and leaves the question of slavery to be decided by the settlers when they apply for statehood. The act infuriates abolitionists because, in effect, it erases the thirty-four-year-old prohibition of slavery above the Mason-Dixon line as established in the Missouri Compromise.

1857 Responding to Dred Scott's lawsuit in which he contended that he and his wife are free from slavery because they lived with their owner in territories where slavery was not allowed, the Supreme Court rules that blacks, free or slave, are not citizens of the United States; that slavery is a property right established by the U.S. Constitution and therefore owners still retain title to their slaves, even when visiting or living on free soil; and that territories are common lands of the United States where the property rights of all citizens—including slaveholders—apply. The court, in effect, declared the Missouri Compromise unconstitutional and opened all territories to slavery.

1859 **John Brown,** a white abolitionist, carries out a raid on Harpers Ferry, Virginia, hoping to capture the federal arsenal and arm slaves for a massive uprising to end slavery. The revolt is crushed, and Brown and his followers are hanged.

1860 There are about 4 million slaves in the United States at this time, 90 percent of them living in the rural South.

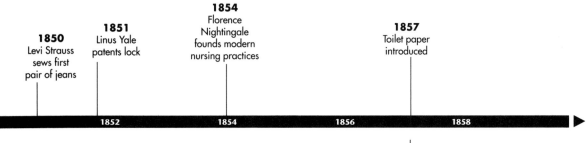

1850
Levi Strauss sews first pair of jeans

1851
Linus Yale patents lock

1854
Florence Nightingale founds modern nursing practices

1857
Toilet paper introduced

1852   1854   1856   1858

The United States is producing more than 5 million bales of cotton annually.

1860–1861 When Republican Party candidate for president, **Abraham Lincoln,** is elected on an antislavery platform in November 1860, seven southern slaveholding states withdraw from the Union and form their own government. Those states—South Carolina, Mississippi, Florida, Alabama, Georgia, Louisiana, and Texas—then form the Confederate States of America.

1861 The Civil War officially begins on April 12, when Confederate soldiers open fire on Fort Sumter, a Union-held fort located in the harbor of Charleston, South Carolina. Union forces surrender after a thirty-one-hour battle. The defeat costs the Union four more slave states, as Virginia, North Carolina, Tennessee, and Arkansas join the Confederacy.

1861 Former slave **Harriet Ann Jacobs** authors *Incidents in the Life of a Slave Girl,* the first full-length autobiography published by an African American woman in the country and the only slave narrative that took as its subject the exploitation of female slaves.

1862 On June 19, the United States abolishes slavery in the territories. On July 19, an act proclaims that all slaves who make it into Union territory from Confederate states are to be set free. On September 22, **Abraham Lincoln** issues a preliminary draft of the Emancipation Proclamation, freeing all slaves held in Confederate states. At the same time, he allows the enlistment of blacks into the Union's armed forces. These acts mark a huge change of policy: the war's goal is no longer just to save the Union, but to crush slavery in the United States.

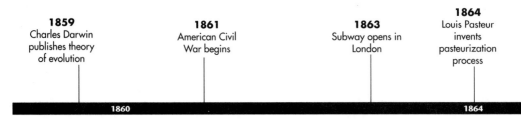

1859
Charles Darwin
publishes theory
of evolution

1861
American Civil
War begins

1863
Subway opens in
London

1864
Louis Pasteur
invents
pasteurization
process

1860

1864

1863   **Abraham Lincoln** issues the final Emancipation Proclamation, declaring approximately 3 million enslaved people in the United States free. (The decree did not apply to salve states that remained loyal to the Union or to areas of the Confederacy that were occupied by Union troops.) The Thirteenth Amendment (passed by Congress in 1865) frees the remaining slaves.

1864   **Sojourner Truth,** former slave, meets with President Abraham Lincoln in the White House, on October 29.

1865   The Civil War ends on April 9, when the Confederate army, led by General Robert E. Lee, surrenders at Appomattox Court House, Virginia.

1865   The Thirteenth Amendment to the U.S. Constitution, which abolishes slavery in America, is ratified by the states on December 18, 1865.

1865–1866 In the post-war South, Black Codes that horribly restrict the rights of blacks become the law of the land.

1866   The Republican-controlled U.S. Congress passes a Civil Rights bill that repeals the Black Codes of the South. The bill grants citizenship to blacks, and equal rights with whites in every state and territory.

1867   The Reconstruction Era begins. Congress passes a series of acts that: divide the former Confederacy into five military districts under the command of army generals; strip the right to vote from most whites who had supported the Confederate government; order elections for state constitutional conventions; and give black men the right to vote, in some states by military order. Black voters soon make up a majority in the states of Alabama, Florida, Louisiana, Mississippi, and South Carolina. Blacks are elected to state legislatures and, in much smaller numbers, to the U.S. House and Senate.

Abraham Lincoln. *(Library of Congress)*

1865
American
Civil War
ends

1866
First transatlantic
telephone cable laid

1867
Russia sells
Alaska to the
United States

1866

1868

1868 The Fourteenth Amendment, which grants U.S. citizenship to blacks, is made law.

1870 The Fifteenth Amendment, guaranteeing the protection of U.S. citizens against federal or state racial discrimination, is ratified by the states.

1876 **Tippu Tib,** a slave and ivory trader of Arab descent, assists British explorer Henry Morton Stanley in his search for the upper reaches of the Congo River in Africa, setting in motion the European takeover and colonization of the Congo River Basin, an area that Tippu Tib and other Arab merchants had controlled for thirty years.

1877 The withdrawal of all federal troops from the South in 1877 marks the end of the Reconstruction period; southern Democrats regain political dominance, and inequality between blacks and whites once again becomes the rule.

1885–1908 After European powers grant **King Leopold II of Belgium** the right to rule over the Congo Basin, his troops in the Congo begin to round up whole communities of Africans in forced labor. The Congo people face inhuman conditions of hard labor and atrocious brutality and violence at the hands of Leopold's forces. Millions die.

1903 **Edmund Dene Morel,** former shipping clerk, founds the Congo Reform Association, the twentieth-century's first international human rights organization. Its mission is to expose to the world —and bring to an end —the use of slave labor by **King Leopold II of Belgium** in the Congo region of Africa.

1927–1953 The Union of Soviet Socialist Republics (USSR), ruled by the dictator Joseph Stalin, enslaves millions of Soviet citizens in labor camps in Siberia, Central Asia, and above the Arctic Circle. Soviet citizen **Aleksandr Solzhen-**

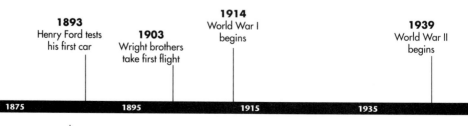

1893
Henry Ford tests
his first car

1903
Wright brothers
take first flight

1914
World War I
begins

1939
World War II
begins

1875   1895   1915   1935

itsyn is falsely accused of political crimes and enslaved from 1945 to 1953.

1941 **Haksun Kim,** a Korean woman, becomes one of an estimated 200,000 "comfort women" who were forced into sexual slavery by the Japanese Army during its Fifteen Year War on eastern Asia (1930–1945). Fifty years later Kim and other Korean comfort women tell their stories publicly for the first time and seek compensation from the Japanese government.

1962 **Aleksandr Solzhenitsyn** publishes his first novel, *One Day in the Life of Ivan Denisovich,* based on his own experiences as a slave in Stalin's labor camps from 1945 to 1953. The book is the first honest portrayal of life under Stalin published in the Soviet Union and launches Solzhenitsyn's instant rise in the worldwide literary community.

1991 After years of silence, **Haksun Kim** becomes one of the first of many surviving "comfort women" to report her story to the public via the Korean Council for Women Drafted for Military Sexual Slavery by Japan. Later in 1991, she is one of three former comfort women to file a lawsuit—on behalf of all comfort women—against the Japanese government for twenty million yen in damages.

1994 After being stripped of his Soviet citizenship in 1974 and being deported to West Germany, **Aleksandr Solzhenitsyn's** Soviet citizenship is restored in 1990. He returns to Russia in 1994, three years after the collapse of the Soviet Union.

1996 to 1998 Japan sets up a private fund to compensate former Korean comfort women. From 1996 to 1998, the Asia Peace National Fund for Women distributes approximately $72,000 to qualified recipients.

Aleksandr Solzhenitsyn.
(AP/Wide World Photos)

Former "comfort women" stage a demonstration in 1998. *(AP/Wide World Photos)*

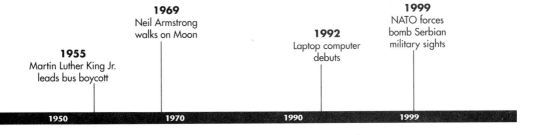

1969
Neil Armstrong
walks on Moon

1992
Laptop computer
debuts

1999
NATO forces
bomb Serbian
military sights

1955
Martin Luther King Jr.
leads bus boycott

1950 1970 1990 1999

Words to Know

A

Abolition: The act of getting rid of slavery. An abolitionist is someone who fights against the institution of slavery.

Agricultural slaves: People owned as property by owners of farms and forced to labor in the fields.

Amnesty: An official act of pardon for a large group of people.

Antebellum: Before the war; particularly before the Civil War (1861–65).

Apprentice: Someone who learns an art or trade by serving for a set period of time under someone who is skilled at the trade.

Assassinate: To murder a public figure by surprise attack, usually politically motivated.

Auction: A sale of property in which the buyers bid on the price, and the property goes to the highest bidder.

B

Baptism: A Christian ceremony marking an individual's acceptance into the Christian community.

Benevolent societies: Organizations formed to promote the welfare of certain groups of people determined by the society's members. In antebellum America, benevolent societies were very important social, cultural, and economic organizations for free blacks.

Black codes: Bodies of law that emerged in the states of the U.S. South that restrictively governed almost every aspect of slaves' lives.

Bondage: The state of being bound by law in servitude to a controlling person or entity.

Branding: Marking something, or someone, usually by burning them with a hot iron with a particular mark that shows ownership.

C

Censor: To remove or prevent from becoming available any materials (books, movies, etc.) that are considered improper or harmful.

Chattel slavery: A permanent form of slavery in which the slave holder "owns" a human being—the slave—in the same way that property (chattel) is owned: permanently and without restrictions. Historically, chattel slaves had no legal rights and were considered property that their owners had the right to possess, enjoy, and dispose of in whatever way they saw fit. Slaves could be bought, sold, given away, inherited, or hired out to others. Slave masters had the right, by law and custom, to punish and, in some times and places, to kill their slaves for disobedience. Slaves were forced to work where and when their masters determined. They could not own property or freely marry whom they chose, and their children were born as slaves.

City-state: An independent political unit consisting of a city and its surrounding lands.

Civil War (American): The 1861 to 1865 conflict between northern states (the Union) and southern states (the confederacy) over issues such as slavery and states' rights.

Coffle: A group of people chained together.

Colonialism: Control by one nation or state over a dependent territory and its people and resources.

Colony : A territory in which settlers from another country come to live while maintaining their ties to their home country, often setting up a government that may rule over the original inhabitants of the territory as well as the settlers.

Commodity: Something that is to be bought and sold for a profit.

Compromise: To arrive at a settlement or agreement on something by virtue of both parties giving up some part of their demands.

Compromise of 1850: A decision by the U.S. Congress to admit California as a free state and leaving the status of territories to be determined when they applied for statehood. It also outlawed the slave trade in the District of Columbia and strengthened the fugitive slave laws.

Concentration camps: Prison camps where inmates are detained, often, historically, under severe conditions and for political or ethnic reasons.

Concubine: A sex slave or mistress.

Confederate States of America: Often called the Confederacy, the government established in 1861 when seven states of the South—South Carolina, Georgia, Louisiana, Mississippi, Florida, Alabama, and Texas—seceded from the Union.

Conspiracy: The act of two or more parties secretly joining together to plan an illegal action.

D

Dark Ages: A period of the Middle Ages in western Europe from 500 to 750 when there was no central government, lords ruled over small territories, and education and the arts were minimal. The term is also used to mean the entire span of the Middle Ages (500–1500).

Debt slavery: A form of forced servitude usually taking place when a person has borrowed money against a pledge, or a promise, of work. If the loan goes unpaid, the borrower or members of his family are enslaved for a period of time to the lender to clear the debt.

Democracy: Government ruled by the people or their representatives.

Democratic party: A party founded by Thomas Jefferson in the early days of the United States favoring personal liberty and the limitation of the federal government. In 1854 the political party names changed to reflect the proslavery forces of the South versus the antislavery forces of the North. The Democrats were the proslavery forces of the South; the Republicans were the antislavery party of the North.

Domestic slaves: Slaves who worked in the homes of the slaveowners, usually cooking, cleaning, serving, or performing child care.

Dysentery: An infection of the lower intestine.

E

Emancipate: To free from bondage.

Emancipation Proclamation: The 1863 order by President Abraham Lincoln during the Civil War that freed all slaves in the rebel states that had seceded and were battling against the Union.

Exile: Enforced removal from one's native country.

Exodus: Departure.

Exploitation: An unfair or improper use of another person for one's own advantage.

F

Free state: A state in which slavery is not permitted.

Freedman's Bureau: Also called the Bureau of Refugees, Freedmen, and Abandoned Lands, an organization formed in 1865 by Congress to provide food, land, clothing, medicine, and education to the newly freed peoples of the South.

Freedpeople: Former slaves.

Fugitive: Someone who is running away or escaping from something.

Fugitive slave laws: Federal acts of 1793 and 1850 that required the return of escaped slaves between states. Thus, a citizen of a free state was required to return an escaped slave to his or her owner in a slave state.

G

Gladiator: Trained fighters in ancient Rome who fought each other—and sometimes wild beasts—to the death in huge arenas in front of crowds of spectators.

Gulag: The penal system of the former United Soviet Socialist Republic (USSR), consisting of a network of labor camps.

H

Holocaust: Mass slaughter.

Human rights: Rights that belong to every person by virtue of their being a human being; the idea that everyone should be provided with the civil, political, economic, cultural, and social opportunity for personal human dignity.

I

Imperial slaves: Slaves owned by the emperor.

Indentured servants: Servants who work under a contract, bound to their masters for terms usually between two and fourteen years. In American history the terms of service were generally part of the deal that paid for an indentured servant's passage from England to the New World. Upon completion of their contract, indentured servants were promised their freedom and perhaps some food, clothing, tools, or land.

Industrial slaves: Slaves who labored in factories, mines, quarries, and other fields of production.

Insurrection: Rebellion.

J

Jim Crow laws: Laws passed in the South after the Reconstruction period (1865–77) that separated black people from white people in many public places.

K

Kansas-Nebraska Act: An 1854 act that organized Kansas and Nebraska as territories and left the question of slavery to be determined by the settlers when they applied for statehood. This act, in effect, erased the prohibition of slavery north of the Mason-Dixon line as established in the Missouri Compromise.

Kidnapping: The holding of captured people for ransom (money or goods paid for the return of the captured person).

Ku Klux Klan: A society formed in the South after the Civil War (1861–65) by white individuals who use terrorist tactics to guarantee white supremacy over non-white ethnic groups.

L

Labor camp: A prison camp in which forced labor is performed.

M

Manumission: Formal release from bondage.

Mason-Dixon line: The boundary between the states of Pennsylvania and Maryland. Before the Civil War the Mason-Dixon line became the boundary between the free states of the North and the slave states of the South.

Massacre: The act of killing a group of people who are not prepared to adequately defend themselves; the word connotes a cruel or atrocious act.

Medieval: Relating to the Middle Ages (500–1500), particularly in Europe.

Middle Ages: A period of European history that dates from about 500 to 1500, beginning after the fall of the Roman empire in 476 and characterized by a unified Christian culture, economy, politics, and military and a feudal hierarchy of power.

Middle Passage: The voyage from Africa to the Americas; the middle stretch of the slave-trading triangle that connected Europe to Africa, Africa to the Americas, and the Americas back to Europe.

Militia: A unit of armed forces that is trained and ready to do battle or patrol in an emergency.

Missionary: A person with a religious mission, usually a minister of the Christian church who tries to convert non-Christians to the faith.

Missouri Compromise: A series of measures passed in 1820 and 1821 admitting to the Union Missouri as a slave state and Maine as a free state and prohibiting slavery in all other territory north of Missouri's southern boundary.

Mulatto: A word—used mainly in past times—meaning a person of mixed white and black ancestry.

Mutilation: The act of cutting something or someone in a way that is permanently disfiguring or removes an essential part of the body.

N

Narratives: Something that is told like a story. Slave narratives in the years before the Civil War were written personal stories about what life was like as a slave. They were either written by former slaves or told out loud by them and then written down by someone else. Either way, they were presented in the manner of a spoken story.

O

Overseer: Person who works for the plantation owner and is the boss of the slaves while they work in the field.

P

Peasants: A class of people throughout the history of Europe and elsewhere who were poor and lived by farming the land, either as small landowners or laborers.

Pharaoh: The supreme ruler, as a king, of ancient Egypt.

Plantation: A vast farming estate that is worked by a large staff living on the premises.

Plebs: Short for plebeians; Rome's majority middle class.

Prostitution: The practice of engaging in sexual activities for payment.

Public slaves: Slaves owned by cities or towns who did administrative, construction, public-safety, or maintenance work or worked in temples.

Q

Quakers: A religious body formally known as the Religious Society of Friends that originated in seventeenth-century England. Its founders believed that people could find the spiritual truth that was provided by the Holy Spirit within themselves, having no need of church services or its hierarchy. The Quakers believed in the equality of all human beings and were staunch abolitionists in the eighteenth and nineteenth centuries.

R

Ratification: The formal approval or confirmation of a document or act, such as an amendment to the Constitution.

Reconstruction acts: Acts passed in 1867 by Congress that divided the former Confederacy into five military districts under the command of army generals. They stripped the right to vote from whites who had supported the Confederate government. Elections were ordered for state constitutional conventions, and black men were given the right to vote. Withdrawal of the federal forces in 1877 marked the end of the Reconstruction period.

Reenslavement: Being forced back into slavery once one has achieved freedom from bondage.

Reparations: Compensation required for damage or injury during a war.

Republic: A form of government run by elected representatives and based on a constitution.

Republican party: A party formed in 1854 by the antislavery forces of the North. The first Republican president was Abraham Lincoln, elected in 1860.

S

Secede: To withdraw

Segregation: The separation of people along racial lines. For example, in many churches before and after the Civil War, black people were forced to sit in separate sections than white people; in public transportation in some places there were separate sections for blacks and whites; in education, there were sometimes separate schools.

Sexual slavery: The control and ownership of one human being by another for the purpose of engaging in sexual activities with that person, often forcibly, or selling the person's sexual services to others.

Slave catchers: Individuals hired by slave owners to track down and return runaway slaves.

Slave codes: The body of laws held by the states governing the slaves themselves and the ownership of them. Many slave code laws severely restricted slaves because of the slaveowner's strong fear of slave uprisings.

Slave raids: Military expeditions for the purpose of capturing slaves.

Slave trading forts: Sometimes called "slave factories," trading posts operated by Europeans mainly on the west coast of Africa with dungeons capable of holding thousands of captured Africans until they could be placed on the next ship to the Americas.

Slaver: A person who is involved in the slave trade for profit.

Stereotype: An oversimplified generalization of people or of ideas.

Supreme Court: The highest court of the United States, and the highest authority on all cases that arise under the Constitution, laws, and treaties of the federal government.

T

Temperance: Abstinence from alcoholic beverages.

Territory: An area, or a vast stretch of land in eighteenth and nineteenth century America that had settlers and local communities but had not yet organized as a state of the Union.

U

Underground Railroad: A secret network of people, black and white, who guided runaway slaves to freedom and sheltered them along their way in the eighteenth and nineteenth century United States.

V

Vigilante group: A group that organizes independently of official authority, setting its task to suppress or punish other people, for real or perceived offenses, without going through the due processes of law.

Afonso I (also Affonso)

Born 1461
Kongo (now Democratic Republic of the Congo)
Died c. 1550
Kongo

Ruler of Kongo Kingdom

Afonso I (pronounced ah-FAHN-so) was a Christian king of Kongo (now Democratic Republic of the Congo) who attempted to found the first Europeanized kingdom in Africa. During his reign (1506 to 1543) he established a partnership with the kings of Portugal, who had been sending explorers and traders to Kongo since the 1480s and 1490s. In 1518 Afonso's son, Henrique, became a bishop in the Roman Catholic church, further strengthening ties between Kongo and Portugal. Yet cultural and religious concerns were soon overshadowed by the slave trade, as Portuguese and Africans alike scrambled to make huge profits on the growing demand for slaves. Although Afonso took a stand against this alarming development, his kingdom was eventually destroyed and his experiment ended in tragedy.

> " . . . we need from your Kingdoms no more than some priests and a few people to teach in schools, and no other goods except wine and flour for the holy sacrament. . . . It is our will that in these Kingdoms there should not be any trade of slaves or outlet for them."
>
> *Afonso I, from letter to King John III of Portugal*

Family converts to Christianity

In the thirteenth century, about 150 years before the Portuguese arrived in Africa, Kongo-speaking invaders from north of the Congo River conquered weaker groups and united

The Myth of Prester John

The myth of an African Christian king named Prester John stimulated Portuguese exploration of Africa. Christian rulers in Europe believed the fabulously wealthy kingdom of Prester John could be found in Ethiopia, so they sent explorers along the Atlantic coast of Africa to find a river route across the continent to his kingdom. Portuguese prince Henrique de Aviz (Henry the Navigator; 1394–1460) set up a school of navigation in 1420 and financed the early expeditions himself. At the time of Prince Henry's death in 1460, Portuguese explorers had reached the western coastal region of Sierra Leone. The hunt for the imaginary king continued, contributing to the discovery of the Americas, the exploration of the Congo River, and the establishment of a sea route around southern Africa to India.

them into the Kongo Kingdom. (Kongo spanned from the Congo River in the north to the Kango River in the east and from the Dande River in the south and the Atlantic Ocean to the west). With its capital in Mbanza, the kingdom consisted of six divisions that were headed by leaders appointed by the *manikongo* (king of the Kongo people).

Afonso was the son of manikongo Nzinga a Nkuwu, who made the first contact with the Portuguese in 1482 when explorer Diogo Cão discovered the place where the Congo River empties into the Atlantic Ocean. After a second visit in 1485 Diogo Cão left behind four Catholic missionaries and took four young Kongo noblemen back to Portugal with him. The Portuguese king, John II (reigned 1477–95), received the Kongolese warmly and assumed responsibility for their education. Likewise, the manikongo welcomed the Portuguese and treated them as royal visitors. When the Portuguese returned home, the two kings agreed to a policy of peace and friendship between Kongo and Portugal.

In 1490 King John established diplomatic relations with Nzinga a Nkuwu, sending three ships, Catholic priests, soldiers, and craftsmen. The priests quickly succeeded in converting Nzinga a Nkuwu and his family to Catholicism. According to some reports, 100,000 people were baptized (initiated into the faith through anointment with water) the following year. Nzinga a Nkuwu took the name of his benefactor, King John, and his wife became Eleanor, after the queen of Portugal. Afonso was named for King John's son.

This swift embrace of a foreign religion was not accepted by all the nobles in the Kongo court. Some refused to be baptized. Among them was Mpanzu a Nzinga, chief of the Mpemba and the king's son by another wife. In time, the

Kongo Christians also resisted the teachings of the church, refusing to give up some of their traditional practices. The priests therefore resorted to violence, destroying Kongo ritual centers and whipping people. As a result, many converts turned away from the church. Eventually, Afonso's father himself abandoned Christianity.

Afonso, however, continued to practice Catholicism. As punishment the king banished him and all remaining Portuguese to Afonso's inherited district of Nsundi in 1495. Afonso lived in exile (forced absence from one's homeland) for about eleven years, during which time he held fast to his Christian beliefs. He also expelled from Nsundi anyone who practiced traditional Kongo rituals.

Afonso takes the throne

The manikongo died in 1505 and Afonso took the throne after winning a battle against Mpanzu a Nzinga, who wanted to be king himself. During the eleven years he spent in exile, he had studied with European priests and absorbed European customs. Afonso had also learned something about court politics. One of his first acts as king was to rid the court of his non-Christian enemies, ordering many to be hanged or sent into exile.

Afonso also took steps to heal the split in the court and agreed to respect certain traditional rituals. He then asked the new Portuguese king, Manuel I (reigned 1495–1521), to send more skilled Europeans to the kingdom. As a gesture of goodwill, Afonso shipped to Portugal some of Kongo's most valued riches: ivory, copper, parrots—and slaves. He also sent his own son, Henrique, and other sons of court nobles to be educated in Lisbon, the capital of Portugal. In return, Manuel dispatched fifteen priests, along with various craftsmen, soldiers, and teachers, to Kongo.

Modernizes Kongo kingdom

Afonso then embarked on his dream of creating a modern, Europeanized Kongo by building several schools in Mbanza. In 1509 four hundred students were enrolled, and within seven years the number had reached nearly a thousand. Afonso also put the craftsmen to work redesigning the capital city, which was renamed São Salvador and had a population of 100,000.

Using the knowledge he had gained from his exposure to Europeans, Afonso helped advance the living conditions in his kingdom. He imported fruit-bearing trees such as guava, lemon, and orange to improve the diet of the people. He also brought in maize (corn), manioc (a tropical plant), and sugar cane for planting from Brazil and Asia. In addition, Afonso taught his people how to use contemporary weapons such as mortars, muskets, swords, and sabers.

Afonso and the Kongo noblemen adopted the dress and manners of the Portuguese. Duarte Lopes, Portuguese representative to the court, reported that they were garbed in "cloaks, capes, scarlet tabards, and silk robes. . . . They also wear hoods and capes, velvet and leather slippers, [with] rapiers [swords] at their sides. . . . The women have adopted the Portuguese fashions, wearing veils over their heads, and above them black velvet caps, ornamented with jewels, and chains of gold around their neck." Members of the court took the titles of Portuguese nobles: princes, dukes, marquises, counts, and barons. Afonso ordered the design of a royal coat of arms (official insignia). Soon, however, the most advanced kingdom in Africa was torn apart by bitter conflict.

Slavery brings ruin

After reaching the African coast in the late 1480s, the Portuguese established sugar plantations on an uninhabited island they called São Tomé. (The island is situated on the equator, about two hundred miles west of Gabon.) Because sugar growing and processing require extensive labor, the Portuguese brought slaves with them from West Africa to do the work. São Tomé quickly became the leading slave trade depot for the Lower Guinea coast (a region in Africa) and the Kongo territory.

A company licensed by the Portuguese king ran the island, but the head of the company did not want the king to interfere in his business. By 1512 São Tomé completely controlled the trade between Kongo and Europe. Rather than deal with African middlemen on the coast, the São Tomé traders went inland to buy their own slaves. They encouraged various African groups to make war on one another and then to take captives to sell as slaves.

Afonso wrote a letter to Manuel describing the horrible conditions in Kongo and requesting that the king send a representative with the power to stop the whites. Manuel responded with assistance, but for his own purposes—he realized that the slave trade was highly profitable and he wanted to keep the São Tomé company out of it. Consequently, he brought the Kongo under government rule, appointing an official representative to protect Portuguese interests.

Manuel also sent five ships loaded with missionaries, teachers, books, tools, and furniture. Most important, he prepared an official document, a *regimento,* which specified Portuguese responsibilities to Kongo and, in turn, Kongo's obligations to Portugal. In exchange for teachers, missionaries, and soldiers, each year Kongo had to fill Portuguese ships with ivory, copper, and slaves. The agents at São Tomé, however, learned of the Portuguese move to cut them out of the trade and went into the Kongo before the *regimento* took effect. They ravaged the countryside for slaves, bribing and threatening local chiefs.

Meanwhile, in Mbanza, two factions had developed—those who favored the alliance with the Portuguese and those who saw an opportunity to make a fortune by siding with the São Tomé agents. Stone masons, carpenters, teachers—even some of the priests—joined in the trade. So many slaves were supplied to São Tomé agents that a corral had to be built to hold them until they could be taken to the coast. Ironically, the corral was located next to the church.

Afonso opposes slave trade

Between 1505 and 1575, nearly 345,000 slaves were exported from Kongo. In 1515 a Portuguese trader described the situation at Mbanza:

> Of all those who go there, few fail to sicken and of those who sicken few fail to die, and those who survive are obliged to withstand the intense heat of the torrid zone, suffering hunger, thirst, and many other miseries, for which there is no relief

save patience. [Patience] is needed . . . not only to tolerate the discomforts of such a wretched place but . . . to fight the barbarity, ignorance, idolatry, and vices which seem scarcely human but rather those of irrational animals.

Afonso wrote several more letters to the king, requesting ships so that Kongo might bypass São Tomé and deal directly with Portugal. His appeals went unanswered. Portugal chose not to honor its agreement with Afonso because its interests lay in the slave trade, not in a modern Christian nation in Africa. In 1522 Portugal managed to take control of São Tomé, and a new king, John III (reigned 1521–27), declared it a colony of the crown.

Alarmed at the ruination of his kingdom, in 1526 Afonso wrote to John III. When he received no reply, he banned the slave trade. So great was the resistance, however, that he was forced to cancel the ban and trading continued. By the 1530s traders were shipping at least five thousand slaves a year out of Kongo.

Afonso's nightmare

By this time only four missionaries remained in the entire kingdom. Afonso's son, Henrique, who had been ordained as the first African bishop in the Roman Catholic church, received poor treatment at the hands of the Portuguese. After thirteen years of religious study in Portugal, he returned to the Kongo to take his position. The white clergy treated him so badly that he became seriously ill. Nevertheless, Afonso did not lose faith in Portugal, and he entrusted twenty young noblemen to the care of the Portuguese for their education. His trust was cruelly betrayed, however, for on the way to Lisbon half of the men were taken captive and enslaved on São Tomé. From there they were sent to Brazil as slaves on plantations.

As Kongo deteriorated into lawlessness, a Catholic priest named Friar Alvaro ordered eight Portuguese traders to kill Afonso as he attended church on Easter Sunday of 1539. They fired a cannonball into the church but it missed him, wounding other worshipers instead. After that event, Afonso became more remote and withdrawn. He is believed to have died around 1550.

Wars over his succession further tore the kingdom apart. With the support of the Portuguese powers in São Tomé, manikongo Pedro I rose to power, but the Kongo people rebelled after several years. They then installed Afonso's Lisbon-educated grandson, Diogo I (reigned 1545–61), as king. Yet Diogo faced the same issues his grandfather had confronted. During his reign the southern kingdom of Ndongo declared independence from Kongo and began dealing directly with the traders on São Tomé. The Portuguese eventually gained total dominance by invading Ndongo and taking the port of Luanda (in present-day Angola). Thus Afonso's remarkable experiment came to a tragic end.

Further Reading

Curtin, Philip, and others, eds. *African History: From Earliest Times to Independence,* 2nd ed. New York: Longman, 1995.

Davidson, Basil. *Africa in History.* New York: Macmillan, 1974.

Dictionary of African Biography. Algonac, Mich.: Reference Publications, 1979.

Forbath, Peter. *The River Congo.* New York: Harper & Row, 1977.

Murphy, E. Jefferson. *The Bantu Civilization of Southern Africa.* New York: Thomas Y. Crowell Co., 1974.

Murphy, E. Jefferson. *History of African Civilization.* New York: Thomas Y. Crowell Co., 1972.

Wilson, Derek. *A History of South and Central Africa.* New York/UK: Cambridge University Press, 1975.

Richard Allen

Born February 14, 1760
Philadelphia, Pennsylvania
Died March 16, 1831
Philadelphia, Pennsylvania

Freedperson, preacher, community leader

Richard Allen was born a slave. At the age of seventeen, Allen became deeply involved in the Methodist religion, a form of Christianity. After gaining his freedom at the age of twenty, he began traveling and preaching to blacks and whites alike. When he was twenty-seven, Allen emerged as a leader in Philadelphia's black community, co-founding the Free African Society as a first step toward establishing the country's first African church in 1794. Allen founded mutual aid societies, helped create numerous schools for black youths, and organized and presided over many conferences and conventions. Allen proved to a doubting society by example that blacks were more than capable of independently creating their own social and economic opportunities.

The founder of the nation's first independent black church. A self-educated leader of national importance who worked for the social, economic, and educational advancement of black people.

Born without a last name

Richard—he had not yet acquired the surname Allen—was born in Philadelphia, Pennsylvania, at a time when slavery was still legal in the North. Slaves were seldom given more than a first name, and if given a surname, it often

Richard Allen.

9

was the same as their master's. Richard's parents were slaves and, like his three brothers and sisters, he was born into slavery by law. Richard and his family were owned by Benjamin Chew, a Philadelphia lawyer and officeholder. In 1768, when Richard was just eight years old, Chew sold the whole family to Stokely Sturgis, a small farmer in Kent County, Delaware, near Dover.

It was probably debt and hard times that forced Sturgis, in 1776, to sell some of his slaves for cash. Unfortunately for Richard, who was only sixteen at the time, his mother and several of his siblings were sold away from the farm. The breakup of families through the sale of some of its members was a common practice during the American slaveholding period. In this case, the sorrow and heartbreak it caused may have led to the religious conversion of Richard and his brother to Methodism, a form of Christianity.

Religion and freedom

In 1777, as Allen recalled in his autobiography, he and his brother (with permission from Sturgis) joined the Methodist Society and attended religious classes that were held in the forest at a nearby farm. A short time later, Sturgis, moved by the religious beliefs and commitments of his young slaves, converted to Methodism himself and invited traveling Methodist ministers to preach at his farm. In the fall of 1779, after hearing one such preacher tell the small farm congregation that slaveholders were acting against God's will, Sturgis offered freedom to Richard and his brother.

Sturgis allowed the brothers to buy their freedom for $2,000 each. The two young men jumped at the chance of gaining their liberty and signed a contract with Sturgis that allowed them to make payments in yearly installments beginning in February 1781. In 1780 at twenty years of age, "Richard Negro" as he was called in his manumission (official release) papers, became Richard the freedperson. He chose Allen as his surname, which was the name of an associate of his original master, Benjamin Chew.

Even though the contract allowed him five years, Allen wanted to pay his purchase price quickly, for if Sturgis, who was in his sixties, died before the terms of the contract were complete, Allen could be sold to the highest bidder. Allen spent the next few years working and preaching at various places on the road. At first Allen chopped wood and labored in a brickyard. He also made shoes, and for a while, hauled salt for the Revolutionary army. Hard work combined with a talent for business paid off when, on August 27, 1783, a year and a half ahead of schedule, Allen paid off Sturgis in full. Allen also gave a gift to the struggling Sturgis of eighteen bushels of salt (equal to about half a year's wages for a common laborer).

A traveling preacher

In 1783, with the Revolutionary War (1775–83) over, the twenty-three-year-old Allen began to work full time as a traveling Methodist preacher. For the next three years Allen traveled by foot over thousands of miles, preaching to black and white audiences in villages, crossroads, and forest clearings. Allen's journeys, sponsored by the Methodist Society, took him into various parts of New York, New Jersey, Pennsylvania, Delaware, Virginia, Maryland, and North Carolina.

It was during this period of time that Allen, with no formal education, gained skills such as reading and writing. Through extensive traveling and preaching, Allen also developed his speaking and leadership skills, and learned how to survive and flourish in a world dominated by white people. Allen became a trusted man in the community. Stories about his honesty and integrity were well known among the public and laid a foundation for his life's work as a minister.

 Building Character

Richard Allen faced many challenges growing up black in a white-controlled world. Perhaps the single greatest test of Allen's character as a young man came in 1783, when he was just twenty-three. Allen tells the story in his autobiography, *The Life Experience and Gospel Labors of the Rt. Rev. Richard Allen*:

> Embarking on a trip to New York from Wilmington, Allen happened upon a heavy trunk "he thought might contain Cash to some Considerable amount." Allen left the trunk with a friend and when he returned to Delaware, they opened it together. Just as he had suspected, it contained a small fortune in French silver and gold. After placing an advertisement in the newspaper, the trunk's owner was found and the contents returned in their entirety. Allen refused the large reward offered to him, and instead accepted a modest new suit of coarse cloth. This episode established Allen as a man of integrity and great character, and the story followed him wherever he went.

Mother Bethel African
Methodist Episcopal Church
in Philadelphia. *(Archive
Photos, Inc. Reproduced by
permission.)*

Founds African Church

In 1786 Allen returned to Philadelphia, his city of birth,
and began his twenty-year battle to establish a black church independent of white authorities. Invited to preach to the small
black congregation at the mostly white Saint George's
Methodist Church in Philadelphia, Allen soon found himself at
odds with the church's segregated seating, a policy that forced
blacks to sit in the back of the church or in the balcony. On a

November Sunday in 1787, Allen and Absalom Jones (1746-1818; the first black ordained as a priest in the Episcopal church) led a small group of blacks to seats in the white section of the church. When the usher tried to remove them, they walked out of the church.

The group then started the process of setting up their own church. Earlier in the year, on April 12, 1787, Allen and Jones had already taken the first steps when they founded the Free African Society, an organization that was dedicated to ending slavery and racial hatred. They bought an abandoned blacksmith shop (for $35) and moved it with a team of six horses to a plot of newly purchased land. Allen led Sunday services at the society until the blacksmith shop was fixed up and dedicated in July 1794, as Bethel African Methodist Episcopal Church, or Bethel A.M.E.. By 1800 Bethel A.M.E. was Philadelphia's largest black church, with more than five hundred members.

The white Methodist authorities opposed Allen's efforts to become independent every step of the way, even contesting the ownership of the church building itself. Finally, on January 1, 1816, the Pennsylvania Supreme Court ruled that Bethel was a legally independent church. A few months later, in April, black ministers from New York, New Jersey, Delaware, Maryland, and Pennsylvania gathered at Allen's Bethel A.M.E. Church for a convention. Together they formed the African Methodist Episcopal (A.M.E.) Church. Allen, at fifty-six years of age, was ordained a church elder and the A.M.E. Church's first bishop.

Empowerment through the church

In the early nineteenth century, the A.M.E. Church was one of the most important institutions for black people—free and enslaved—because it demonstrated that blacks could organize themselves without charity or interference from the white people who were in power. Just as important, the A.M.E. Church played a crucial role in the everyday lives of blacks by providing a place where they were safe and welcome in a very hostile world. The A.M.E. Church helped many slaves make the transition from bondage in the South to daily life as freedpersons in the North.

The A.M.E. Church was very active in the antislavery movement. The voices of abolitionist leaders, such as Frederick Douglass (1817–95) , were heard from the church's pulpits on a regular basis. The Bethel A.M.E. Church played host to runaway slaves, housing them in its basement as part of the Underground Railroad (a secret network that helped slaves escape to the North). The church's congregation also collected money to secretly feed, clothe, and educate fugitive slaves as they made their way to freedom.

Leads by example

Richard Allen dedicated his life to the advancement of social, economic, and educational oportunities for his people. In addition to founding the A.M.E. Church, Allen helped to create many schools for black youths and mutual aid societies that helped blacks escape from being dependent on whites for their own improvement. Allen organized many conferences and conventions, always with the goal of improving the social, political, and economic status of blacks. Allen was also the author of an autobiography, a hymnal, and many antislavery and antiracism sermons and pamphlets.

Allen's reputation as a national figure in the black community was well established by 1830 when he was given the honor of presiding over the first Free People of Color Congress in Philadelphia. At that gathering, black delegates from six states formed what came to be known as the National Negro Convention Movement. Yearly conventions were held in different cities until the Civil War (1861–65). The conventions organized boycotts of slave-produced goods, developed strategies for ending segregated travel on public coaches and steamboats, and worked to improve educational opportunities for blacks.

Richard Allen's death in 1831 was marked by a funeral that was well attended by many black and white admirers. By then, Allen's A.M.E. Church had grown into an international organization with members in Canada, West Africa, and Haiti. The A.M.E. Church continued to be a very important black institution throughout the nineteenth and twentieth centuries, playing an especially significant role in establishing black schools and colleges. In 1997, membership in the A.M.E. Church, founded by Richard Allen in 1794, was estimated at 2.5 million people, attending some eight thousand churches in twenty-nine countries.

Late in life, Richard Allen related pieces of his life story to his son, John Allen, who wrote them down and collected them. A year after Richard Allen's death in 1831, his autobiography was published in Philadelphia entitled, *The Life Experience and Gospel Labors of the Rt. Rev. Richard Allen.*

Further Reading

Books

Allen, Richard. *The Life Experience and Gospel Labors of the Rt. Rev. Richard Allen.* New York: Abingdon Press, 1960.

Encyclopedia of African-American Culture and History. New York: Macmillan Library Reference, 1996.

Miller, Basil. *Ten Slaves Who Became Famous.* Grand Rapids, Mich.: Zondervan Publishing House, 1951.

Periodicals

Nash, Gary B. "New Light on Richard Allen: The Early Years of Freedom." *William & Mary Quarterly,* April 1989: 332–40.

John Brown

Born May 9, 1800
Torrington, Connecticut
Died December 2, 1859
Charlestown, Virginia

Abolitionist, Underground Railroad
conductor, revolutionary

In October 1859, John Brown, a white abolitionist (someone who fights against the institution of slavery), led a raid on Harpers Ferry, Virginia, in what many historians refer to as the "first shots" of the American Civil War (1861–65). To most abolitionists, Brown became a great martyr, an almost saint-like figure who gave his life in a holy crusade to end slavery. In the South, Brown was despised. His violent raids and plans of a large-scale revolt—and rumors of more trouble to come—threatened the security of the South and inspired war preparations as far away as Georgia.

Born into the cause

John Brown's parents, Owen and Ruth Brown, opposed slavery. They were hardworking, sober, religious people who were happy when their home state of Connecticut abolished slavery by law in 1784. In Connecticut, Owen Brown was known as an outspoken opponent of slavery, and when he moved his family to Ohio in 1805, he put his views into practice. After the family became settled, the Browns used

The most radical of abolitionists, Brown believed that slavery in the United States amounted to one part of society—the slaveholders—waging war on another part of society—the slaves. In that context, Brown advocated the use of violence in obtaining or defending the freedom of slaves, ex-slaves, and free blacks.

John Brown. (*National Archives and Records Administration*)

17

their home to illegally shelter runaway slaves as they made their way further north or into Canada using a secret network of safe houses known as the Underground Railroad.

John Brown was just five when his family made the long trip west, taking with them their furniture and equipment on wagons drawn by teams of oxen, as well as their livestock, horses, and cows. The Brown family settled in Hudson, Ohio, a small village carved out of the wilderness about twenty-five miles south of Cleveland. The Browns suffered through a hard winter in a drafty log cabin only to have their spring plantings ravaged by wild animals and a late frost. They lived on wild game and borrowed food from their neighbors.

Owen Brown eventually earned some money at tanning leather and making shoes and harnesses. John learned how to make shoes, hunt, trap, and cure the skins of rabbits, squirrels, and deer, and the hides of cattle and sheep. Owen Brown was also a farmer and John helped on the farm as well. By the age of ten, John was tall and thin but could carry the workload of a grown man.

Frontier life

John Brown's mother died when he was eight years old, the first of many losses he would endure throughout his lifetime. Brown had learned how to read from his mother, and at the age of ten had access to a neighbor's library. Brown had very little formal schooling but he read a great deal and preferred to work on the farm with his father. At the age of twelve, Brown often was responsible for driving a herd of cattle over one hundred miles to the quartermaster depot by himself. His interactions with the federal army led him to a great dislike for military affairs. When he came of age for military duty, Brown paid fines rather than train or drill for service.

When Brown was sixteen, he tried to enter the ministry. He traveled to Massachusetts to secure the necessary education but an eye inflammation forced him to return to Hudson and work in his father's tanning business. He soon became the foreman of the shop and in his spare time taught himself arithmetic and land surveying. At age twenty, Brown set up his own tannery and began to deal in sheep and cattle as well. He also married Dianthe Lusk and began a family.

The Brown family struggles

In 1826 Brown moved his wife and three children to northwest Pennsylvania. He built a large house and a barn with a secret room to hide fugitive slaves, as his father had done. Brown became a leader in the small community of Randolph. He helped start both a school and a post office, where he was the postmaster from 1828 to 1835.

In 1831, however, troubles for the Brown family began. One of his sons died and Brown was sick with fever and unable to work. In 1832, Brown's wife died after giving birth to their seventh child, who also died a few hours later. A year later Brown married seventeen-year-old Mary Ann Day, and in the years to follow they added seven sons and six daughters to their family (only six would live to adulthood).

In 1835, John Brown, ill and without money, moved his family back to Ohio, to Franklin Mills, a village near Hudson. With borrowed funds, he organized a cattle company and began to speculate in land. Unfortunately, the country's economy was suffering and in 1842, Brown was forced to file bankruptcy. The family moved from one home to another as Brown took different jobs to keep them financially afloat. In Hudson, Brown tried breeding racehorses. In Richfield, Ohio, he bred cattle and sheep. He twice drove herds of cattle to be sold in the East. To make matters worse, in the middle of the family's worst financial hardships, in 1843, three of the Brown children died in an epidemic of dysentery (an infection of the lower intestine). And in the same year, another Brown child died from scalding in a kitchen accident.

A turning point

In 1844 John Brown started his last major business venture as a partner in the wool business. He moved his family to Springfield, Massachusetts, where they worked at the company's warehouse. Throughout Brown's travels, and especially during his stay in the New England area, he constantly sought the company of other abolitionists, especially the black leaders of the movement. In 1847, Brown met Frederick Douglass (1817-95; publisher of the abolitionist newspaper, the *North Star*) and invited him for a meal at his house. Brown had read Douglass's newspaper and trusted him enough to reveal for the first time to anyone his plan to attack Harpers Ferry and incite a general slave rebellion.

John Brown could also count among his friends two black women who were very influential in the abolition of slavery: Harriet Tubman (c. 1820-1913), an ex-slave and Underground Railroad conductor; and Sojourner Truth (c. 1797-1883), speaker and organizer for the abolition movement, also an ex-slave. Tubman declared her support for Brown's plans but was too sick at the time to directly participate.

In 1848 Brown bought 244 acres of land at North Elba, New York, from Gerrit Smith (1797-1874), a wealthy white abolitionist landowner. Smith had set aside 120,000 acres of land in northeastern New York as a colony for ex-slaves and free blacks to live and farm. Brown—farmer, stockman, surveyor—offered to help Smith in his project in exchange for a good price on the land.

Call to action

In 1850 Congress enacted regulations that further strengthened the Fugitive Slave Laws of 1787 and 1793. The new law required federal marshals to arrest—or face a $1,000 fine—any black person who was accused of being a runaway slave. If individuals were accused, they were given no right to a jury trial and they could not give testimony in their own defense. Anyone caught helping a fugitive slave was subject to six months in jail and a $1,000 fine.

The abolitionists were furious. The fugitive slave laws directly threatened the freedom of approximately fifty thousand runaway slaves in the North. Thousands of blacks immediately fled across the border to Canada. As slave catchers came North to find runaways, white and black abolitionists defended many fugitives from capture and even rescued a few already in the custody of federal marshals.

Brown urged his black friends in both North Elba and Springfield to resist the new law with violence if necessary. In Springfield, Brown organized the League of Gileadites, a small group of radical whites, free blacks, and runaway slaves who pledged to fight to defend themselves and other blacks.

Bloody Kansas

The Kansas-Nebraska Act of 1854 organized Kansas and Nebraska as territories and left the question of slavery to be decided by the settlers when they applied for statehood. The act, in effect, erased the thirty-four-year-old prohibition of slavery above the Mason-Dixon line as established in the Missouri Compromise of 1820. Once again the abolitionists were fighting mad.

In 1855 Brown quit his partnership in the wool business to devote his time and energy to fighting slavery. In June he moved his family for the last time, to the land at North Elba, where he had been living and working off and on since 1849. In the fall of 1855, at the age of fifty-five, Brown moved to Kansas in order to help establish the territory as free soil.

He joined five of his sons who had settled there in the spring. Brown and his followers fought many armed and bloody battles in Kansas and Missouri for antislavery principles. For example, in May of 1856, Brown and his group killed five proslavery settlers in revenge for the destruction of Lawrence, Kansas, a free-state town. The massacre proved to be a turning point in the struggle for Kansas

Brown left Kansas shortly after proslavery forces were defeated in elections in August 1858. Kansas was now a free state but Brown had paid a heavy personal price. One of his sons was killed and two had been captured by the enemy. Brown's heart was heavy but he became even more determined to wage his personal war against slavery, believing that he was wielding the "sword of the spirit."

Showdown at Harpers Ferry

Before leaving Kansas for good, Brown made one more daring raid. In December 1858, Brown and ten recruits ventured into Missouri and by force of arms liberated eleven slaves. A slaveholder was shot and killed in the process. Brown then personally led the slaves on an 82-day, 1,100-mile journey to Canada and freedom.

Brown's most famous act was his leadership in the October 16, 1859, raid on Harpers Ferry, Virginia. Brown had planned the raid for years, collecting funds from supporters,

Tributes to John Brown

John Brown's personal sacrifices and his display of character and dignity as he faced death led some of his countrymen to publicly declare their admiration. The following are taken from Lorenz Graham's *John Brown: A Cry for Freedom:*

- "His zeal in the cause of my race was far greater than mine," commented Frederick Douglass. "I could live for the slave but he could die for him."

- Essayist and poet Ralph Waldo Emerson (1803-82) said that John Brown's execution "made the gallows glorious like the cross."

- According to Unitarian minister and orator Reverend Theodore Parker (1810-60), for Brown "The road to heaven is as short from the gallows as from a throne."

- In the words of writer Henry David Thoreau (1817-62), "John Brown was such a man as it takes ages to make, and ages to understand."

recruiting and training fighters, and stockpiling arms and ammunition. The plan was put into action in April 1859. Members of Brown's raiding party secured a farmhouse about six miles from Harpers Ferry, where they secretly shipped firearms and ammunition. Brown arrived in July, and his son Oliver and his wife Mary soon joined the group to give the farm a peaceful look.

With all his men in place, including three of his sons, Brown ordered the strike to begin on Sunday, October 16. They marched to the armory under cover of night, cut the telegraph wires, captured the Potomac bridge, took about fifty hostages, and then holed up in the armory. By evening of the next day, about four hundred Virginia militiamen had engaged the rebels in battle and forced Brown and his men to retreat into the engine house. Of the original twenty-one, only four men remained unwounded. Two of his sons were killed in battle.

Final days

The next morning a company of U.S. Marines, commanded by General Robert E. Lee (1807–70), surrounded the engine house. Brown refused to surrender. The Marines stormed the building and in three minutes the battle was over. During the scuffle, one Marine struck Brown in the face with a saber and another ran a bayonet through his body. One of Brown's men was shot and two Marines were wounded.

According to an account in Eve Marie Iger's *John Brown: His Soul Goes Marching On,* as Brown lay wounded in jail awaiting his trial on charges of treason and murder, he

A wounded John Brown awaits trial on charges of treason and murder.

was interviewed by two congressmen and a senator. "Why did you do it?" they asked. "To free the slaves," Brown answered. The governor of Virginia also visited Brown and had this to say about him: "They are mistaken who take [John Brown] to be a madman. He is a bundle of the best nerves I ever saw, cut & thrust & bleeding, and in bonds."

Brown was carried to his trial on a stretcher, but managed to stand and tell the court, "Gentlemen, it is no use whatever to hold the mockery of a trial over me. Take me out and hang me at once!" On November 2 the jury found Brown guilty as charged and set his hanging date for one month later.

On the morning he was to be hung, Brown wrote a message to his countrymen and passed it on to a guard at the jail: "I, John Brown am now quite certain that the crimes of this guilty land will never be purged away but with Blood." Seventeen months later the Civil War began, resulting in great bloodshed and the loss of 600,000 American lives—all over the question of slavery.

Further Reading

Graham, Lorenz. *John Brown: A Cry for Freedom.* New York: Thomas Y. Crowell, 1980.

Iger, Eve Marie. *John Brown: His Soul Goes Marching On.* New York: Young Scott Books, 1969.

Meltzer, Milton. *Slavery: A World History.* New York: De Capo Press, 1993.

Stavis, Barrie. *John Brown: The Sword and the Word.* New York: A. S. Barnes and Co., 1970.

Joseph Cinque

Born c. 1810
Present-day Sierra Leone
Died c. 1880
Sierra Leone

Slave, revolt leader

Cinque, sometimes referred to as Joseph Cinque (pronounced sink-AY), led a slave revolt in 1838 aboard the ship *Amistad,* which was carrying captured Africans. Tried for his part in the mutiny, Cinque was defended by former U.S. president John Quincy Adams (1767–1848). Adams won the case before the U.S. Supreme Court in 1841, and Cinque and the other mutineers were freed and returned to Africa.

The details of Cinque's early life in Africa are uncertain, and the facts of his death are likewise clouded in mystery. But in the years between his capture and his return to Africa in 1842, Cinque became a celebrated figure among both African American slaves and abolitionists (people who wanted slavery to be abolished). Since then, Cinque has remained a powerful symbol of the eternal desire for freedom. In 1997 the movie *Amistad* told the story of the revolt and the subsequent trial.

Sold into slavery

Historians know little about Cinque's early life. He was born in the 1810s in what is now the African country of

Leader of the first and only successful mutiny in the history of the American slave trade.

Joseph Cinque. *(Archive Photos, Inc. Reproduced by permission.)*

25

Sierra Leone. His name, in the Mende language of his tribe, was actually Sengbe Pieh (pronounced sing-BAY pea-AH). At the time of his capture by slave traders, he was in his twenties and had a wife and three children.

Unfortunately, Cinque lived in a part of Africa with an active slave trade. He was captured by members of an enemy tribe and sold to Spanish slave traders who owned a so-called "slave-factory" (a holding facility for captives awaiting shipment to the New World) on the island of Lomboko. They in turn sold him to a Portuguese slaver on his way to Cuba.

Human cargo

The voyage from Africa to the Americas was called the Middle Passage because it was the middle stretch of the slave trading triangle that connected Europe to Africa, Africa to the Americas, and the Americas back to Europe. In pursuit of higher profits, slave traders overloaded their ships with slaves, packing in as many Africans as possible for the two-month voyage.

Thrown in with the human cargo aboard the Portuguese slave ship *Técora,* Cinque was subjected to extraordinarily cruel treatment. The slaves were crowded into the cargo hold and chained to one another and to the sides of the ship. Spoiled food, stagnant water, diseases such as smallpox and dysentery, and dark, damp, and dirty quarters typically killed up to twenty-five percent of the slaves on the Middle Passage voyage. The fact that Cinque survived is a tribute to his strength, both physically and mentally.

In the Spanish colony of Cuba, the importation of slaves was illegal, but slavery itself was not. Therefore the slavers gave their captives Spanish names to make it look as though they had been born in Cuba. Sengbe became José, or Joseph, Cinque. Cinque and forty-eight other adult males were sold to a Cuban planter named Ruiz. Sailing from the Cuban capital of Havana, Ruiz and his partner, Pedro Montes, planned to take the adults, along with three little girls and a boy, to a plantation a short distance away. The name of their ship was *Amistad,* which means "friendship" in Spanish.

Mutiny

Conditions on board the *Amistad* were no better physically than on the *Técora,* and psychologically they were even worse. A cook used sign language to tell the slaves that when they got to their destination, the Spaniards would slaughter them and eat them. The Africans, who had no way of knowing otherwise, believed him, and the cook's cruel joke ultimately triggered the famous *Amistad* mutiny.

Cinque seems to have quickly emerged as the leader of the slaves. He reportedly told the others, "We might as well die in trying to be free as be killed and eaten." Cinque somehow managed to break free of his chains and then freed other slaves from their chains. Their captors had foolishly stored a large number of knives for harvesting sugar cane. These knives now became weapons in the mutineers' hands.

The first person the slaves killed was the cook, who Cinque himself handled with a single blow. They also killed the captain and all but two members of the crew, who managed to escape in a lifeboat. The only ones left were Ruiz and Montes, who themselves became captives when the mutineers placed them in chains.

Tricked and captured

Although Cinque and his fellow mutineers controlled the *Amistad,* no one but the two Spaniards knew how to sail the ship. If they wanted to get back to Africa, Cinque and the others would have to keep their former captors alive. Knowing that they had sailed west to the New World, which meant sailing away from the rising sun, Cinque ordered Montes to sail toward the sun. But Montes managed to trick the Africans. He sailed east by day but northwest at night. Montes hoped to steer the ship to the southern United States, where slavery was legal, but when the ship finally pulled into a harbor six weeks later, it was on Long Island, New York, where slavery was against the law.

The U.S. Coast Guard captured the *Amistad.* At first Cinque tried to escape by jumping overboard, but he finally allowed himself to be captured. By that point, there were only

Slave revolt leader Cinque (played by Djimon Hounsou, center) is portrayed in the 1997 Steven Spielberg movie *Amistad*. *(The Kobal Collection. Reproduced by permission.)*

forty-three African men alive on the ship, along with the four children. They were placed in jail.

Humans or property?

The slaves might have been returned to Cuba had it not been for a group of abolitionists. Among the abolitionists who supported the cause of the *Amistad* prisoners were lawyer Joshua Leavitt and Lewis Tappan, a New York businessman. Like many abolitionists, they were Christians, opposed to slavery on moral grounds.

U.S. president Martin Van Buren (1782–1862), however, was no abolitionist. Ruiz and Montes initiated a court case to secure the return of the slaves to them. They argued that the Africans were their property, and that by revolting, Cinque and the others had in effect "stolen" themselves from their rightful owners. Van Buren was inclined to agree, especially because he wanted to maintain good relations with the Spanish authorities. To fight for Cinque and the others, the abolitionists hired attorney Roger S. Baldwin (1793–1863), who set out to prove in court that the slaves were not "property" at all, but kidnapped human beings, and therefore Montes and Ruiz were the true criminals.

Lower court victory

The trial began in Hartford, Connecticut, on September 19, 1839. When Cinque testified in court, aided by a Mende language interpreter, he gave a stirring account of his capture and treatment. In a powerful display, he graphically illustrated the way he and the other slaves had been crammed into the ship's hold by sitting on the floor with his hands and feet pulled tightly together.

In a move that surprised the White House, Judge Andrew T. Judson (1784–1853) of the Connecticut district court ruled on January 13, 1840, that the slaves had indeed been kidnapped, and should be returned to their homes in Africa. President Van Buren filed an appeal, which meant that the case would go before the highest court in the land, the U.S. Supreme Court in Washington, D.C.

Supreme Court decision

Prospects did not look good for the Africans. A majority of the Supreme Court, five of its nine justices—including Chief Justice Roger Taney (1777–1864)—were slaveholders from the South. By now the Africans' supporters had formed the Amistad Committee, which consisted of both whites and free blacks. The committee hired former U.S. representative and president John Quincy Adams to argue the case on behalf of the Africans.

Although in his seventies and almost deaf, Adams was still a powerful orator (speaker), and the case of the Africans had moved him deeply. Adams argued before the Supreme Court for eight hours over the space of two days. On March 9, 1841, the Supreme Court ruled that the Africans had been kidnapped, and that their mutiny had been an act of self-defense.

Amistad Brought to the Big Screen

In 1978, almost exactly a century after Cinque's death, actress Debbie Allen (1950–) became inspired by the *Amistad* story. Then a student at Howard University in Washington, D.C., Allen would later receive acclaim as a dancer and the star of the hit TV series *Fame.* In 1984 she purchased the film rights to a 1953 book about Cinque called *Black Mutiny,* but it would be many years before she would achieve her dream of bringing the story to film.

In 1994 Allen "found [her] John Quincy Adams in Steven Spielberg." Allen and Spielberg (1947–), one of the most successful directors of all time, teamed up to make the movie *Amistad.* The film starred Djimon Hounsou (1964–), an actor from the West African country of Benin, as Cinque; Academy Award winner Anthony Hopkins (1937–) as Adams; and many others, including Morgan Freeman (1937–). A descendant of Cinque in Sierra Leone, Samuel H. Pieh, served as a consultant in the making of the movie.

Return to Africa

By this time Van Buren was no longer president. His stand on the *Amistad* issue, which infuriated northern members of his party, the Democrats, helped lead to his defeat to William Henry Harrison (1773–1841) in the 1840 election. Even with Van Buren out of office, the Amistad Committee had to raise money for the former captives' return trip to Africa. U.S. president John Tyler (1790–1862) refused to fund the voyage. (Tyler became president when Harrison died after only one month in office.)

On November 25, 1841, Cinque and the other former captives set sail for Africa aboard a British vessel, the *Gentleman.* They were now traveling as free human beings, not slaves. When they arrived in Sierra Leone nearly two months later, a British government official welcomed them.

Little is known about Cinque's later years. He returned to his home, but found that many of his family members had been killed in tribal fighting. In subsequent years, African American missionaries set up a mission in Sierra Leone. One day in 1879, an old man who said he was Cinque arrived at the missionary's compound. He said he was dying and asked to be buried on the grounds of the mission. He died soon afterward, and was buried at the American Missionary Association compound.

Further Reading

Books

Cable, Mary. *Black Odyssey: The Case of the Slave Ship* Amistad. New York: Penguin USA, 1998.

Hudson, Wade, and Valerie Wilson Wesley. *Afro-Bets Book of Black Heroes From A to Z.* East Orange, N.J.: Just Us Books, 1997.

Jones, Howard. *Mutiny on the* Amistad. New York: Oxford University Press, 1997.

Jurmain, Suzanne. *Freedom's Sons: The True Story of the* Amistad *Mutiny.* New York: Lothrop Lee & Shepard, 1998.

Owens, William A. *Black Mutiny: The Revolt of the Schooner* Amistad. New York: Plume, 1997.

Zienert, Karen. *The* Amistad *Slave Revolt and American Abolition.* North Haven, Conn.: Linnet Books, 1997.

Periodicals

Brailsford, Karen. "Don't Give Up the Ship." *People,* December 22, 1997, p. 22.

"Samuel Pieh Applauds 'Amistad' Movie About His Ancestor, Slave Revolt Leader Joseph Cinque." *Jet,* February 23, 1998, p. 39.

Web sites

Amistad: An Extraordinary Tale of Courage, Justice, and Humanity. [Online] http://www.penguinputnam.com/amistad/ (accessed on September 22, 1999).

Amistad Trial Home Page. [Online] http://www.law.umkc.edu/faculty/ projects/ftrials/amistad/amistd.html (accessed on September 22, 1999).

Levi Coffin

Born October 28, 1798
New Garden, North Carolina
Died September 16, 1877
Cincinnati, Ohio

Teacher, merchant, abolitionist, reformer, relief worker, author

Levi Coffin was born and raised in the southern United States at a time when slavery was legal and widespread. However, the Coffin family had been practicing Quakers (religious body formally known as the Religious Society of Friends) for generations, and long opposed to slavery. Like many other people who wanted to see slavery abolished, the Coffins moved north in the 1820s, at first to Indiana and then to Ohio—where slavery was illegal. Levi Coffin quickly established profitable businesses, which allowed him to engage, at his own expense, in many antislavery activities. This included turning his home into a "station" for fugitive slaves fleeing north on the Underground Railroad. Over the years Coffin assisted an estimated three thousand fugitive slaves.

Much of what historians know about Levi Coffin and his work comes from Coffin's 1876 autobiography, *Reminiscences of Levi Coffin*. The book immediately became popular and today remains one of the most reliable sources for information about the Underground Railroad and its role in the abolition of slavery in the United States.

Abolitionist who personally assisted thousands of runaway slaves on their flight to freedom.

Levi Coffin.

Young abolitionist

Levi Coffin was born the sixth of seven children, and the only son of Levi Coffin, a schoolteacher and farmer, and Prudence (Williams) Coffin. As the only male child on a farm, Coffin had little time for formal schooling while growing up. His father tutored him and his sisters when there wasn't outdoor work to be done. He sometimes attended classes at a school where his father taught during the winter months. Levi Coffin was raised a farmer until he was twenty-one. He then enrolled in school to obtain a formal education.

Coffin's parents, and his grandparents, were members of the Society of Friends (Quakers). They were farmers but did not own slaves because they were morally opposed to slavery. In his autobiography, Coffin claims he was converted to abolitionism (the movement to end slavery) at the age of seven. One day, while chopping wood by the roadside with his father, a gang of slaves passed by, handcuffed and chained together, driven by a man on horseback with a long whip. Coffin's curiosity and sympathy were deeply aroused. When Coffin was fifteen he had his first chance to act on those feelings and took it. He helped free a black man who had been kidnapped into slavery. Coffin then made it his business to aid fugitive slaves who used to conceal themselves in the woods and thickets around his home of New Garden, North Carolina.

Teacher and merchant

In the summer of 1821 Coffin and his cousin, Vestal Coffin, obtained permission from some of the area's slaveholders to open a Sunday school, where slaves would be taught how to read the Bible. Other slaveholders in the area became upset. It was against the law in the South to teach slaves how to read. They threatened to enforce the law against the Coffins and those who allowed their slaves to attend the school. The school was closed down after only a couple of months.

In 1822 Coffin and his young Quaker friends started another school (not for slaves). Coffin taught there for three years. During that time Coffin helped to organize a manumission society (an organization dedicated to gaining freedom for slaves). In 1824, on his twenty-sixth birthday, Coffin married fellow Quak-

er and antislavery worker Catherine White. They had at least four children, although the exact number is unclear.

A group of escaped slaves at a stop along the Underground Railroad in Virginia. *(Library of Congress)*

Slave laws in the South became more harsh every year and many southern Quaker families decided to move to the North rather than live where slavery was tolerated. In 1825 Coffin's parents and siblings moved to Indiana. One year later, Coffin, his wife, and their one-year-old son, Elias, joined them. The Coffin family settled in the small village of Newport, in Wayne County. There Coffin opened a small store, which soon grew into a large retail business offering a wide assortment of goods. Coffin also became director of a bank, and in 1836 built a mill to manufacture linseed oil.

Underground Railroad conductor

In the winter of 1826-27, the Coffins' Newport house became an active "station" on the Underground Railroad,

The Underground Railroad

The network of people, black and white, who guided runaway slaves to freedom and who sheltered them along the way came to be known as the Underground Railroad. The system began to take shape as early as the 1780s when Quakers in a number of towns in Pennsylvania and New Jersey began assisting slaves in their escape to freedom. By 1819 towns in Ohio and North Carolina were acting as way-stations and shelters for fugitive slaves. Long before the militant era of abolitionism began in 1831, the Underground Railroad was an established antislavery institution. Historians estimate that in the fifty years before the Civil War (1861–65), at least 3,200 "conductors" helped about 75,000 slaves escape to freedom.

The term "Underground Railroad" was probably invented after 1831, about the time that steam railroads became popular.

Some of the Underground Railroad's "lines" shared names with the nineteenth-century railroads that ran the same routes. In the early days, the railroad to freedom for fugitive slaves (mostly men) was a route traveled on foot, mostly at night, through swamps, up creek beds, across rivers, and over hills, using only the North Star as a guide.

As the traffic got heavier and more women and children slaves fled the South, escorts were provided and vehicles such as covered wagons and carriages were used to transport the human cargo from one station to the next. During the day, the fugitive slaves were hidden in barns and attics, where they would rest, eat, and prepare for the next stretch of their journey. The activities of the Underground Railroad were illegal and people risked fines, jail, and sometimes death for participating.

which was a network of abolitionists who helped fugitive slaves escape to freedom in Canada. It was against the law to aid runaway slaves but Coffin never hid the fact that fugitives were welcome at his house.

Coffin was a prosperous merchant who chose to use the profits from his ever-growing retail business to provide fugitives with food, clothing, and temporary housing. For the Coffins—who aided an average of 100 fugitive slaves a year for over twenty years while in Indiana—that was no small expense. Among abolitionists in the region, Coffin's leadership and long-time service earned him the informal title of "President of the Underground Railroad."

Coffin was also active on other antislavery fronts. In 1838 he helped to found the Indiana State Anti-Slavery Society. In 1842 differences over antislavery strategies led to a split among the Quakers. Not all Quakers approved of helping runaway slaves so Coffin and others left the Indiana Yearly Meeting of Friends to found their own Yearly Meeting of Anti-Slavery Friends.

Reformer

By the mid-1840s Coffin had become a leader in the movement to boycott products made from slave labor and to support free labor in the South. With help from the Philadelphia Free Labor Association, Coffin sold free-labor goods, such as cotton, grown without slave labor by independent southern farmers and processed by a Quaker family in Mississippi. The demand for such goods was so high that Coffin was unable to supply all of his customers. In 1847, with encouragement from a Quaker organization, Coffin moved his family to Cincinnati, Ohio, to open a business center that sold only goods made without the use of slave labor. Coffin sold the store after a decade.

The Coffins continued their work with the Underground Railroad in Cincinnati. Coffin established a network similar to the one he had organized in Newport and his house quickly became a temporary refuge for fugitive slaves on their way further north. The Coffin home also became the meeting place for the Anti-Slavery Sewing Society, which provided essential clothing for the runaway slaves coming through the city.

Relief worker

In addition to his antislavery work, Coffin was active in the temperance movement (the crusade to abolish the use of alcoholic beverages) and in efforts to improve the conditions of free blacks and former slaves. In 1844 Coffin made the first of several trips to Canadian settlements of former slaves. He found their living conditions better than had been reported but determined that there was still a great need for clothing and other essential items for new arrivals. After returning home Coffin raised money and collected clothing for the refugees.

The 1850s brought an increase in Coffin's Underground Railroad work. The passage of the Fugitive Slave Law in 1850 made it easier for slave catchers to pursue and apprehend runaways in the North, causing thousands of fugitives to flee northern cities like Cincinnati and head even further north into Canada, where slavery was illegal. Coffin was so well known for his fugitive slave relief work that he was said to have inspired the character of Simon Halliday in Harriet Beecher Stowe's popular 1852 antislavery novel, *Uncle Tom's Cabin.*

The Civil War years and beyond

During the Civil War (1861–65), which he viewed as divine punishment for slavery, Coffin gave no direct aid to the North's (the Union) military effort. Instead he provided supplies only to those forces prepared to defend Cincinnati from attack by Confederate forces. Coffin's war efforts were entirely nonviolent. He cared for the wounded and visited former slaves behind Union lines, making trips home to collect money for warm clothing and bedding for the refugees.

In 1863 Coffin organized the Western Freedman's Aid Commission to assist the thousands of former slaves who were now on their own due to their liberation by Union armies. Coffin toured northern cities to raise money and then made many trips down the Mississippi to distribute supplies and money to the freedpeople. In 1864 Coffin traveled to England to raise money for the freedpeople. There he helped organize the London Freedman's Aid Society, an organization that raised over $100,000 within a single year. In 1867 Coffin attended the International Anti-Slavery Conference in Paris, France, as a delegate from the Western Freedman's Aid Commission.

Coffin unofficially began his retirement in 1867, but waited until the passage of the Fifteenth Amendment in 1870, which gave black males the right to vote, to officially close down his Underground Railroad activities. During his retirement, Coffin wrote his autobiography, which was published in Cincinnati in 1876, a year before his death.

Further Reading

Bowden, Henry Warner. "Coffin, Levi," In *Dictionary of American Religious Biography.* Westport, Conn.: Greenwood Press, 1977.

Coffin, Levi. *Reminiscences of Levi Coffin: The Reputed President of the Underground Railroad,* Third Edition. Cincinnati: The Robert Clarke Co., 1898; New York: Arno Press, 1968.

Garraty, John A., and Marc C. Carnes, eds. *American National Biography.* New York: Oxford University Press, 1999.

Garraty, John A., and Marc C. Carnes, eds. "Coffin, Levi," In *American Reformers.* H. W. Wilson Co., 1985.

Ellen Craft

Born c. 1826
Clinton, Georgia
Died 1897
Charleston, South Carolina

William Craft

Born 1824
Macon, Georgia
Died January 28, 1900
Charleston, South Carolina

Slaves, freedpeople, abolitionists, teachers

The story of the Crafts' 1848 escape from slavery illustrates the great lengths slaves were willing to go in order to be free. Escaping slavery was never easy, but the odds against the Crafts were especially steep because they lived in the state of Georgia—a thousand miles away from the nearest free soil. Their journey to freedom did not end, however, until they were many thousands of miles away, in England, where slavery was illegal. After the Civil War (1861–65), their homesickness for the land where they grew up led them back to Georgia and farming.

Ellen's childhood

Ellen Craft was born in 1826 on a cotton plantation in Clinton, Georgia. Ellen's mother was a house slave of African descent named Maria. Her father was Major James Smith, the white owner of the plantation. Ellen resembled her father more, and to all appearances was white. Black or white, being born to a slave mother made Ellen a slave according to the law.

Through their daring escape from slavery in the Deep South, followed by their activities in Boston, Massachussetts, in England, and again in the South, the Crafts greatly contributed to the abolition of slavery in the United States and the elevation of freedpeople in society.

William Craft. *(Fisk University Library. Reproduced by permission.)*

Growing up, Ellen felt like she could do nothing right in the eyes of her mistress, the wife of Major Smith. She tried to be helpful with the household work—dusting, polishing, sewing, and setting the table—but her mistress was always scolding her, often slapping or hitting her. What Ellen didn't realize was that her mistress saw her as a constant reminder that her husband had fathered a child with a slave woman. Ellen complained to her mother how unhappy she was but Maria could do nothing more than remind her child that at least she was not a field slave and that the two of them were together.

In 1837, when Ellen was eleven years old, she was given as a wedding present to her half-sister Eliza when Eliza married Dr. Robert Collins, of Macon, Georgia. Although Ellen was very sad to leave her mother, and angry that she could be given away as a present, she was glad to leave the abuse of her jealous mistress. Ellen's new masters were very kind to her. They were also very wealthy and Ellen grew up in a beautiful mansion as her mistress's personal maid and seamstress.

William's childhood

William Craft was born in 1824 on a cotton plantation in Macon, Georgia. Both of his parents were slaves as were his two brothers and two sisters. William had to endure a number of painful separations from his family as he was growing up. When his master, Mr. Craft, decided that William's parents were too old to be of any use to him he sold them at different times to different owners. When Mr. Craft found himself in need of money he sold one of William's brothers and one of his sisters, again to different owners.

Another way for a slave owner to make income from their slaves besides selling them was to have them trained in a trade and then to collect their wages. William was apprenticed to a cabinetmaker and his brother to a blacksmith. When Mr. Craft needed money to start growing cotton, however, he sold William's brother even though his apprenticeship was not over. And when Mr. Craft couldn't repay a loan, William and his sister became the property of the bank, which sold them separately on the auction block. William watched the last member of his family taken away in a wagon, helpless to do anything about it.

Husband and wife

William was bought by Mr. Ira Taylor, an employee of Ellen's master, Dr. Collins. Taylor allowed William to return to his work as a cabinetmaker. Some years later, William and Ellen met and fell in love. Both hesitated to get married as they feared it would then be more painful if they were ever separated by sale. But in 1846 they asked for, and received, permission from their masters to live together as husband and wife (slaves were not allowed by law to have a religious or civil wedding ceremony).

Ellen and William Craft's lives as slaves were not as bad as most of the three million slaves in the southern United States at the time, yet they dreamed of being free—of having no master to claim their time or wages. They knew from their earliest experiences that the practices of slavery could be very cruel. Masters were free to do virtually anything they wanted with their slaves: work them in the fields or house, starve them, punish them, have them sold—even kill them. Although neither Ellen nor William was ever a field slave or severely punished by their masters, they experienced other horrible realities of slavery, the kind that do not necessarily leave physical scars but that can be as painful and long-lasting as any beating.

The plan for escape

William and Ellen had heard many stories about slaves who tried to escape to the North. Chased by bloodhounds and men on horseback, many runaways were caught and returned to their owners, who punished them severely as examples to others. Finally, in December 1848 William came up with an idea: the two would travel north together on public transportation—Ellen disguised as "Mr. Johnson," a white Southern gentleman accompanied by William, "his" slave.

For four days William and Ellen prepared for their journey. William secretly bought Ellen a shirt, a coat, and a hat. Ellen sewed her own trousers. When it was time to go, William cut Ellen's hair. In addition to wearing men's clothes, Ellen added props to make it look as if she were ill. She put her arm in a sling so that she would not be forced to write or sign anything (neither of them could read or write). To cover

Ellen Craft disguised as a man; a trick that helped her and husband William escape to the North. *(The Granger Collection, New York. Reproduced by permission.)*

her whiskerless face Ellen also tied a bandage about her head, pretending to have a bad toothache. And for a final touch, Ellen wore green-tinted eyeglasses to hide her eyes.

Over the years William had been able to sometimes earn extra money that he did not have to pay his master. This money now came in handy as the couple would need it to buy tickets for their train and boat rides north, and food and lodging along the way. The first test of Ellen's disguise was at the train station in Macon where she stepped up to the window just as the train was about to leave and bought two tickets, one for herself ("Mr. Johnson") and one for Mr. Johnson's "slave" William.

The journey

Ellen and William traveled by train to Savannah, Georgia, where they boarded a steamer to Charleston, South Carolina. After an overnight stay in the city they were taken by boat to Wilmington, North Carolina; then by train to Richmond, Virginia; then by another steamer to Baltimore, Maryland; and finally by a train to the free soil of Philadelphia, Pennsylvania.

Ellen's disguise was tested again and again by ticket-sellers, hotel clerks, customs officials, and by her daily interactions with other travelers. As the train was leaving the station from Macon, Ellen noticed a man frantically running alongside the train, peering into the windows. The man was William's master, who had become suspicious and was looking for his slave. He did not find him: William was already in the windowless baggage car with the other slaves, and Ellen sat in disguise in the carriage for whites. But who should sit next to Ellen but Mr. Cray, a man who was a friend of her master's and who had known her for years. Ellen was so afraid that if she spoke her voice would give her away, so when Mr.

Cray greeted her she pretended not to hear him. Mr. Cray soon assumed that "Mr. Johnson" was deaf and gave up trying to hold a conversation.

The greatest crisis of their trip occurred in Baltimore, their last stop in the slaveholding South. A Maryland customs officer demanded that "Mr. Johnson" produce papers proving that he owned William, otherwise they would be detained and questioned further. To the Crafts' surprise, a young military officer who befriended "Mr. Johnson" on the trip stepped forward and vouched for the couple, claiming he had known "Mr. Johnson" all of his life!

Almost free

On Christmas Day 1848, only eight days after William first devised their plan, the Crafts arrived in Philadelphia. The couple immediately went to a boarding house run by an abolitionist (a person who wanted to end slavery), an address William was given by a free black person on the trip. After a few weeks the Crafts went on to Boston, where with the help of prominent abolitionists such as William Lloyd Garrison (1805–79) and the Rev. Theodore Parker (1810–60), William found work as a cabinetmaker and Ellen as a seamstress.

Henry "Box" Brown

Henry Brown, like William and Ellen Craft, gained fame through an extraordinary escape to freedom. In 1848, when Brown was thirty-two years old, his master sold his wife and three children away from him so he decided to make a daring and dangerous escape to the North. He had a carpenter make a wooden box, two feet by two-and-a-half feet by three feet. With the help of a white friend, a shoemaker, the crate was marked "right side up with care," labeled with an address in Philadelphia, Pennsylvania, and shipped on March 29, 1849—with Henry Brown inside.

Brown took a container of water with him and had three small holes for air. He thought he would die at one point when the crate was loaded wrong and he had to travel upside down. The trip ended twenty-seven hours later when the box was retrieved and opened by four abolitionists (someone who fights against the institution of slavery) in Philadelphia.

Henry Brown moved to Boston where he joined the abolition movement and became known as Henry "Box" Brown for his escape.

During their two-year stay in Boston, the Crafts spoke frequently at antislavery meetings about their years in slavery and their escape. When an article about one of their Boston appearances ran in a Macon, Georgia, newspaper, Dr. Collins and Mr. Taylor learned of the whereabouts of their missing slaves. In September 1850, after Congress passed the Fugitive

Slave Act making it easier for fugitive slaves to be captured in the North, a slave catcher was sent to Boston armed with arrest warrants for William and Ellen.

Exile in England

Reverend Parker and other abolitionists provided protection for the Crafts and thwarted the attempts by the slave catchers to seize the two. The Crafts no longer felt safe in Boston, however, and left for Maine, then went on to Nova Scotia, Canada, where they boarded a steamer to Liverpool, England. Before they left for England, William and Ellen had Reverend Parker marry them.

The Crafts remained in exile in England for nineteen years, returning to the United States only after the Civil War (1861–65) and the abolition of slavery. During that time the Crafts made friends with many leaders of the English abolition movement. Although slavery was made illegal in the British Empire in 1833, abolitionists continued to fight against slavery elsewhere in the world, including the United States. In England the Crafts studied writing, grammar, and scriptures at a trade school where they eventually became teachers. Ellen taught needleworking and William taught cabinetmaking.

The Crafts went on a speaking tour of England sponsored by abolitionists. They told of the cruelties of slavery in the United States and how they managed to escape but were still hunted down in the North. In 1860 the Crafts published *Running a Thousand Miles to Freedom,* an account of their dramatic escape to freedom.

Home again

Ellen and William Craft had five children while they were in England. When the couple decided to move back to the United States in 1869 two of their children stayed behind to finish their education. After a brief visit to Boston the family moved south to "Hickory Hill," a plantation in South Carolina near the Georgia border. There they opened an industrial school for blacks. Ellen taught day classes and her daughter taught at night. After the school was burned down in 1870 by the Ku Klux Klan (a society formed in the South after the Civil War by white individuals who used terrorist tactics to guarantee white supremacy), the couple established the Woodville Cooperative Farm School in a nearby county. William was often away raising funds for the project while Ellen taught classes and managed the seventy-acre plantation of rice, cotton, and peas.

Mounting debts and angry white neighbors forced the school to close in the 1880s. The Crafts then moved to be with their daughter in Charleston, South Carolina, where Ellen died in 1897 and William three years later.

Further Reading

Craft, William and Ellen. *Running a Thousand Miles to Freedom; or The Escape of William and Ellen Craft From Slavery.* Miami, Fla.: First Mnemosyne Publishing Co., Inc., 1969 (reprint of the 1860 edition).

Freedman, Florence B. *Two Tickets to Freedom: The True Story of Ellen and William Craft, Fugitive Slaves.* New York: Simon and Schuster, 1971.

Garraty, John A., and Marc C. Carnes, eds. *American National Biography.* New York: Oxford University Press, 1999.

Logan, Rayford W., and Michael R. Winston, eds. *Dictionary of American Negro Biography.* New York: W. W. Norton & Co., 1982.

Rodriguez, Junius P., ed. *The Historical Encyclopedia of World Slavery.* Santa Barbara, Calif.: ABC-CLIO, Inc., 1993.

Frederick Douglass

Born 1817
Tuckahoe, Maryland
Died 1895
Washington, D.C.

Chattel slave, fugitive slave, freedman, abolitionist, orator, journalist, reformer, public servant

Frederick Douglass was born a slave but rose to great heights by the end of his life. After gaining his freedom Douglass devoted his life to abolishing slavery and fighting for equal rights for African Americans as well as women. He was one of the finest writers and speakers of his time and greatly influenced the development of American democracy. Douglass published three book-length autobiographies as well as a weekly newspaper, the *North Star*. His printing office in Rochester, New York, also served as a way station in the Underground Railroad, a secret network that helped runaway slaves escape to freedom in Canada.

The most prominent black American of his day due to his tireless devotion and effective leadership in the causes of abolition of slavery and civil rights for black Americans and women.

Humble beginnings

Frederick Douglass never knew who his father was, and barely remembered his mother. He did not even know his own birthdate. Soon after Douglass was born in 1817, his mother, a slave named Harriet Bailey, was sent by her master to work on a farm some distance from her child. At the time, it was common for slaveholders to part children from their

Frederick Douglass. *(Library of Congress)*

mothers at a very early age—usually within the first twelve months. The only thing Frederick knew for sure about his father was that he was white. If the rumors that he heard while growing up were true, his father was most likely the same man who owned his mother and who now owned him—Captain Aaron Anthony.

Harriet Bailey named her child Frederick Augustus Washington Bailey. Frederick Bailey later changed his name to Frederick Douglass when he gained his freedom. Douglass lived with his grandparents, Betsey and Isaac Bailey, for his first seven years in a two-story windowless cabin with a clay floor in the little town of Tuckahoe, Maryland. The Baileys were responsible for raising the children of the plantation slaves so that their parents could work in the fields. Douglass only saw his mother a few times because she lived so far away and risked being whipped if she was not back to her plantation on time for work in the morning.

Plantation life

As was customary for slave children, when Douglass reached the age of seven, he was forced to move from his grandparents' house to the plantation, known as the Big House Farm. Too young to labor in the fields, Douglass was kept busy tending the cows and chickens, keeping the barnyard clean, and running errands. The care of his loving grandmother was replaced by the watchful eyes of a household slave named Aunt Katy, whose job was to supervise the slave children.

Aunt Katy and Douglass did not get along well at all. She had a quick temper and often hit Douglass with a stick or kicked him when she was angry. She also used starvation as a punishment, forcing Douglass sometimes to go a whole day without any food. Even when he was fed it was just corn mush (boiled cornmeal) in a large wooden tray set on the ground for the children to fight over like pigs at the trough. Douglass suffered much more from the cold than hunger, he wrote later, as he had no shoes, socks, pants, or jacket—only a coarse cloth shirt that hung to his knees. On the coldest nights he slept, headfirst, in a burlap corn storage bag on a dirt floor.

City life

When Douglass was seven years old his mother died. A year later, in 1825, Douglass was sent away from Aunt Katy and the Big House Farm to the city of Baltimore, Maryland. His master's relatives, Hugh Auld and his wife Sophia, needed a servant to help look after Tommy, their little son. Douglass was given food, clothing, and a warm bed to sleep in. Miss Sophia, as she was called, treated him with kindness. She read to Tommy and Frederick, taught them the alphabet and how to count to ten. After about two years Mr. Auld found out about the lessons. He told Miss Sophia that it was against the law to educate a slave and he told Frederick that he was forbidden to read. Douglass did just the opposite. He read everything he could get his hands on including newspapers from trash cans—all in secret, of course.

The last straw

Douglass lived with the Aulds in Baltimore until 1833 when he was ordered back to the plantation by a new master. He was sad to leave the Aulds and his friends—black and white—in the bustling port city. The farm was now owned by Thomas Auld who was both greedy and cruel, working his slaves to near exhaustion and starvation. When the other slaves found out that Douglass knew how to read they begged him to start a Sunday school for black children. One Sunday morning, the lessons were broken up by an angry mob of local white men, including his master, Thomas Auld. A week later, Douglass was sent to the farm of Edward Covey, who was considered the best slave breaker (one who "tamed" slaves into submission by breaking their spirit) in the state.

After six months of abuse, which included being worked seven days a week, starved, and beaten, Douglass ran away briefly from Covey's farm. He knew he would be whipped, perhaps beaten to death, when he returned. The day after Douglass came back Covey attacked him in the barn, only this time Douglass did not turn the other cheek. He fought back, and after two hours Covey gave up. Douglass did not get whipped again in his remaining six months at Covey's farm. It was Covey, not Douglass, who had been broken.

Freedom bound

On January 1, 1834, Douglass was sent by his master, Thomas Auld, to work at the farm of William Freeland. There he was given enough to eat and wear. As he got stronger, Douglass began making plans to escape. His plan included five other slaves but somehow the plan was discovered and they were all arrested and thrown in jail.

Thomas Auld, fed up with his rebellious slave, sent Douglass to Baltimore, back to Hugh and Sophia Auld. Mr. Auld found Douglass a job in the shipyards where he learned to be a skilled caulker (applying waterproof material to the seams of ships). On Saturdays Douglass would hand over his week's wages to Mr. Auld, sometimes as much as six dollars. Mr. Auld sometimes gave Douglass a portion of his wages back as an allowance—usually about six cents.

Douglass was very unhappy that he had to work all week and then turn over his wages to his master. He was also unhappy that he was not free to live with the woman he loved and wanted to marry, a free black woman named Anna Murray. On September 3, 1838, instead of going to work, Douglass went to the house of a friend, a free black sailor who agreed to help him escape. With his friend's papers that said he was a free man, and his friend's clothes that made him look like a sailor on shore leave, Douglass boarded a train heading north. When the train reached New York City, Douglass got off and for the first time set foot on free ground.

A new life

The first thing Douglass did as a free man was to write to Anna Murray and ask her to join him. Douglass then wandered the streets of New York City for three days and nights, penniless, hungry, and tired. On the fourth day, he was taken in by Mr. Ruggles, an abolitionist and conductor on the Underground Railroad. Douglass stayed in New York just long enough for Anna to arrive. Mr. Ruggles arranged for a minister to marry them and then sent the two on their way to New Bedford, Massachusetts, where Douglass would be safer from the slave catchers who were sure to be sent looking for him.

In New Bedford, the slave born Frederick Bailey became the fugitive slave named Frederick Douglass. He began a family and in two years' time had a daughter (Rosetta, b. 1839) and a son (Lewis Henry, b. 1840). Douglass worked hard to support his family doing odd jobs for low wages but he took pleasure and pride in keeping what he earned.

Abolitionist and orator

During their first year in New Bedford the Douglass family joined the Methodist church, where they met other free blacks and Frederick learned more about the antislavery movement. Douglass began to subscribe to *The Liberator,* an abolitionist newspaper published and edited by William Lloyd Garrison (1805–79) since 1831. Douglass greatly admired Garrison, a white man who publicly declared that all slaves should be freed immediately and given full rights as U.S. citizens.

On August 11, 1841, Douglass unofficially began a new career as a traveling speaker for the abolitionist cause. Douglass was urged to take the speaker's platform at a Massachusetts Anti-Slavery Society convention in Nantucket that night by a man who had heard him speak about slavery in New Bedford's Methodist Church. Douglass was nervous but when he was done the audience of five hundred people stood and cheered. Douglass was hired by the society to travel throughout the northern states and make speeches against slavery.

Douglass faced great odds on the lecture circuit. As a black man in the "free" North he had to travel and lodge in segregated quarters from his white companions. He was sometimes mobbed and beaten by anti-abolitionists. Douglass was even accused of being too smart and well-spoken to have ever been a slave.

Author and journalist

In May 1845, Douglass published his *Narrative of the Life of Frederick Douglass,* a small book that told his life story through 1841. The book was a success, so much so that Douglass feared for his safety now that his whereabouts were

Frederick Douglass, center, on a "Heroes of Black History" lithograph. (Corbis-Bettmann. Reproduced by permission.)

known to his former master. With his new book in hand, in August 1845, Douglass left for a speaking tour of England, Ireland, and Scotland. He returned to the United States in the spring of 1847 with enough money to buy his freedom and start a newspaper.

In November 1847, Douglass moved his family to Rochester, New York, and on December 3 the first issue of the *North Star* was printed. The articles in the newspaper were mostly about slavery and many of them were written by black writers. There were also articles about other groups of people who needed help such as poor people who were hungry and homeless, children who were forced to work in factories, and women who were fighting for the right to vote. Douglass published the *North Star* until the start of the Civil War (1861–65), and during that time over four hundred runaway slaves found refuge at his printing shop on their way to freedom in Canada.

Reformer and public servant

Douglass was very active in the turbulent 1850s, the decade leading up to the Civil War. He published the *North Star* and reported on the important issues of the day. The Compromise of 1850 and the Kansas-Nebraska Act of 1854 were among the issues he spoke about from black America's perspective. He lectured, supported women's suffrage (the right to vote), participated in politics, tried to start an industrial school for black youth, and counseled with other abolitionists, such as the revolutionary John Brown (1800–1859). In fact, in October 1859 when John Brown's rebellion at Harpers Ferry, Virginia, failed, Douglass left the country for Canada for fear of being accused as an accomplice.

Douglass was back in the United States when the Civil War began. He welcomed it and once the Emancipation Proclamation went into effect on January 1, 1863, and blacks were allowed to enlist in the Union army, Douglass vigorously recruited soldiers for the all-black regiments of Massachussetts. Two of his own sons were the first to enlist. Douglass provided counsel to U.S. president Abraham Lincoln (1809–65) during the war, and during Reconstruction (1865–77) fought for suffrage and civil rights for freed blacks.

The last years of Douglass's life were spent in comfort and honor. He enjoyed three successive government appointments, the last being the U.S. minister to Haiti. In 1884 Douglass married for a second time (his first wife, Anna, died in 1882). When criticized for marrying Helen Pitts because she was white, Douglass replied that his first wife "was the color of my mother, and the second, the color of my father."

In His Own Words

The following excerpt is from Frederick Douglass's first book, *Narrative of the Life of Frederick Douglass, An American Slave* (1845):

> *I am filled with unutterable loathing when I contemplate the religious pomp and show, together with the horrible inconsistencies, which everywhere surround me. We have men-stealers for ministers, women-whippers for missionaries, and cradle-plunderers for church members. The man who wields the blood-clotted cowskin during the week fills the pulpit on Sunday, and claims to be a minister of the meek and lowly Jesus. The man who robs me of my earnings at the end of each week meets me as a class leader on Sunday morning, to show me the way of life, and the path of salvation.*

Other books by Douglass include: *My Bondage and My Freedom* (1855) and *Life and Times of Frederick Douglass* (1881).

Further Reading

Davidson, Margaret. *Frederick Douglass Fights for Freedom*. New York: Four Winds Press, 1968.

Douglass, Frederick. *The Narrative of the Life of Frederick Douglass, An American Slave*. Cambridge, Mass.: Harvard University Press, 1988.

Logan, Rayford W., and Michael R. Winston, eds. *Dictionary of American Negro Biography*. New York: W. W. Norton & Co., 1982.

Malone, Dumas, ed. *Dictionary of American Biography*. New York: Charles Scribner's Sons, 1936.

McKissack, Patricia, and Frederick McKissack. *Frederick Douglass: The Black Lion*. Chicago: Children's Press, 1987.

Olaudah Equiano
(also Gustavus Vassa)

Born c. 1750
Nigeria, Africa
Died 1797
England

African slave, writer, abolitionist

Olaudah Equiano (pronounced ek–wee–AHN–o; also called Gustavus Vassa) led a remarkable life. When he was a child living in Nigeria, he was captured by African slave traders. After being sent first to the West Indies and then to a plantation in Virginia, Equiano was bought by British Naval officer Michael Henry Pascal. While serving Pascal, he received many advantages, including an education. He also became a skillful sailor during the Seven Years War (1756–63; a worldwide conflict fought in Europe, North America, and India). After the war, Equiano was traded to Robert King, who was a Quaker (member of the Society of Friends, a Christian group). King provided Equiano with the experience to begin his own trading business, which enabled him to save enough money to buy his freedom. After writing *The Interesting Narrative of the Life of Olaudah Equiano* (1789), Equiano became a prominent abolitionist (a person who opposes slavery).

"The closeness of the place and the heat of the climate, added to the number in the ship, which was so crowded that each had scarcely room to turn himself, almost suffocated us."

from The Interesting Narrative of the Life of Olaudah Equiano

Kidnapped by slave traders

Olaudah Equiano was born in Africa around 1750. He was the son of an Ibo chief (the Ibos were an East-Nigerian

Olaudah Equiano. *(Library of Congress)*

tribe of Africans). As a child, Equiano experienced the security of a close community. This security was shattered when, at age eleven, he was captured along with his sister by African tribesmen who participated in the slave trade. (Africa had a long history of slavery before European slave traders reached the continent in the fifteenth century.) In his narrative Equiano described this frightening event:

> One day, when all our people were gone out to their works as usual, and only I and my dear sister were left to mind the house, two men and a woman got over our walls, and in a moment seized us both; and, without giving us time to cry out, or to make resistance, they stopped our mouths, tied our hands, and ran off with us into the nearest wood, and continued to carry us as far as they could, till night came on, when we reached a small house, where the robbers halted for refreshment, and spent the night.

> We were then unbound, but were unable to take any food; and, being quite overpowered by fatigue and grief, our only relief was some sleep, which allayed [reduced] our misfortune for a short time. The next morning we left the house, and continued traveling all the day. For a long time we had kept to the woods, but at last we came into a road which I believed I knew. I now had some hopes of being delivered, for we had advanced but a little way before I discovered some people at a distance, on which I began to cry out for their assistance; but my cries had no other effect than to make them tie me faster, and stop my mouth, and then they put me into a large sack. They also stopped my sister's mouth, and tied her hands. And in this manner we proceeded till we were out of the sight of these people. . . .

Slavery firsthand

Equiano was soon separated from his sister, whom he never saw again. He was traded from village to village, where he worked for a variety of African masters. When he was taken to the coast of West Africa he was purchased by a European trader. He was then chained together with many other captives in the cramped hold of a slave ship. There Equiano witnessed firsthand the brutal treatment of slaves by the white traders:

> The stench of the hold while we were on the coast was so intolerably loathsome that it was dangerous to remain there for any time. . . . The closeness of the place and the heat of the climate, added to the number in the ship, which was so crowded that each had scarcely room to turn himself, almost suffocated us. This produced copious perspirations, so that the air soon be-

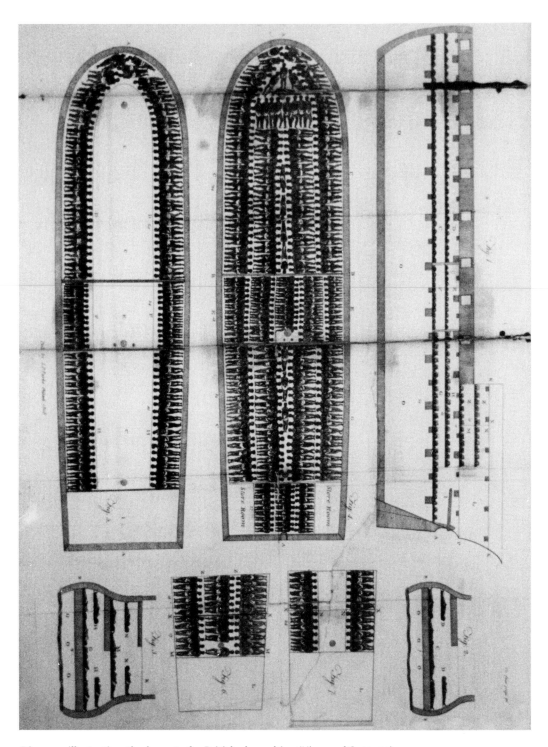

Diagram illustrating the layout of a British slave ship. *(Library of Congress)*

The Middle Passage

Sailors referred to the shipboard experience of enslaved Africans across the Atlantic Ocean as "the middle passage." During the voyage men were usually chained, while women and children were allowed some freedom of movement on the ship deck. Captains chose one of two methods for transporting slaves: tight packing or loose packing. Tight packing squeezed in as many slaves as possible. Male slaves lay in spaces six feet long, sixteen inches wide, and two and one-half feet high. Female slaves lay in spaces five feet long, fourteen inches wide, and two and one-half feet high. This method prevented the slaves from moving about or even sitting up. Captains who chose this style of storage did not want to waste space. They believed their net receipts were higher from the larger cargo even if many slaves died. Part of the profit derived from less food and a smaller crew.

Other captains chose loose packing. They believed that more room, better food, and a degree of freedom reduced the death rate of slaves. Healthy slaves increased the profit. Some captains insured their stock of slaves against drowning. Because insurance did not cover the loss of slaves who died aboard a ship, some captains dumped dying slaves overboard and claimed they drowned in order to collect insurance benefits.

came unfit for respiration from a variety of loathsome smells, and brought on a sickness among the slaves, of which many died. . . .

Equiano was then transported thousands of miles to the Caribbean island of Barbados, where sugar plantations made it the richest British colony of the eighteenth century. When none of the planters in Barbados purchased Equiano, he was taken to the American colony of Virginia and there worked briefly on a tobacco plantation. His job was to pull weeds and collect stones.

Cheated out of his freedom

Only a few weeks after being purchased in Virginia, Equiano was sold again, this time to Michael Henry Pascal, a lieutenant in the British Royal Navy. Pascal renamed Equiano after the sixteenth-century Swedish king Gustavus Vasa (Equiano spelled his own name "Vassa"). During the voyage to England in 1757, Equiano met a thirteen-year-old Virginian named Richard Baker, who taught him to read and write. Equiano subsequently took every opportunity to improve his reading and writing skills and to add to his knowledge. In 1759, while living with some friends of Pascal in London, England, Equiano was baptized (admitted to the Christian faith through anointment with water) at St. Margaret's Church.

During the Seven Years War, Pascal encouraged Equiano to become a skillful sailor. He served on several naval vessels in the Atlantic Ocean and the Mediterranean Sea. For instance, he was a steward (one who assists passengers) on board the *Aetna* in 1761. Toward the end of the year the *Aetna* returned to England. Although Equiano said he had no specific promise from the captain that he would be given his freedom when they landed, he certainly expected it. Instead, the captain forced Equiano onto a barge and later onto a ship sailing for the West Indies.

Buys his freedom and seeks adventure

Under instruction from Pascal, the captain sold Equiano when the ship reached the island of Montserrat in 1763. His new master was a Quaker merchant, Robert King, who had a reputation as a kind and charitable man. Equiano was valuable to King because of his skills as a sailor and his ability to read, write, and do arithmetic. Equiano assisted King in shipping sugar and other agricultural goods between the Caribbean, Georgia, and South Carolina. Once he was even forced to transport slaves.

Equiano also did a little trading of his own: he would buy an item in the Indies and resell it for a small profit in North America. Likewise he would make yet another profit by purchasing something in North America and then selling it in the Indies. In this way he eventually earned enough money to buy his freedom. Despite the fact that the Quakers had renounced slavery as part of their religion in 1761, King still required Equiano to pay forty pounds sterling (British silver coins). Equiano became a free man in 1766.

Equiano went to London, where he worked for a short time as a hair dresser, a skill he had learned aboard ship. Unable to make ends meet in London, in 1768 he signed up again as a sailor on a ship going to Turkey. He spent several more years sailing in the Mediterranean and making trips to the West Indies. Equiano soon found, however, that the life of a freed man in the islands could be dangerous. Black people had no protection under the law and might easily be kidnapped and taken away on a ship as a slave.

In the early 1770s he returned to England and worked for a Dr. Irving, whose business was purifying salt water into drinkable water. Equiano acted as Irving's assistant, purifying between twenty-six and forty gallons a day. When a Captain Phipps invited Equiano to accompany him on an expedition to the Arctic (the icy region around the North Pole), Irving asked to join Equiano on the trip. Equiano wrote that in their four-month voyage they explored farther north than any previous navigation team

Upon returning to London, Irving bought a 150-ton sloop (sailing boat) that he planned to sail to Jamaica to establish a plantation there. In 1775 Equiano accompanied him on this venture. After spending several months with the doctor along the coast of Nicaragua and Honduras, Equiano left and returned to Jamaica. He planned to go back to England, but in several instances of bad judgment, he put his trust in people who duped and cheated him. Finally, in 1777, he settled in England and began working on his autobiography.

Becomes prominent abolitionist

During the previous decade Equiano's life had taken another important turn. While visiting Savannah, Georgia, he had attended a religious service led by the famous English preacher George Whitfield. The clergyman's powerful sermon greatly influenced Equiano, who continued to think about the sermon's message of heaven, hell, and salvation for several years. In 1774 he experienced a religious conversion in Cadiz, Spain, and began to attend worship services and to read the Bible. Through his religious activities he came into contact with Quakers, Anglicans, and Methodists who were involved in the abolitionist movement. Soon Equiano became committed to ending the slave trade.

Equiano was a valuable contact person for the early abolitionists as he carried news of the horrors of slavery between England and America. In 1785 during a journey to Philadelphia, Pennsylvania, he was pleased to observe that the Quakers had emancipated (freed) their slaves and founded a free school in the city. Because of his involvement in the antislavery movement, naval authorities in England appointed him Commissary for Provisions and Stores for the Black Poor, a position in which he supervised supplies sent to Africans in Sierra Leone.

In 1787 British abolitionists, humanitarians, and church groups established the Sierra Leone Company, a community for freed slaves in Sierra Leone, a small British colony on the west coast of Africa. It started as an experimental colony with 411 freed slaves from Britain. Their goals were to "introduce civilisation among the natives and to cultivate the soil by means of free labour."

Equiano never made the trip back to Africa. He quarreled constantly with the company agent and wrote a public letter to the newspaper accusing the promoters of the expedition of corruption and deception. In response the agent accused him of disobedience to authority and disrespectful behavior toward his superiors. The navy dismissed Equiano from his post and the expedition went ahead without him.

Gains international fame

In 1789 Equiano published *The Interesting Narrative of the Life of Olaudah Equiano,* which increased his status as an abolitionist spokesman. Nine editions of the autobiography were printed during his lifetime, and the book quickly brought him to international fame. In his narrative Equiano compared the experiences of African slaves with the stories of Hebrew slaves in the Bible (see Moses entry). He also expressed his own antislavery views. The book is now ranked with such great slave narratives as the *Narrative of the Life of Frederick Douglass* (1845) and others that were written around the time of the American Civil War (1861–65).

In 1792 Equiano married Susan Cullen, an English-woman with whom he had two daughters, Anna Maria and Johanna. Susan Cullen Vassa died only months after Johanna's birth, and Equiano died in 1797. Johanna died two months after her father, but Anna Maria survived him into adulthood.

Further Reading

Edwards, Paul, ed. *Equiano's Travels: His Autobiography. The Interesting Narrative of the Life of Olaudah Equiano or Gustavus Vassa the African Life.* London: Heinemann, 1967.

Jones, G. I. "Olaudah Equiano of the Niger Ibo." In *Africa Remembered: Narratives by West Africans from the Era of the Slave Trade,* edited by Philip D. Curtin. Madison: University of Wisconsin Press, 1977.

Stiles, T. J., ed. *In Their Own Words: The Colonizers.* New York: Berkeley Publishing Group, 1998, pp. 349–60.

William Lloyd Garrison

Born December 10, 1805
Newburyport, Massachusetts
Died May 24, 1879
New York , New York

Journalist, abolitionist leader, social reformer

William Lloyd Garrison.
(Library of Congress)

Publisher of an antislavery newspaper, *The Liberator,* and leader of a group of radical abolitionists. A tireless advocate and activist for racial equality and integration, women's rights, temperance, and other social causes.

William Lloyd Garrison was born into a very poor family in New England but was determined from a very early age to make something out of his life. He got his lucky break at the age of twelve when he became an apprentice with the owner and editor of the local newspaper. At twenty years old he started his own newspaper and although it didn't last long he knew he had found his calling. After a series of jobs as editor of different publications he also knew that he had found his cause: ending slavery in the United States. In 1831 Garrison created *The Liberator,* a weekly newspaper devoted to abolishing slavery, which he edited for thirty-four years.

Garrison's role in the abolition of slavery in the United States was especially important in the 1830s and 1840s when people in the North were still, as a group, undecided on the question of slavery. Garrison's greatest accomplishment in these decades—as a journalist and lecturer for the abolition movement—was that he forced people to think about slavery. To his credit, by the 1850s, a decade before the Civil War (1861–65), the topic of slavery was on everyone's mind—and virtually everyone's tongue—as well.

Hard times

William Lloyd Garrison was born in Newburyport, Massachusetts, the third child of Abijah and Fanny Garrison. Lloyd, as his mother called him, lived with his siblings—four-year-old James and two-year-old Caroline—and his parents in a rented room in the poorer section of the small port town. Abijah Garrison was a sailor and often left Fanny to care for the family while he was at sea.

When Garrison was just an infant the Garrison family suffered two serious misfortunes. The local shipping economy came to a standstill and Abijah could not find work. Then in the summer of 1808, five-year-old Caroline died after eating poisonous flowers. Abijah took to drinking heavily and after a heated quarrel with Fanny, who was a Baptist and firmly against the use of alcohol, he deserted his family never to be heard from again.

With the birth of Maria Elizabeth in July 1808, Fanny had three children under the age of seven to support. She found work nursing sick people, leaving her children with a neighbor while she made her rounds. When Fanny had a hard time finding steady work she sent Garrison to the public square to sell molasses candies that she had made. Other times, she sent him with a small pail to the back doors of the town's mansions to beg for scraps of food. When he had the time Garrison attended the nearby primary school where he learned—after many blows on his knuckles—to write using his right hand despite being left-handed.

Failed apprentice

In 1812 Fanny moved to Lynn, Massachusetts, hoping to find more regular work. She took eleven-year-old James with her so that he could learn the shoemaking trade. Maria Elizabeth was left with a neighbor and Garrison, now seven, was sent to live with Deacon Ezekial Bartlett and his family, members of the same Baptist church as the Garrison family. Life with the Bartletts was better. Garrison had to do chores around the house and odd jobs but in exchange he was fed and clothed and even had a little more time for school. On Sundays he sang in the Baptist church choir.

When Garrison was nine he joined his mother in Lynn where she apprenticed him to a shoemaker. The work was too much for Garrison and after a few months and an illness he was happy to be sent back to the Bartletts. After several failed attempts by Fanny to place her son as an apprentice (someone who studies under a skilled tradesperson) to a shoemaker and a cabinetmaker, Garrison was allowed to return to the Bartletts in Newburyport where he found the time to finish his formal grammar school education.

Beginnings of a newspaperman

On October 18, 1818, just weeks before his thirteenth birthday, William Lloyd Garrison had the good fortune to be apprenticed to Ephraim Allen, the editor and owner of the Newburyport *Herald.* As an apprentice Garrison moved into the Allen home where he had access to a well-stocked library. By the time he was fifteen Garrison was the best typesetter (the job of arranging pieces of lead type on a page) and was made the foreman of the print shop. Garrison was also doing editorial work at fifteen, clipping articles of interest from other newspapers for publication in the *Herald.*

At nineteen, Garrison tried his hand at writing. To his surprise his anonymously written articles to the *Herald* were published. And when he revealed his secret to Mr. Allen, Garrison was rewarded with a month's vacation!

Freelance editor

When Garrison turned twenty his apprenticeship ended. He turned down a job offer from Mr. Allen in order to start his own newspaper. He called it the *Free Press.* After just six months the paper had to close. Garrison was out of money and had managed to alienate his subscribers and supporters— even Mr. Allen who had been so kind to him—by his strongly worded articles on the issues of the day, including slavery.

Garrison then moved to Boston and worked a few years on and off as a printer's helper. On July 4, 1828, Garrison became the editor of the *National Philanthropist,* a publication devoted to temperance (abstinence from alcohol). He was fired six months later because he refused to limit his writings to the subject of the evils of alcohol. He also wrote about religion, conditions among the poor, and slavery.

At the end of 1828, Garrison was invited to Baltimore by antislavery activist and newspaper publisher Benjamin Lundy (1789-1839), to co-edit *The Genius of Universal Emancipation*. In the first issue of the new *Genius* (September 2, 1829), Garrison demanded the immediate and unconditional end to slavery, a position that was considered very bold and radical at the time. While Garrison's views raised some eyebrows in the emerging abolitionist movement, the general public in New England appeared indifferent.

Jail, journalism, and fame

In 1830 Garrison finally got the public to pay attention to him and to his message. Garrison was sued for libel (a printed statement that unjustly damages a person's reputation) for one of his editorials. When he refused to pay a fine he spent forty-nine days in jail. During his incarceration Garrison sent out letters to newspaper editors explaining that his only crime was in speaking the truth when he called a local slave trader a "murderer" in *The Genuis*. As a result, more than one hundred newspapers wrote about Garrison and the issue of slavery. In a matter of a few weeks, William Lloyd Garrison was a well-known name in New England.

After returning to Boston in 1830 Garrison began his next publishing project—his own newspaper, in which the doctrine of immediate emancipation would be the central theme. The first issue of *The Liberator* came out on January 1, 1831. Relying on seed money mainly from the free black community, *The Liberator* slowly grew in the number of subscribers and the area of its distribution, North and South.

Garrison soon became one of the most hated men in the country. The South blamed unrest among their slaves on the availability of abolitionist newspapers like *The Liberator*. An incident that caused particular concern was the violent rebellion led by slave leader Nat Turner (1800–31) in August 1831, in which almost sixty whites were killed. Garrison published many articles praising Turner as a hero. Several states

OFFICERS

OF THE

AMERICAN ANTI-SLAVERY SOCIETY,

ELECTED MAY, 1859.

PRESIDENT.

WILLIAM LLOYD GARRISON, MASSACHUSETTS.

VICE PRESIDENTS.

PETER LIBBEY, Maine.	THOMAS WHITSON, Pennsylvania.
LUTHER MELENDY, New Hampshire.	JOSEPH MOORE, "
JOHN M. HAWKS, " "	ROWLAND JOHNSON, New Jersey.
JEHIEL C. CLAFLIN, Vermont.	ALFRED GIBBS CAMPBELL, "
FRANCIS JACKSON, Massachusetts.	THOMAS GARRETT, Delaware.
EDMUND QUINCY, "	THOMAS DONALDSON, Ohio.
ASA FAIRBANKS, Rhode Island.	SARAH OTIS ERNST, "
JAMES B. WHITCOMB, Connecticut.	BENJAMIN BOWN, "
SAMUEL J. MAY, New York.	WILLIAM HEARN, Indiana.
CORNELIUS BRAMHALL, " "	WILLIAM HOPKINS, "
AMY POST, " "	JOSEPH MERRITT, Michigan.
PLINY SEXTON, " "	THOMAS CHANDLER, "
LYDIA MOTT, " "	CYRUS FULLER, "
LUCRETIA MOTT, Pennsylvania.	CARVER TOMLINSON, Illinois.
ROBERT PURVIS, "	CALEB GREEN, Minnesota.
EDWARD M. DAVIS, "	GEORGIANA B. KIRBY, California.

CORRESPONDING SECRETARY.

CHARLES C. BURLEIGH, PLAINFIELD, CT.

RECORDING SECRETARY.

WENDELL PHILLIPS, BOSTON.

TREASURER.

FRANCIS JACKSON, BOSTON.

EXECUTIVE COMMITTEE.

WILLIAM LLOYD GARRISON.	ANNE WARREN WESTON.
FRANCIS JACKSON.	SYDNEY HOWARD GAY.
EDMUND QUINCY.	SAMUEL MAY, JR.
MARIA WESTON CHAPMAN.	WILLIAM I. BOWDITCH.
WENDELL PHILLIPS.	CHARLES K. WHIPPLE.
ELIZA LEE FOLLEN.	HENRY C. WRIGHT.

Officers as listed in the 1859 American Anti-Slavery Society's annual report.

in the South passed laws making it a crime to possess a copy of *The Liberator* and Garrison received a great deal of hate mail and a number of threats on his life.

Abolitionist and activist

Early in 1831, Garrison helped found the Boston-based New England Anti-Slavery Society, an organization dedicated to fighting for complete social equality for all persons regardless of race. In December 1833, Garrison also helped found the American Anti-Slavery Society. Its main purpose was to promote the formation of abolitionist societies throughout the North with the goal of convincing the public that slavery was morally wrong.

Garrison was a leader in the abolition movement for thirty years but his ideas were not always popular among its members. For example, Garrison's idea that slaves should not only be freed but granted equal rights with whites was considered extreme by the mainstream abolitionist movement. In 1840 Garrison's insistence that female abolitionists be allowed to participate fully in antislavery activities led some members to quit the American Anti-Slavery Society and form their own male-dominated organization.

Garrison further alienated some people in the 1840s when he called for the North to secede (formally withdraw) from the Union, adopting the new motto "No Union with Slaveholders!" In 1854 he even went so far as to burn a copy of the U.S. Constitution at a public Fourth of July celebration. But in the explosive decade of the 1850s, Garrison's protests drew little attention. Articles about slavery were now in every newspaper, not just the abolitionist publications. People argued about it on street corners, in churches, and in the halls of Congress. People were even fighting and dying over the issue of slavery in the western territories.

Garrison's rewards

For thirty years or so Garrison divided his time between publishing *The Liberator,* organizing and leading abolitionist and women's rights activities, and traveling around the northern states making speeches against slavery. Somewhere along the way he also found time to be a husband and a father. Garrison married Helen Benson in September 1834, and together they raised five sons and one daughter in their Boston home. The Garrison family never had much money but their house had many guests—people who needed a meal or a place to sleep.

Garrison always said that if he had wanted to be rich he would have chosen a different line of work. Instead of wealth, Garrison was rewarded in other ways. Although he was against the use of violence he welcomed the Civil War as a means to end slavery. Although against participating directly in electoral politics, Garrison supported U.S. president Abraham Lincoln (1809–65) after he issued the Emancipation Proclamation on January 1, 1863, freeing about three-fourths of all slaves. Garrison was even Lincoln's guest at the White House following the convention that nominated him for a second term as president.

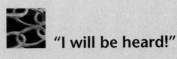 **"I will be heard!"**

William Lloyd Garrison chose to use words, not violence, to try to change what he saw as an unjust world. The major weapon in his fight to end slavery in the United States was his weekly newspaper, *The Liberator.* For thirty-four years Garrison kept the promises he made on the subject of slavery in the very first issue of *The Liberator,* on January, 1, 1831:

> *I will be as harsh as truth, as uncompromising as justice. On this subject I do not wish to think, or speak, or write with moderation. No! No! Tell a man whose house is on fire to give a moderate alarm; tell him to moderately rescue his wife from the hands of the ravisher; tell the mother to gradually extricate her babe from the fire into which it has fallen—but urge me not to use moderation in a cause like the present. I am in earnest—I will not equivocate—I will not excuse—I will not retreat a single inch—and I will be heard.*

Garrison had the distinction of going from one of America's most hated men in 1835 to one of the country's most honored men in 1865. With the end of the Civil War and the passage of the Thirteenth Amendment by Congress abolishing slavery, Garrison was invited to many celebrations in honor of his lifelong work. He was the guest of honor in his hometown of Newburyport—where fifty years before he had begged for food scraps—and in his adopted city of Boston. On April 14, 1865, Garrison traveled to Charleston, South Carolina, for a banquet in his honor and a parade the following day. Thousands of liberated slaves lined the route and offered presents to Garrison as he passed by, an experience that Garrison later described as the proudest moment in his life.

The right to rest

When Garrison published the last issue of *The Liberator* on December 29, 1865, he was as penniless as when he began his project thirty-four years earlier. Garrison lived out the rest of his life in relative comfort, however, thanks to the generosity of his supporters who raised thirty thousand dollars to support him in retirement. Garrison continued to lecture occasionally and write essays for the *New York Independent* newspaper on various social reforms until his death in 1879.

Further Reading

Faber, Doris. *I Will be Heard: The Life of William Lloyd Garrison.* New York: Lothrop, Lee & Shepard Co., 1970.

Garraty, John A., and Marc C. Carnes, eds. *American National Biography.* New York: Oxford University Press, 1999.

Merrill, Walter, M. *Against Wind and Tide: A Biography of William Lloyd Garrison.* Cambridge, Mass.: Harvard University Press, 1963.

Thomas, John L. *The Liberator: William Lloyd Garrison.* Boston: Little, Brown & Co., 1963.

Sarah Grimké

Born November 26, 1792
Charleston, South Carolina
Died December 23, 1873
Hyde Park, Massachusetts

Angelina Grimké

Born February 20, 1805
Charleston, South Carolina
Died October 26, 1879
Hyde Park, Massachusetts

Abolitionists, women's rights activists

Sarah and Angelina Grimké were among the very first women to publicly speak out against slavery in the United States. They may also have been the first Americans to argue in print for women to receive the same legal and social rights as men. The Grimké sisters crusaded for the emancipation of slaves and women during a time in America when women could not vote, run for office, or go to college. No organized religion except the Quakers allowed women to speak out or participate in church affairs. It was a time when women were expected to have their names in the newspapers only three times in their lives: when they were born, married, and died.

Aristocratic roots

Sarah and Angelina Grimké were born into a wealthy slaveholding family in Charleston, South Carolina. Angelina was the fourteenth and last child of John Faucheraud Grimké and Mary Smith, and twelve years younger than Sarah. John Grimké was the chief judge of the South Carolina Supreme Court. Mary Smith came from one of the wealthiest families in the state and her family tree included two colonial governors.

As speakers and writers, the Grimké sisters were pioneers and leaders in the abolition and women's rights movements. Not only should slavery be abolished, they argued, but women should be given the same legal and social rights as men.

Sarah Grimké. *(Library of Congress)*

The Grimké family lived in a large house in the city of Charleston. Judge Grimké owned other properties including a plantation in Beaufort on the Carolina coast. He also owned hundreds of slaves—some as servants for his city residence but most of them as field workers for his farm. Judge Grimké was a member of the Episcopal church and every Sunday the family attended services and the children went to Sabbath school. A formal education, including the study of law, Greek, Latin, and philosophy was readily available for the sons of the Grimké family but not the daughters, who were only expected to prepare themselves for marriage.

Sarah's childhood

While the education of Sarah's brothers was designed to prepare them for professional lives as lawyers and doctors, Sarah's instructions focused on making her a better homemaker and a "lady." Reading, writing, a little arithmetic, and French were the basics; drawing, piano, and voice lessons rounded out the curriculum. But Sarah wanted to learn more and she spent much of her time until she was twelve studying the lessons of her older brother Thomas: mathematics, geography, history, Greek, natural science, and botany.

Sarah was exposed to some of the practices of slavery at an early age. She was just four years old when she accidentally witnessed the whipping of a slave woman at the Grimké plantation. It affected her so much that she ran away from the house and had to be searched for by her nurse. Whenever Sarah heard that a slave was to be punished she shut herself up in her room and prayed for the whipping not to happen. As was the custom of the time in the South, Sarah was given a slave girl by her father to be her servant and companion. Sarah became very fond of Kitty and treated her as an equal. When the little girl died after just a few years Sarah refused to have another slave replace her.

Sarah's rebellion

Sarah was just twelve when she committed her first act of rebellion against the slave system that surrounded her. Like the other Grimké girls Sarah had taught Bible classes for black children, slave and free, every Sunday afternoon since she was eight. Sarah asked for permission to teach her students how to *read* the Bible and was told by her father that it was against the law to do so. Teaching slaves how to read, he told her, might make them restless and rebellious. Sarah later recalled her response to the situation in an 1827 diary entry:

> My great desire in this matter would not be totally suppressed, and I took an almost malicious satisfaction in teaching my little waiting-maid at night, when she was supposed to be occupied in combing and brushing my long locks. The light was put out, the keyhole screened, and flat on our stomachs, before the fire, with the spelling book under our eyes, we defied the laws of South Carolina.

Life in the South

One of the reasons Sarah Grimké left her life of privilege in the South to become an abolitionist in the North was her frustration with the practices of slavery, especially the law that prevented her from legally teaching slaves to read and write (from the Statute Book of South Carolina):

> *AN ACT FOR THE BETTER ORDERING AND GOVERNING OF NEGROES AND SLAVES . . . 1740. SECT. 45. And whereas, having slaves taught to write, or suffering them to be employed in writing, may be attended with great inconveniences . . . that any person who shall teach a slave to write or to employ any slave as a scribe in writing, shall forfeit 100 pounds [monetary currency].*

A turning point

Sarah was almost thirteen when it was time to baptize her new sister, Angelina. Although it was an unusual request for a girl of her age, her parents consented to Sarah being Angelina's godmother. Sarah pledged to cherish, protect, and train her sister, a promise that she spent her life fulfilling.

Sarah spent her teenage years doting on her younger sister and yearning to be allowed to go off to law school like her older brother Thomas. She also led the leisurely life of a young and wealthy southern belle. Her days were made up of long meals, walks in the garden, shopping, visiting friends, writing letters, horseback riding, and strolling in town in the evening. Meanwhile, Angelina benefitted from a better formal education than Sarah had as she attended a seminary school for daughters of Charleston's upper class.

In 1819, at age twenty-six, Sarah accompanied her ill father on a trip north to seek medical treatment. Her father died on the trip and when Sarah was traveling back home she met a Quaker family who gave her a copy of the writings of a

Angelina Grimké. *(The Granger Collection, New York. Reproduced by permission.)*

Quaker abolitionist. Despite her life of privilege in Charleston, Sarah was not happy with many aspects of her life—especially the contradictions she saw between the preachings of the Episcopal church and the practices of its slaveholding members. In 1821 Sarah left her family and moved north to Philadelphia, Pennsylvania, where she worked and studied with Quakers.

Angelina's choices

Angelina had the same problems with her family's choice of religion as Sarah, and at the age of thirteen refused confirmation in the Episcopal church. At twenty, Angelina converted to the Presbyterian church. She taught Bible classes, organized prayer meetings, and urged every church member to speak out against slavery. Like her sister, Angelina was unhappy with Christianity as practiced in the South, especially the mistreatment of slaves by her own family, mostly by her brothers. In 1829 Angelina moved to Philadelphia to join Sarah who had become a member of the Society of Friends (the Quakers).

By 1831 Angelina had also become a member of the Society of Friends. The Grimké sisters were drawn to the Friends' movement because of its history in the antislavery struggle. American Quakers had opposed slavery since 1688. They helped establish many of the earliest organizations designed to abolish slavery and aid free blacks. But the Grimké sisters ultimately found the Quakers to be too moderate in their practices when it came to race relations. They noted that there were a fair number of blacks who had converted to Quakerism but relatively few who were full-fledged members. And, blacks who attended the same Quaker meetings as Sarah and Angelina were seated in the "Negro benches" in the back of the room.

About this time Angelina began reading abolitionist literature, including *The Liberator,* a Boston-based weekly newspaper established by editor and abolitionist William Lloyd Garrison (1805–79). She was very attracted to Garrison's call for the immediate emancipation of all slaves. She attended her first antislavery lecture in February 1835, and a few months later joined the Philadelphia Female Anti-Slavery Society.

Recruited to the cause

Angelina first came to the attention of the organized abolition movement in the summer of 1835 when she wrote a letter to Garrison praising his work and condemning slavery. On September 19 Angelina's letter appeared in *The Liberator* without her permission. It caused outrage among the Quaker elders and an uproar in her home state of South Carolina. The newspaper was burned when it arrived at post offices in South Carolina and a warrant was issued for Angelina's arrest. Instead of remaining silent, Angelina responded in 1836 by writing a 36-page antislavery pamphlet, *Appeal to the Christian Women of the South.*

In 1836 Angelina was asked to become a speaker for the American Anti-Slavery Society. The society planned to send speakers all over the North to drum up support for the cause of abolition. They invited seventy recruits to New York City for training. Angelina Grimké was the only woman in the group. Sarah soon joined Angelina in New York and the two were trained in November as speakers by abolitionist Theodore Weld (1803-95). In December Sarah wrote her own antislavery pamphlet, *Epistle to the Clergy of the Southern States,* which was published by the American Anti-Slavery Society. In it she attacked the many biblical arguments used by the southern clergy in their Sunday sermons in support of slavery.

In the public eye

In early 1837 Sarah and Angelina began their speaking tour of the state of New York, telling people about their experiences with slavery in the South and why the practice should be abolished everywhere. Their positions on slavery enraged the South but the North was offended almost as much by the fact that women were speaking in public to "mixed audiences" of women *and* men. They were criticized in the press and by the clergy, even denied permission to give their talks in churches throughout the North.

In May 1837 the Grimké sisters went on a speaking tour of New England. Women and men flocked to hear them speak. In five months Sarah and Angelina separately visited sixty-seven towns and addressed more than forty thousand people in eighty-eight meetings. In February 1838 Angelina became the first woman to ever speak before the state legislature in Massachusetts, a talk that lasted for three sessions over three days before a packed house each time. At the same time she presented a petition to the government calling for an end to slavery—signed by twenty thousand Massachusetts women.

Slavery and women's rights

The Grimké sisters were powerful messengers in the antislavery cause. Their southern roots and firsthand experiences made their stories of the brutal treatment of slaves more believable. The fact that they were women added to their draw, as very few people could say they ever heard a woman speak in public on any subject. The sisters took full advantage of this fact and used their lectures to advocate for the equality of women as well as blacks. According to the Grimkés, women should not only be able to be doctors, lawyers, and ministers but they should be able to vote and make laws as well.

In 1838 Sarah wrote what amounted to the first statement in the United States of a woman's rights to equality. Her *Letters on the Equality of the Sexes* was published in the newspaper, the *Spectator,* and in pamphlet form. In it she argued that non-males and non-whites held very similar positions in U.S. society. For example, the law upheld the right of a man to beat his wife or his slave. A husband, or master, also owned all the personal property of his wife or slave, and if wages were earned by either they also belonged to him. Education, Sarah pointed out, was also very limited or nonexistent for both women and slaves.

In their speeches the Grimkés also used the realities of slavery to discredit some of the myths that were common about women in the times. If women were too weak to work as equals with men why was it that black women were able to work side by side with black men in the fields? If women who had sexual relations outside of marriage either committed suicide or went mad why were black women able to become pregnant—often by white men—work, give birth, and return to work?

Marriage and retirement

In May 1838 Angelina married Theodore Weld, the man who had trained her as a speaker in New York. The Society of Friends expelled Angelina for marrying a Presbyterian and Sarah for attending their wedding. Two days after her wedding Angelina and a number of other women gave speeches to the Philadelphia Anti-Slavery convention. An angry mob threw stones through the windows and later burned the building to the ground.

Angelina, Theodore Weld, and Sarah withdrew from the lecture circuit and moved to Fort Lee, New Jersey. There the sisters compiled articles on slavery clipped from southern newspapers for a book they published in 1839, *American Slavery As It Is: Testimony of a Thousand Witnesses*. The book was an important source for author Harriet Beecher Stowe's explosive antislavery novel, *Uncle Tom's Cabin* (1852).

Angelina Grimké and her husband Theodore Weld had three children, whom Sarah helped raise because of her sister's poor health. For a while the Grimké sisters and Weld ran a successful boarding school in New Jersey before relocating to Hyde Park, Massachusetts, near Boston. Although they remained in the background of the abolition and suffrage (women's right to vote) movements the sisters never lost interest in their causes. In 1868 the Grimké sisters and Weld served as officers of the Massachusetts Woman Suffrage Association. Two years later the sisters led a group of Hyde Park women in an attempt to illegally cast ballots in a local election.

Further Reading

Birney, Catherine H. *Sarah and Angelina Grimké: The First Women Advocates of Abolition and Women's Rights*. Boston: Lee and Shepherd Publishers, 1885.

Ceplair, Larry, ed. *The Public Years of Sarah and Angelina Grimké: Selected Writings 1835–1839.* New York: Columbia University Press, 1989.

Frost, Elizabeth, and Kathryn Cullen-Dupont. *Women's Suffrage in America: An Eyewitness History.* New York: Facts on File, Inc., 1992.

Garraty, John A., and Marc C. Carnes, eds. *American National Biography.* New York: Oxford University Press, 1999.

Lerner, Gerda. *The Grimké Sisters from South Carolina: Rebels Against Slavery.* Boston: Houghton Mifflin Company, 1967.

Nies, Judith. *Seven Women: Portraits from the American Radical Tradition.* New York: The Viking Press, 1977.

Hammurabi

Birthdate unknown
Babylon
Died 1750 B.C.E.
Babylon

King of Babylonia

Hammurabi was the king of Babylonia, an empire in ancient Mesopotamia. (Mesopotamia was a region located between the Tigris and Euphrates Rivers in southwest Asia; in the Greek language, Mesopotamia means "between the rivers.") He developed a set of 282 laws called the Code of Hammurabi, which controlled nearly every aspect of Babylonian society. Several of the laws related to the ownership of slaves, who were considered the property of their masters. Nevertheless the code gave certain rights to the children of male slaves who married free-born women. Although Hammurabi was a humane and just ruler, his laws involved strict punishments of offenders in all levels of society. He is best known today for the concept of "an eye for an eye," which means the punishment should be equal to the crime.

Builds a great kingdom

Hammurabi (pronounced ham-uh-ROB-ee) was born in Babylon, a city-state that was located about fifty miles south of present-day Baghdad, Iraq, on the Euphrates River.

"... then Anu and Bel called by name me, Hammurabi, the exalted prince, who feared God, to bring about the rule of righteousness in the land, to destroy the wicked and the evil-doers; so that the strong shall not harm the weak. ...."

"Prologue," Code of Hammurabi

Hammurabi. *(Library of Congress)*

He was the son of Sin-muballit, the ruler of Babylon. Around 1792 B.C.E., Hammurabi succeeded his father to the throne. At that time larger city-states with more powerful kings surrounded Babylon. Seven years into his rule, Hammurabi started to expand his empire, which he called Babylonia (also known as the Old Babylonian Kingdom). He conquered the neighboring cities of Uruk and Isin, and then, two years later, the small country of Emutbal.

During an eighteen-year period Hammurabi ruled in relative peace. In 1764 B.C.E., however, a number of neighboring cities in the northeast formed an alliance and launched attacks on Hammurabi's kingdom. His forces easily defeated the invaders and strengthened his empire. Hammurabi then moved against an old enemy to the south, the powerful Rim-Sin of Larsa. Hammurabi emerged triumphant, and by 1762 B.C.E. the empire of Babylonia, with Babylon as its capital, included all of southern and central Mesopotamia.

Hammurabi was more than a conquering military ruler. He personally supervised the expansion and improvement of Babylonia, digging canals, building and restoring temples, and revising the calendar. Archaeologists (scientists who study the remains of ancient cultures) have discovered that the streets of Babylon were laid out in a grid pattern (straight lines that intersect at right angles), a sign that Hammurabi had planned the design of the city. They also believe that the king began building the tower of Babel, which is now identified with Etemenanki, a temple-tower in Babylon. (The famous story of the tower of Babel, a symbol of the confusion caused by people speaking many different languages, appears in the book of Genesis in the Old Testament of the Bible.)

Creates famous Code

Hammurabi's greatest achievement was forming a strong central government that established law and order in Babylonia. Greatly concerned with helping the poor and oppressed, he issued many laws and regulations that protected them. Near the end of his reign he had these laws—the Code of Hammurabi—carved into an eight-foot-tall black diorite (a type of rock somewhat like coal) column called a stele. He

The eight-foot-tall Code of Hammurabi column. The figure of Hammurabi is carved into the top of the stone; the laws are carved along the front and back of the column. *(Corbis-Bettmann. Reproduced by permission.)*

then ordered the column to be erected in Babylon so that all his subjects could read the laws.

In the twelfth century B.C.E. the Elamites (inhabitants of Elam in present-day western Iran)—Hammurabi's enemies in the northeast—conquered Babylon and took the stele to Susa (an ancient city in southwestern Iran). Discovered by French archaeologists in Iran in 1902, the column is now exhibited in the Louvre Museum in Paris, France.

At the top of the well-preserved stele is a finely sculptured scene that shows Hammurabi praying before Shamash, the Babylonian god of law and of justice. Appearing below this scene is the prologue (introductory statement), in which Hammurabi stated that he developed the code "to cause justice to prevail in the land." The laws are carved in cuneiform (pronounced KYOO-nee-uh-form; wedge-shaped characters used to represent words or ideas) under the prologue, both on the front and back of the column. (The text of laws sixty-six through ninety-nine is missing.) The code deals with a wide range of social matters: marriage, divorce, private property, wages, trade, theft, assault, slavery, and many others. Although Hammurabi's Code was not the first set of laws established in the ancient world, his emphasis on justice was an advance over previous legal systems.

"An eye for an eye"

The Code of Hammurabi had two important features. The first was the *lex talionis,* or the practice of giving a punishment equal to the crime committed. For example, law 196 states that "If a man has put out the eye of another man, they shall put out his eye." The second characteristic was the extreme harshness of the penalties, which included drowning, burning, and mutilation (cutting off of body parts).

The code reflected three basic social classes in Babylonia: *awilum* were free men (the highest class); *mushkenum* were citizens responsible to the government; and *wardum* were slaves. Punishments were given out according to one's social rank. If an awilum lost an eye, then the aggressor also lost an eye. If the injured party was a mushkenum, however, the aggressor simply had to pay the victim a fee. The aggressor paid even less if the victim was a wardum. Justice was the main concern of the code. The first law states that "If a man accuses another man of murder and it proves to be false, the accuser shall be put to death." According to the last law, "If a slave say to his master: 'You are not my master,' if they convict him his master shall cut off his ear."

Slaves are valuable property

At least twenty-two of Hammurabi's laws had to do with slaves, defining them as property and protecting the rights of their owners. In fact, slaves were so valuable that stealing a slave or harboring a runaway was punishable by death. For instance, law fifteen states that "If any one take a male or female slave of the court, or a male or female slave of a freed man, outside the city gates, he shall be put to death." The next law was equally harsh: "If any one receive into his house a runaway male or female slave of the court, or of a freedman, and does not bring it out at the public proclamation of the major domus, the master of the house shall be put to death." Law seventeen granted a good citizen a reward of two shekels (coins) of silver for returning a slave to his or her master.

Owners were compensated if a slave was injured or died. Law 199 states that "If [a person] put out the eye of a man's slave, or break the bone of a man's slave, he shall pay one-half of its value." Even doctors were responsible for the injury or death of a slave. According to law 219, "If a physician make a large incision in the slave of a freed man, and kill him, he shall replace the slave with another slave."

Barbers could also suffer stiff penalties. Before a slave was sold, a barber would carve a mark on the slave's body indicating that he or she was for sale. Law 226 stated that "If a barber, without the knowledge of his master, cut the sign of a slave on a slave not to be sold, the hands of this barber shall be cut off." The next law went on to specify, however, that "If any one deceive a barber, and have him mark a slave not for sale with the sign of a slave, he shall be put to death, and buried in his house. The barber shall swear: 'I did not mark him wittingly [knowingly],' and shall be guiltless."

Exceptions for some children

Although the Code of Hammurabi did not give slaves any rights, exceptions were made for the children of a male slave who married a free-born woman. According to law 175, "If a State slave [one owned by the government] or the slave of a freed man marry the daughter of a free man, and children are born, the master of the slave shall have no right to enslave the children of the free." In other words, a child could not be held in slavery if his or her mother was not a slave. The next law, which is more complex, made it possible for the children of a free-born woman and a slave to inherit property.

Hammurabi died around 1750 B.C.E. Shortly thereafter the Elamites attacked and defeated his son, Samsuiluna. The Babylonian Empire fell, and the capital city of Babylon was eventually burned to the ground. Hammurabi had instructed future kings to rely on his great code, but there is no historical evidence that it was ever used after his death.

Further Reading

Books

Cook, Stanley Arthur. *The Laws of Moses and the Code of Hammurabi.* A. and C. Black, 1903.

Knapp, A. B. *The History and Culture of Ancient Western Asia and Egypt.* Dorsey Press, 1988.

Oates, J. *Babylon.* Thames & Hudson, 1979.

Saggs, H. W. F. *Civilization Before Greece and Rome.* New Haven, Conn.: Yale University Press, 1989.

Web sites

King, L. W., translator. "Hammurabi's Code of Laws," in *Exploring Ancient World Cultures.* [Online] http://eawc.evansville.edu/anthology/hammurabi.html/ (accessed on September 6, 1999).

Sally Hemings

Born 1773
Bermuda Hundred, Virginia
Died 1835
Charlottesville, Virginia

American mulatto slave

The general story of the life of Sally Hemings—a mulatto (a person of mixed black and white ancestry) slave who served her master as a domestic servant and possibly his concubine (mistress)—was not all that unusual in late-eighteenth- and early-nineteenth-century United States. What makes Sally Hemings's tale especially interesting is that her white master, and some argue, the likely father of her seven children, was Thomas Jefferson (1743–1826), the third president of the United States (1801–1809). Hemings's relationship with Jefferson probably began sometime in 1788, when the two of them were in Paris, France, and lasted until his death in 1826.

The relationship between Thomas Jefferson and Sally Hemings has caused controversy and debate among their descendants—as well as historians and scholars—for almost two hundred years.

Hemings's early years

Although she was three-fourths white, Sally Hemings was born a slave. In colonial America, the status of the mother—free or slave—determined the status of the child. Sally Hemings's father, John Wayles, was white but her mother, Elizabeth Hemings, was a mulatto slave, the child of a white father (Captain Hemings) and a full-blooded African mother (a slave owned by John Wayles). Elizabeth Hemings was John Wayles's slave from birth, and after the death of Wayles's wife, she became his concubine. Together they had six children: Robert, James, Peter, Critty, Sally, and Thena.

John Wayles died in 1773, the same year that his illegitimate (out of wedlock) daughter Sally was born. Sally Hemings, her mother, and her five siblings (along with about 125 other slaves and 11,000 acres of land), were inherited at that time by John Wayles's legitimate daughter, Martha. At the time, Martha Wayles was the wife of Thomas Jefferson (a wealthy Virginia planter and statesman). Sally Hemings was Martha Wayles Jefferson's half-sister, both having been fathered by the same man.

The Hemings were brought to Monticello (pronounced mon-teh-CHELL-oh), Thomas Jefferson's Virginia farming estate, and given the privileged position of house slaves. James Hemings, Sally's older brother, became Thomas Jefferson's personal servant.

Jefferson and Hemings in Paris

In September of 1782, Martha Jefferson died, leaving Thomas Jefferson a widower at the age of thirty-nine, and the father of two girls, Martha (about to turn ten years old) and Maria (four years old). In 1784 Thomas Jefferson was sent as a diplomat to France by the American colonial government. James Hemings went with him. Jefferson's eldest daughter Martha joined him in Paris a short time later, and was enrolled in a convent school for a formal education. In 1787 Jefferson sent for his other daughter, Maria, who made the voyage from Virginia escorted by Sally Hemings, who was either fourteen or fifteen at the time.

It is impossible for historians to say with any certainty exactly what happened in Paris between Thomas Jefferson and Sally Hemings. Legally, Sally Hemings was a free person in Paris, and so was her brother James, as slavery had been abolished in France. While in France, Jefferson paid Sally and James a monthly salary for their services. James Hemings, with Jefferson's support, apprenticed under French cooks and became a skilled chef.

One historical witness

In the fall of 1789, Jefferson and his two daughters, as well as Sally and James Hemings, returned to America. By all accounts, Sally Hemings was visibly pregnant at the time of their homecoming to Monticello. Many years later, in 1873, Madison Hemings (1805-77), the sixth child of Sally Hemings, described the circumstances of his mother's return from Paris. His account was published in the *Pike County Republican,* a newspaper in Ohio.

Madison Hemings grew up at Monticello and after Jefferson's death in 1826, he and his younger brother, Eston, rented a house in a nearby county where they lived with their mother, Sally, until her death in 1835. Madison is considered the most important historical witness in this story by some, but others point to minor errors and inconsistencies in his rendering of the facts. The following excerpt from Madison's published story sheds light on his mother's trip to France and its result:

Thomas Jefferson holding the Declaration of Independence. *(Library of Congress)*

Their stay (my mother's and Maria's) was just about eighteen months [it was really twenty-six months]. But during that time my mother became Mr. Jefferson's concubine, and when he was called back home she was *enciente* [pregnant] by him. He desired to bring my mother back to Virginia with him but she demurred. She was just beginning to understand the French language well, and in France she was free, while if she returned to Virginia she would be re-enslaved. So she refused to return with him. To induce her to do so, he promised her extraordinary privileges, and made a solemn pledge that her children should be freed at the age of twenty-one years. In consequence of his promises, on which she implicitly relied, she returned with him to Virginia. Soon after their arrival, she gave birth to a child, of whom Thomas Jefferson was the father.

Promises kept

Between 1790 and 1808, Sally Hemings gave birth to seven children, all the time while residing at Monticello: Thomas, Harriet, Edy, Beverly, Harriet, Madison, and Eston. Hemings's firstborn took the name Thomas Woodson and is conspicuously absent from Jefferson's personal records. He was born in 1790, shortly after Hemings and Jefferson returned from France. Thomas Woodson was probably gone from Monticello by the time Madison was born in 1805, although the age of his departure is unknown. Hemings's second child, Harriet, was born in 1795 but only lived two years. Edy was born in 1796 and died in her infancy. Hemings's second son, Beverly, was born in 1798, followed by Harriet in 1801, Madison in 1805, and Eston in 1808.

Harriet and Beverly were listed as "runaways" in Thomas Jefferson's personal records from 1822. The reality was that they were allowed to walk away and, because of their light-colored skin, blend into the free white world of Washington, D.C. Madison and Eston were freed in Jefferson's will at his death in 1826. Sally Hemings was not mentioned in Jefferson's will, and a year later was listed on the official slave inventory as worth $50. Jefferson's daughter, Martha, freed Sally Hemings, who spent her remaining years living in a rented house with her sons Madison and Eston.

A 200-year debate

The public first learned of Sally Hemings in 1802, during the second year of Jefferson's first term as president, when the *Richmond Recorder* published an article that contained the following: "It is well known that the man, whom it delighteth the people to honor, keeps and for many years has kept, as his concubine, one of his slaves. Her name is Sally. The name of her eldest son is Tom. His features are said to bear a striking though sable resemblance to those of the president himself. . . . By this wench Sally, our president has had several children."

The possibility that one of America's founding fathers had a long-term sexual relationship with one of his slaves that resulted in the births of several children caused great controversy in 1802. At the time, the charge against Jefferson was neither proven true nor false. Jefferson himself never denied or confirmed the relationship. The result was that the question has been debated by historians and scholars ever since.

Until recently many historians argued, supported by the claims of some of Jefferson's white descendants, that Thomas Jefferson could not have fathered Hemings's children because he wasn't around when conception must have taken place. On the other side, descendants of Sally Hemings have claimed from the very beginning that Thomas Jefferson was the father of all of her children. They based their arguments on a well-kept oral family history, and an 1873 memoir written by one of Hemings's seven children, Madison Hemings.

Historians have more recently acknowledged that Jefferson, who traveled widely and often, was present at his Virginia plantation home, Monticello, eight or nine months before the birth of all but one of Hemings's children. That child, Thomas Woodson, was conceived when Jefferson was minister to France and Sally Hemings was living with him in Paris.

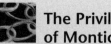

The Privileged Slaves of Monticello

Life at Monticello (Jefferson's plantation) for the Hemings family is best described by Madison Hemings (Sally Hemings's sixth child) in his 1873 memoir:

> My brothers, sister Harriet and myself were used alike. They were put to some mechanical trade at age fourteen. Till then we were permitted to stay about the 'great house,' and only required to do such light work as going on errands. Harriet learned to spin and weave in a little factory on the home plantation. We were free from the dread of having to be slaves all our lives long, and were measurably happy. We were always permitted to be with our mother, who was well used. It was her duty, all her life which I can remember, up to the time of our father's death, to take care of his [Jefferson's] chamber and wardrobe, look after us children and do such light work as sewing, &c. Provision was made in the will of our father that we should be free when we arrived at the age of 21 years.

Science muddies the waters

For some, the results of a 1998 DNA test on known descendants of both Jefferson and Hemings adds great weight to the historical evidence for a Jefferson-Hemings connection. The purpose of the study was to compare Jefferson's Y chromosome—a genetic marker passed from father to son—with those of Hemings's family to see if there was a match. Since Jefferson had no adult sons, the blood from a descendant of one of his male cousins, who would have had the same Y chromosome as their mutual grandfather, was used for the study. From the Hemings side, blood samples were tested from the descendants of two of Hemings's children, Thomas Woodson, the first born, and Eston Hemings, the last born.

The results showed a definite Jefferson-Hemings genetic link, only instead of providing a clear answer to the question, the scientific evidence further complicated the debate. First, the DNA tests found a genetic match between Jefferson and Eston Hemings, but not between Jefferson and Thomas Woodson. This finding has disappointed the descendants of Thomas Woodson, who have a very detailed oral family history that claims otherwise. Second, the test only confirms that *a Jefferson,* not necessarily *Thomas* Jefferson, fathered a child with Sally Hemings (other possible Jefferson candidates include his brother, Randolph, and his two sons, who both spent some time at Monticello).

Obviously, more tests are going to be needed before any definitive scientific findings can prove Jefferson's paternity one way or another. Historians and scholars, and descendants of both Jefferson and Hemings, will continue to debate the issue for years to come. Meanwhile, the Thomas Jefferson Memorial Foundation, which runs tours of Jefferson's Monticello plantation, have adjusted their version of what their guides tell visitors about the Jefferson-Hemings controversy. Within twenty-four hours of the release of the study results, according to the foundation's director, "guides were telling visitors that new DNA evidence indicated a sexual relationship between Sally Hemings and Jefferson."

Further Reading

Books

Brodie, Fawn M. *Thomas Jefferson: An Intimate History.* New York: W. W. Norton & Co., 1974

Encyclopedia of African-American Culture and History. New York: Macmillan Library Reference, 1996.

Gordon-Reed, Annette. *Thomas Jefferson and Sally Hemings: An American Controversy.* Charlottesville, VA: University of Virginia Press, 1997.

Smith, Page. *Jefferson: A Revealing Biography.* New York: American Heritage Publishing Co., Inc., 1976.

Periodicals

Ellis, Joseph J. "When a Saint Becomes a Sinner." *U.S. News & World Report,* November 9, 1998.

Lord, Lewis. "The Tom-and-Sally Miniseries (cont.)" *U.S. News & World Report,* January 18, 1999.

Marshall, Eliot. "Which Jefferson Was the Father?" *Science,* January 8, 1999.

Randolph, Laura B. "The Thomas Jefferson/Sally Hemings Controversy." *Ebony,* February 1999.

Harriet Ann Jacobs

Born autumn 1813
Edenton, North Carolina
Died March 7, 1897
Washington, D.C.

Slave, fugitive in the South and North, freed slave,
writer, antislavery activist, reformer

The story of Harriet Jacobs's life as a slave in the nineteenth-century United States, from her birth in 1813 to her freedom in 1852, was published in 1861 as *Incidents in the Life of a Slave Girl: Written by Herself*. Although the Civil War (1861–65) was about to begin and many slave narratives had already been published, *Incidents* was the first full-length autobiography published by an African American woman in the United States. It was also the only slave narrative that took as its subject the sexual exploitation of female slaves; and the only slave narrative that identified its targeted audience as female.

Jacobs's first-person slave narrative strengthened the antislavery cause with its comprehensive depiction of a slave woman's desperate struggle for freedom, her battles against sexual oppression, and her fight to protect her children and maintain her role as mother of a family.

Making the private public

Writing about her own private sexual history was not easy for Jacobs. She felt, however, that by telling her story in the public arena, the issue of sexual abuse of female slaves would become part of the country's political debate about slavery. Jacobs also felt that even though society's notions of acceptable sexual behavior for single women did not apply to slave women (Jacobs herself had two children out of wedlock

Harriet Ann Jacobs.

with a white man), they were still entitled to sympathy for the unwanted sexual advances from their white masters.

"Slavery is terrible for men; but it is far more terrible for women," Jacobs writes in *Incidents*. "I have not written my experiences in order to attract attention to myself. . . . Neither do I care to excite sympathy for my own sufferings. But I do earnestly desire to arouse the women of the North to a realizing sense of the condition of two millions of women at the South, still in bondage, suffering what I suffered, and most of them far worse.

In *Incidents,* Jacobs writes her story in the first-person narrative style but she changes the names of her characters, including herself, whom she refers to as Linda Brent. Although the names of characters and places have been changed to spare innocent people possible embarrassment, Jacobs tells readers in the preface to her book: "Reader, be assured this narrative is no fiction."

Fond memories

As her story is told in *Incidents,* Jacobs was born a slave in Edenton, a small town in North Carolina. Both of her parents were mulattoes (people of mixed black and white ancestry). Her father, Daniel Jacobs, was a carpenter and the slave of Dr. Andrew Knox. Daniel Jacobs had a fairly rare arrangement with his master. As long as he paid a yearly fee to Dr. Knox he was allowed to work at his trade and manage his own affairs. Harriet Jacobs's mother, Delilah Horniblower, was owned by Margaret Horniblower and worked as her household servant.

Jacobs lived with both her parents (they were unmarried, as it was against the law for slaves to marry) in a comfortable home for the first six years of her life. Jacobs's maternal grandmother, Molly Horniblower, lived nearby. "Though we were all slaves," Jacobs writes, "I was so fondly shielded that I never dreamed that I was a piece of merchandise, trusted to them for safe keeping, and liable to be demanded of them at any moment." When her mother died in 1819, Jacobs was taken to live with her mother's mistress, Margaret Horniblower, who taught her how to read, spell, and sew.

The real world

When Margaret Horniblower died in July 1825, she willed Jacobs and her ten-year-old brother, John S. Jacobs, to her niece, Mary Matilda Norcom. Since Mary Matilda was only three years old, Jacobs and her brother came under the control of their mistress's father, Dr. James Norcom. After just a few weeks with her new masters, Jacobs heard the cries of one of Dr. Norcom's slaves—who was brought to town from the doctor's rural plantation—as he was beaten by his master. "Never before, in my life, had I heard hundreds of blows fall, in succession, on a human being," she writes in *Incidents*. "His piteous groans, and his 'O, pray don't, massa,' rang in my ear for months afterwards."

When Jacobs was fifteen, Dr. Norcom began to sexually harass her, constantly pressuring her to have sexual relations with him. "My master began to whisper foul words in my ear," she writes in *Incidents*. "Young as I was, I could not remain ignorant of their import . . . I turned from him with disgust and hatred. But he was my master . . . . He told me I was his property; and that I must subject to his will in all things."

LETTERS FROM A SLAVE GIRL

THE STORY OF HARRIET JACOBS

Can Harriet create her own life within the bounds of slavery?

BY MARY E. LYONS

This 1992 work, based on a true story, describes Harriet Jacobs's ordeals as she attempts to win her freedom. *(Cover illustration ©1992 by Todd L.W. Doney. Reproduced by permission of Todd L.W. Doney)*

War of wills

Dr. Norcom was set on having his way with Jacobs, and she, in turn was set on refusing his advances. When Dr. Norcom learned that Jacobs was in love with—and wanted to marry—a free-born black man whom she had met at her grandmother's house, he struck her and threatened to have her thrown in jail. (Slaves could not legally marry but a free-born black could marry a slave with a master's permission.) Fearing for her lover's safety due to threats from her master, Jacobs encouraged him to move north where she hoped to join him later.

To get back at Dr. Norcom for making her life so miserable, Jacobs engaged in a sexual relationship with Norcom's white neighbor, Samuel Sawyer, a lawyer. Jacobs gave birth to two children by Sawyer, Joseph in 1829 and Louisa Matilda in 1833. "I knew nothing would enrage Dr. Flint [Dr. Norcom] so much as to know that I favored another," she writes in *Incidents*, "and it was something to triumph over my tyrant even in that small way."

Enraged, but still persistent, in 1835 Dr. Norcom threatened to send Jacobs to work as a field slave on his plantation if she did not become his concubine (mistress). She refused to give in and was sent to Auburn (the name of his plantation), a few miles outside of town. When Jacobs learned that Dr. Norcom planned to move her children from her grandmother's house, where they had been living, to Auburn to be "broken in," she set in motion a series of events that would eventually lead to her escape to the North and freedom for her children.

Saving her children

Believing that she could save her children from plantation slavery, in June 1835 Jacobs ran away from Auburn and was temporarily sheltered by black and white friends. In August, after hiding in a swamp for several days, Jacobs secretly moved into a tiny crawlspace above a storeroom in her grandmother's house where she hid for nearly seven years.

Jacobs's trick was successful. Dr. Norcom looked everywhere for her. He even posted a $100 reward for her capture. Jacobs chose the cramped quarters of her grandmother's storeroom attic over her master's bed, and as a result, Dr. Norcom lost interest in her children and sold them to their father, Samuel Sawyer. Sawyer allowed the children to continue to live with their grandmother. While in hiding, Jacobs sewed, practiced writing, and read—mostly the Bible.

Reward: $100

When Harriet Jacobs was twenty-one years old she disappeared from the plantation of her owner, Dr. James Norcom. For seven years Jacobs hid in her grandmother's attic to escape her cruel master. Dr. Norcom, thinking she had fled to the North, placed an advertisement in the newspaper offering a reward for the return of his missing slave, which read as follows:

$100 REWARD . . . Will be given for the apprehension and delivery of my Servant Girl HARRIET . . . She is a light mulatto, 21 years of age, about 5 feet 4 inches high, of a thick and corpulent habit, having on her head a thick covering of black hair that curls naturally, but which can be combed straight. She speaks easily and fluidly and has an agreeable carriage and address. Being a good seamstress, she has been accustomed to dress well, has a variety of very fine clothes, made in the prevailing fashion, and will probably appear, if abroad, tricked out in gay and fashionable finery. As this girl absconded from the plantation of my son without any known cause or provocation, it is probable she designs to transport herself to the North.

The above reward, with all reasonable charges, will be given for apprehending her, or securing her in any prison or jail within the U. States.

All persons are hereby forewarned against harboring or entertaining her, or being in any way instrumental in her escape, under the most rigorous penalties of the law.

Fugitive in the North

In 1842, with the aid of family and friends, Jacobs escaped to the North. She first went to Philadelphia, Pennsylvania, then New York City, where she found work as a nursemaid with the Willis family. In New York, Jacobs met up with her daughter, Louisa Matilda, who had earlier been brought north by Sawyer. With slave catchers (people who were paid to capture fugitive slaves) hired by Dr. Norcom on her trail, in 1843 Jacobs fled briefly to Boston, Massachussetts, where she arranged for her son, Joseph, to be sent from her grandmother's Edenton home.

Jacobs returned to New York, and after another close call with slave catchers, in October 1844 fled with her daughter and settled in Boston, where she worked as a seamstress. In the spring of 1845 Mrs. Willis died, and Jacobs traveled to England with Mr. Willis as a nurse for their child,

Imogen. Back in New York in 1846, Jacobs learned that her son had fled his job as a printer's apprentice and had shipped out to sea.

After enrolling her daughter in a boarding school in Clinton, New York, in 1849 Jacobs moved to Rochester, New York, to join her brother, John Jacobs, a fugitive slave now lecturing for the abolitionist movement. Harriet Jacobs lived for a while with Quaker reformers, Isaac and Amy Post. Amy Post was a participant in the first Women's Rights Convention at Seneca Falls in 1848, and an abolitionist. Jacobs worked in the Anti-Slavery Office and Reading Room, located above the offices of Frederick Douglass's (1817–95) abolitionist newspaper, the *North Star*.

Free to write

In 1850 Congress passed the Fugitive Slave Law, making all citizens subject to fines or punishment for harboring fugitive slaves—even in states where slavery had been abolished. Under the provisions of the new law, Mary Matilda Norcom (now an adult) and her husband, Daniel Messmore, traveled to New York repeatedly to seize Jacobs and her children. Jacobs, who had returned to New York City to take a job with Mr. Willis and his new wife, Cornelia Willis, again went into hiding in Massachusetts. With help from the American Colonization Society, in 1852 Cornelia Willis arranged to buy Jacobs from the Messmores for $300, and at the same time gained assurances for Jacobs of the safety of her children (who had been legally sold to Sawyer).

Freed at last, in 1853 Jacobs moved with the Willis family to Idlewild (an eighteen-room estate) in Cornwall, New York, where she worked during the day and wrote at night. Jacobs, who had maintained her connections to the organized antislavery movement, was encouraged to write her life story by one of her abolitionist friends. Jacobs sought help for the task from writer and abolitionist Harriet Beecher Stowe (1811–96) who, in 1852, had authored the best-selling antislavery novel, *Uncle Tom's Cabin*. Stowe refused, so Jacobs decided to write her own story.

Author, activist, and reformer

Jacobs finished the manuscript for *Incidents* in 1858. She tried unsuccessfully for several years to get the book into print. Finally, in early 1861, after a Boston book publisher went bankrupt on the eve of publishing her book, Jacobs somehow obtained the funds to have her book printed. The book (which received good reviews), and Jacobs, became well known among abolitionists. A year later, the British edition of Jacobs's book was published in London under the title *The Deeper Wrong; Or, Incidents in the Life of a Slave Girl.*

Historians have traced Jacobs's life after the publication of *Incidents*. In 1863, during the Civil War (1861–65), Jacobs's work was sponsored by the Philadelphia and New York Quakers in Alexandria, Virginia, where she distributed clothing, taught classes, and provided health care to war refugees. After the war, Jacobs and her daughter moved to Savannah, Georgia, to do relief work. Jacobs abandoned her plans to build an orphanage in Savannah, and in 1870 moved to Cambridge, Massachusetts, where she ran a boarding house. In 1885 Jacobs and her daughter moved to Washington, D.C., where she lived until March 7, 1897.

Further Reading

Encyclopedia of African-American Culture and History. New York: Macmillan Library Reference, 1996.

Gates, Henry Louis, Jr. *The Classic Slave Narratives.* New York: Penguin, 1987.

Starling, Marion Wilson. *The Slave Narrative: Its Place in American History.* Boston, Mass.: G. K. Hall and Co., 1981.

Yellin, Jean Fagan. "Text and Contexts of Harriet Jacobs' *Incidents in the Life of a Slave Girl: Written by Herself.*" In Charles T. Davis and Henry Louis Gates, Jr., eds. *The Slave's Narrative.* New York: Oxford University Press, 1985, pp. 262–82.

Yellin, Jean Fagan. Introduction to *Incidents in the Life of a Slave Girl: Written by Herself,* by Harriet Jacobs. Cambridge, Mass.: Harvard University Press, 1987.

Haksun Kim

Born 1924
Manchuria, China

Comfort woman (prostitute)
for the Japanese military

Haksun Kim was one of an estimated 200,000 women who were forced into sexual slavery by the Japanese military during its Fifteen Year War on eastern Asia (1930–45). The story of Kim's tragic life as a Korean "comfort woman" was originally published in Korea in a 1993 book, *The Korean Comfort Women Who Were Coercively Dragged Away for the Military*. It is one of nineteen life stories that were collected and published by the Korean Council for Women Drafted for Military Sexual Slavery by Japan. Kim relates her abduction and enslavement by the Japanese military in a chapter of the English version of the book (*True Stories of the Korean Comfort Women*), "Bitter Memories I Am Loath To Recall."

One of the first Korean comfort women to publicly tell her story of being forced to serve as a prostitute for the Japanese military in Asia during World War II.

Early years in Korea

Haksun Kim was born in 1924 to Korean parents living in China (who were there to escape the Japanese occupation of their country). When Kim was three months old her father died. Two years later Kim returned with her mother to Pyongyang, a village in present-day North Korea. Kim's newly

Haksun Kim.

widowed mother was at first forced to beg from her brothers and sisters in order to survive. Eventually she found work as a domestic servant, a farmhand, a washerwoman, and a sock-maker.

Kim and her mother were very poor but Kim remembers her early years as happy ones. She regularly attended church with her mother, and from age seven to eleven attended a missionary school run by the church. There she recalls enjoying her lessons, sports, and playing with friends. After school Kim often went home and helped her mother knit woolen socks on a rented knitting machine.

Kim's mother remarried in 1938 when Kim was fourteen. Kim did not get along very well with her stepfather. When she was fifteen she was sent as a foster child to a family that trained *kisaeng* (girls who entertain men by singing and dancing). Kim sang for an audition; then her mother received money from the foster father and made a contract that Kim would stay with the foster family for a number of years.

Abducted by the military

For two years Kim attended classes with three hundred other pupils, including another girl who lived with her foster family. They learned how to dance, to sing, and to tell epic stories through song. Kim was seventeen when she graduated but could not obtain a license as a *kisaeng* until she was nineteen. Unable to make money from his foster children in Korea, Kim's foster father decided to take his two foster children north to China to find work.

The year was 1941, however, and a dangerous time to be Korean and traveling in East Asia. The Japanese Imperial Army, seeking to establish an empire for the island of Japan on mainland Asia, occupied Korea and much of eastern China. The travelers were detained for hours at the Korean border for questioning by the Japanese military police. Finally, they were allowed to board a train to Beijing, China.

When they reached the city they went to a restaurant for lunch. There they were confronted by a Japanese military officer who accused them of being spies because they were

Korean. The officer led Kim's foster father away and other soldiers forced Kim and her foster sister into a truck loaded with about fifty soldiers. Terrified and in shock, the two girls crouched in the corner of the truck and wept as they were driven for hours to an abandoned house. There Kim and her foster sister were each raped by a Japanese officer, one of whom was the man who had abducted the two from Beijing.

Comfort women

Thus Kim began her life as a comfort woman—one of an estimated 200,000 women who were forced to sexually serve the Japanese military from 1930 to 1945. Like Kim, as many as eighty percent of the comfort women were Korean; their ages ranged from eleven to thirty-two. And like Kim, most came from very poor families. Kim found herself a prisoner in what was known as a comfort station. She was given a bed and some food, and forced to service as many as eight Japanese soldiers in a day. She also had to clean, cook, and wash clothes.

Kim had been abducted into slavery directly by the Japanese military. Many other comfort women were tricked into service by false promises of employment in Japan. Sometimes civilians were involved but it was mostly soldiers and the military police that recruited comfort women, with the military controlling the operation and providing the trucks or boats for transport of the women captives to comfort stations.

Sexual slavery

Haksun Kim spent four months as a sex slave for the Japanese military before she managed to escape. For the first three months she lived at a Chinese village called Tiebizhen; she spent another month at a remote countryside location. In the first comfort station, Kim, at seventeen, was the youngest of five women. All were Koreans who were given Japanese names. Kim was renamed Aiko; her foster sister, Emiko. Because of her age Kim was given more washing and cooking to do than the others, and because they were new, the other women sent the roughest and most violent soldiers to Kim and Emiko.

How a Comfort Station Operated

The Japanese military began setting up comfort stations for their soldiers as their armies advanced on the Asian mainland in the early 1930s. They saw them as necessary for the morale of their soldiers and as a way to control the spread of sexually-transmitted diseases by forbidding their soldiers access to civilian brothels (houses of prostitution). The Japanese also saw them as a way of limiting the violence and rapes randomly committed by their occupying forces against the civilian (non-military) population. To that end, the Japanese military imported Korean women as sex slaves throughout the areas of Japanese military campaigns, from Siberia to the South Pacific.

Comfort stations were strictly for the use of soldiers, although they were sometimes run by civilians, who then paid a fee to the military authorities. The hours for visitation and fees paid by the soldiers were fixed by army regulations and posted at each comfort station. Officers were charged more than the rank and file soldier, and in some comfort stations, they were serviced exclusively by Japanese comfort women. Sometimes the fees were set according to the nationality of the women: a Japanese woman would receive 2 yen, a Korean 1.5 yen, and a Chinese 1 yen. (Yen is the basic currency of Japan.) The soldiers paid in cash or in tickets, which the women had to turn over to the managers of the stations. More often than not the fees were paid directly to the managers and the women never saw any money at all.

In an attempt to curb the spread of sexually-transmitted diseases, the military authorities ordered soldiers to use condoms that were supplied to them by the army (in some cases comfort women were also given a supply of condoms). Surviving comfort women reported that some soldiers refused to use protection. Regular medical checkups of the women for sexually-transmitted diseases were also part of official regulations dictated by the military.

Kim had to be available for the soldiers at whatever hours—and in whatever condition—they were given permission to show up. Usually soldiers would visit in the afternoon but sometimes they would arrive early in the morning after returning from a nighttime expedition, or in the evening, drunk and rowdy. Although violence against the women was officially forbidden, Kim and other surviving comfort women reported that they were frequently treated roughly and threatened with beatings if they refused a soldier's sexual demands.

In spite of strict controls, sexually-transmitted diseases were common. When a woman was found to be infected she received an injection and did not serve soldiers for a few days. Medical records of comfort women show that many had to be hospitalized for more serious infections. Women suffered other ailments as well, such as malaria, jaundice, mental disorders, and vaginal swelling; many suffered with lifelong health problems as a consequence.

A miraculous escape

After three months at the Tiebizhen comfort station, the soldiers moved to a new location deep in the countryside, taking Kim and the other comfort women with them. Kim's life continued as before except there were fewer soldiers and fewer disease examinations by the military doctor. Kim had thought about escape from the first day of her captivity but the Tiebizhen comfort station was next to the army base and so well guarded that it was impossible for her to attempt it.

After a month in the new house, a Korean man visited Kim in her room. With the soldiers away on an expedition, the man somehow sneaked past the guard as no one but Japanese soldiers were allowed inside the comfort station. Kim threatened to scream if the man did not take her when he left, and at about two o'clock in the morning the two managed to miraculously escape the grounds undetected. The couple traveled all over China posing as husband and wife. According to Kim, the man knew the country's every nook and cranny and was most likely a dealer of opium (an addictive drug derived from a variety of poppy) for the Chinese.

Kim became pregnant in the winter of 1942 and the couple settled in the French judicial district in Shanghai. On September 20, 1943, Kim gave birth to a girl and in 1945, at age 21, she gave birth to a boy. The couple ran a pawn shop, and with help from a Chinese investor, acted as moneylenders.

Return to Korea

In 1945, at the end of World War II (1939–45), Kim returned to a liberated Korea with her "husband" and children

In 1994, former South Korean comfort women, including Haksun Kim (left), staged a 33-hour hunger strike demanding compensation from the Japanese government for their suffering during World War II. *(AP/Wide World Photos. Reproduced by permission.)*

on board a ship loaded with fellow refugees and Liberation Army soldiers. An outbreak of cholera forced the boat's passengers into a refugee camp where Kim's daughter died of the disease. The family eventually settled near Seoul, the capital of South Korea, where Kim sold vegetables and her husband worked in construction, and then as a deliveryman for the military. After the end of the Korean War (1950–53) in 1953, Kim's husband was killed in an accident. Tragedy continued to haunt Kim when she took her son, a fourth-grade student, to the sea for a summer vacation. He suffered a heart attack and died while swimming.

In 1961 Kim moved away from Seoul to the Cholla province where she says for twenty years she performed odd jobs and drank and smoked away her earnings. Kim tried to commit suicide a number of times before finally returning to Seoul. With the help of a friend she found steady work until 1987, when she retired with the money she had saved over the years.

Breaking the silence

For years Kim, as well as the thousands of other surviving comfort women in Korea, lived in silence and shame. Despite the widespread knowledge in Korea after World War II about comfort women, little was done to seek prosecution of the perpetrators or reparations (compensation) for the victims. Part of the problem was that comfort women were afraid to go public with their stories due to the shame that they and their families would endure in a society that so highly values female purity.

It wasn't until August 1991 that Kim became one of the first of many surviving comfort women to report her story to the public through the Korean Council for Women Drafted for Military Sexual Slavery by Japan. In December 1991, Kim was one of three South Korean comfort women to file a lawsuit—on behalf of all comfort women—in Tokyo District Court against the Japanese government. The lawsuit demanded twenty million yen in damages.

After many years of silence, the Japanese government finally admitted in 1993 that the Imperial army was involved in setting up and running wartime brothels, and forcibly kidnapping women into sexual slavery. Japan, however, has refused to pay any direct compensation to the victimized women, arguing that postwar treaties settled all wartime claims. Instead it has set up a private fund to compensate former Korean comfort women. From 1996 to 1998, the Asia Peace National Fund for Women distributed around $72,000 to qualified recipients.

Further Reading

Chin Sung Chung. "Korean Women Drafted for Military Sexual Slavery by Japan." In *True Stories of the Korean Comfort Women,* edited by Howard Keith. London: Cassell, 1995.

Hicks, George. *The Comfort Women.* St. Leonards, Australia: Allen & Unwin, 1995.

Howard, Keith. "A Korean Tragedy." In *True Stories of the Korean Comfort Women,* edited by Howard Keith. London: Cassell, 1995.

Kim, Haksun. "Bitter Memories I Am Loath To Recall." In *True Stories of the Korean Comfort Women,* edited by Howard Keith. London: Cassell, 1995.

Abraham Lincoln

Born February 12, 1809
Hardin County, Kentucky (near Hodgeville, Kentucky)
Died April 15, 1865
Washington, D.C.

U.S. President

In 1863, during the height of the American Civil War (1861–65), sixteenth president of the United States Abraham Lincoln issued the Emancipation Proclamation, a presidential order that granted freedom to slaves held in Confederate (southern) states. Hailed as the "Great Emancipator," Lincoln set in motion the turning point that ultimately ended the bloodiest conflict in American history. He did not live, however, to see the reconciliation of a divided nation. In 1865, five days after the Confederate surrender, Lincoln became the first U.S. president to be assassinated. He has since become a legendary figure not only in the United States but throughout the world. His story—the rise from humble frontiersman to one of the greatest presidents in U.S. history—is now regarded as a symbol of democracy.

Rises from humble origins

Abraham Lincoln was born in a log cabin in the backwoods of Hardin County, Kentucky, on February 12, 1809. His parents, Thomas Lincoln and Nancy Hanks Lincoln, were

" . . . I do order and declare that all persons held as slaves within said designated States, and parts of States, are, and hence forward shall be free; and that the Executive government of the United States, including the military and naval authorities thereof, will recognize and maintain the freedom of said persons."

Abraham Lincoln, The Emancipation Proclamation

Abraham Lincoln. *(Library of Congress)*

poor, illiterate farmers. He had a sister, Sarah; his brother Thomas died in infancy. In 1816 the family moved to southwestern Indiana.

Abraham was especially close to his mother, and he was grief-stricken when she died in 1818. About a year later his father married Sarah Bush Johnston, a widow with three children, whom Abraham called his "angel mother." Since Thomas thought his son would become a farmer, Abraham received less than a year of formal schooling. His stepmother encouraged him to educate himself, however, so he read and reread a few books, such as a biography of George Washington, *Pilgrim's Progress* by English writer John Bunyan (1628–88), and *Fables* by the ancient Greek poet Aesop.

After his sister's death in 1828, Lincoln joined a flatboat expedition down the Mississippi River. In 1831, after his family had resettled in Illinois, he volunteered in the state militia (citizen army) to fight Native Americans in a conflict known as the Black Hawk War. Although Lincoln never participated in battle, he was elected captain by his company. He left the militia in 1832, moved to New Salem, Illinois, and worked at a variety of jobs, including general store owner, town postmaster, and surveyor (one who measures the geographic features of land).

In 1834, as a member of the Whig Party (a political group that supported the power of Congress over the president), Lincoln was elected four times to the Illinois state legislature, serving until 1841. During his first term he taught himself law and earned his license to practice as an attorney in 1836. The following year he relocated to Springfield, the capital of Illinois, and traveled throughout the state trying court cases. Lincoln proved to be a successful lawyer, eventually earning $1,200 to $1,500 a year (a sizable sum in those days). On November 4, 1842, he married Mary Todd, and over the next eleven years they had four sons: Robert, Edward, William, and Thomas, who was nicknamed Tad (only Robert survived into adulthood).

Forms views on slavery

Lincoln began forming his views on slavery after an event that occurred during his second term in the legislature.

In 1837 Elijah Lovejoy, an abolitionist newspaperman in Alton, Illinois, was hanged by a mob. Several legislators then introduced resolutions that condemned abolitionist groups (groups that opposed slavery) and upheld the right of southern states to practice slavery. Refusing to support these resolutions, Lincoln and one of his colleagues issued a protest in which they stated that slavery was based on "injustice and bad policy."

Lincoln was elected to the U.S. House of Representatives (one of two branches of Congress, the legislative body of the U.S. government) in 1847, but he accomplished very little and served only a single term. A disappointed Lincoln returned to Springfield, vowing to stay out of politics. The growing issue of slavery in America, however, soon pulled him back.

In 1820 Congress had passed the Missouri Compromise, which permitted Missouri to be admitted as a slave state while banning slavery in the remaining northern portions of the Louisiana Purchase (territory west of the Mississippi River acquired from France by the United States in 1803). The compromise was overturned when Congress passed the Kansas-Nebraska Act in 1854. Sponsored by Illinois senator Stephen A. Douglas (1813–61), the act allowed settlers in the new territories of Kansas and Nebraska to reject or allow slavery. Angered over the possible spread of slavery, Lincoln ran unsuccessfully for the U.S. Senate (the second, and highest, legislative branch of the U.S. government) in 1851.

"A house divided against itself"

A group of people who opposed the Kansas-Nebraska Act formed the Republican Party in 1854. Identifying with the Republican position, Lincoln joined the party in 1856 and quickly became a leader. When Douglas, a member of the Democratic Party, ran for re-election as U.S. senator from Illinois in 1858, the Republicans nominated Lincoln to run against him. The two men then engaged in a series of seven debates at various locations throughout the state. Their fiery discussions drew large crowds and national press coverage. Neither Lincoln nor Douglas was an abolitionist, but both opposed slavery. They differed, however, on the question of whether slavery should be permitted in the new territories.

Douglas did not believe there was a need for special legislation to prevent the expansion of slavery in the West. His reason was that the land in the West was poor and would not support crops, such as cotton, that traditionally supported a slave economy. Lincoln disagreed, making the famous speech in which he warned that the United States was in danger of splitting in two over the issue of slavery. "A house divided against itself cannot stand," he declared. "I believe the government cannot endure permanently half slave or half free." Nevertheless, Lincoln did not advocate totally abolishing slavery; instead he felt that it should not be expanded beyond the existing southern states. The election of 1859 was close, but Douglas kept his senate seat.

Confronts crisis as new president

Lincoln's performance in the debates, however, earned him the Republican nomination for U.S. president in May 1860. After he was elected, panic immediately swept through the South. Many, believing Lincoln would do away with slavery after he took office, urged the southern states to secede (break away) from the Union. South Carolina became the first state to do so, on December 20. Mississippi, Florida, Alabama, Georgia, Louisiana, and Texas soon followed.

On February 4, 1861, these states formed the Confederate States of America, drew up a new constitution, and elected Jefferson Davis as president. (Arkansas, North Carolina, Virginia, and Tennessee later joined the Confederacy.) Lincoln had not yet set foot in the White House, the official home of the president in Washington, D.C., the nation's capital.

Tries to hold nation together

After his inauguration in March 1861, Lincoln tried to hold on to all U.S. government property in Confederate territory. In retaliation, the Confederates attacked Fort Sumter on April 12, giving Lincoln no choice but to declare war. The Union (northern) army, unprepared for war, performed badly,

Lithograph of the Emancipation Proclamation.

and the president was frustrated because he could not find a general competent enough to lead successful battles.

At the same time members of Lincoln's cabinet (his top officials) were not working with him, and instead were attempting to make their own policy decisions. Lincoln was also being harshly criticized from all sides. Many people thought he acted like a dictator when he limited the freedom of the press (newspapers) and allowed the army to arrest suspected traitors without proof of their guilt. Lincoln believed these actions were necessary to achieve his main goal—keeping the United States together.

The second goal, the abolitionist campaign to outlaw slavery, was not shared by most northerners. Lincoln therefore did not push any antislavery measures while the Confederacy was gaining an advantage in the war. However, historians report that he remained personally troubled by slavery. In 1855, for instance, he had written a letter to his friend Joshua Speed, recalling a steamboat trip they had taken together on the Ohio River in the 1840s. Lincoln wrote: "From Louisville to the mouth of the Ohio there were, on board, ten or a dozen slaves, shackled together with irons. That sight was a continual torment to me; and I see something like it every time I touch the Ohio, or any slave-border."

Issues Emancipation Proclamation

On August 22, 1862, journalist Horace Greeley (1811–72) wrote an editorial in the *New York Tribune,* calling upon Lincoln to use his powers immediately. Lincoln gave this reply: "My paramount object is to save the Union, and it is not either to save or to destroy slavery. If I could save the Union without freeing any slave I would do it; and if I could save it by freeing all the slaves I would do it; and if I could save it by freeing some and leaving others alone I would also do that."

Lincoln then offered a plan: slaves would be gradually freed by individual state legislatures and slave owners would be repaid, with some funds being provided by the federal government. The freed slaves would be sent abroad to live in specially created colonies. Lincoln's idea was not sup-

Excerpt from The Emancipation Proclamation

And I do order and declare that all persons held as slaves within said designated States, and parts of States, are, and henceforward shall be free; and that the Executive government of the United States, including the military and naval authorities thereof, will recognize and maintain the freedom of said persons.

And I hereby enjoin upon the people so declared to be free to abstain from all violence, unless in necessary self-defence; and I recommend to them that, in all cases when allowed, they labor faithfully for reasonable wages.

And I further declare and make known, that such persons of suitable con-dition, will be received into the armed service of the United States to garrison forts, positions, stations, and other places, and to man vessels of all sorts in said service.

And upon this act, sincerely believed to be an act of justice, warranted by the Constitution, upon military necessity, I invoke the considerate judgment of mankind, and the gracious favor of Almighty God. . . .

Source: *The Emancipation Proclamation: January 1, 1863.* Washington D.C.: National Archives Records Administration.

ported by the border states, however, and African American leaders did not want freed slaves to leave the country.

In September 1862, Union forces stopped the Confederates from moving north at the battle of Antietam in Maryland. Since the war had now turned in the Union's favor, Lincoln took a decisive step. Using his presidential war powers, he issued a preliminary Emancipation Proclamation on September 22 and freed all slaves held in Confederate states. The decree did not apply to slave states that had remained loyal to the Union or to areas of the Confederacy that were occupied by Union troops. On January 1, 1863, Lincoln signed the final Proclamation. By the end of the Civil War around 3 million slaves had been freed.

Delivers famous address

Lincoln believed his most notable act as president was the signing of the Emancipation Proclamation. Yet he is remembered today for the Gettysburg Address, a speech he delivered at the dedication of a national military cemetery at

Gettysburg, Pennsylvania, on November 19, 1863. He was not the main speaker, and many in the audience felt his brief speech—just 272 words—was dull and made no real contribution to the occasion. People later realized that, through his clear and vivid language, Lincoln honored not only the men who had died in battle but also expressed the ideals set forth in the U.S. Constitution.

Lincoln finally found a capable general in Ulysses S. Grant (1822–85), whom he gave command of the Union forces in March 1864. At this time, however, Lincoln was still battling his critics. While some northerners accused him of putting too much emphasis on the issue of slavery, others thought he had not gone far enough. Many people simply wanted an end to the war. Lincoln's re-election was therefore not guaranteed at the end of 1864. Even Lincoln, himself, placed little hope of being re-elected. However, the fall of Atlanta, Georgia, to Union general William Tecumseh Sherman (1820–91) on September 2 helped boost northern hopes that the war would soon be over. Lincoln won the November election.

Assassinated after Confederates surrender

As Lincoln prepared to serve his second term, he lobbied Congress to adopt the Thirteenth Amendment to the Constitution, which would permanently ban slavery throughout the United States. Passed by Congress on January 31, 1865, the amendment states: "Neither slavery nor involuntary servitude, except as punishment for crime whereof the party shall have been duly convicted, shall exist within the United States, or any place subject to their jurisdiction."

For the next two months Lincoln worked tirelessly on a peace plan. Even though southern leaders refused his initial offers, he remained hopeful. Finally, Confederate general Robert E. Lee (1807–70) surrendered his troops to General Grant at Appomattox Court House on April 9, 1865. The Civil War was over. Lincoln had been sworn in as president only a month earlier, but historians can only speculate about how he would have handled the rebuilding of the divided nation.

On April 14, while watching a play at Ford's Theater in Washington, Abraham Lincoln was shot by John Wilkes Booth (1838–65), an actor who sided with the South. Lincoln died early the next morning, becoming the first U.S. president to be assassinated. Secretary of War Edwin M. Stanton, who had been standing by Lincoln's bedside, reportedly said to others gathered in the room, "Now he belongs to the ages."

Further Reading

Books

Ayres, Alex, ed. *The Wit and Wisdom of Abraham Lincoln.* Penguin, 1992.

Bruns, Roger. *Abraham Lincoln.* Chelsea House, 1986.

Ito, Tom. *Abraham Lincoln.* Lucent Books, 1997.

Jacobs, William Jay. *Abraham Lincoln.* New York: Scribner, 1991.

Judson, Karen. *Abraham Lincoln.* Enslow, 1998.

Lowenfels, Walter, ed. *Walt Whitman's Civil War.* Knopf, 1960.

McPherson, James M. *Abraham Lincoln and the Second American Revolution.* Oxford University Press, 1991.

McPherson, James M. *Battle Cry of Freedom.* Oxford University Press, 1988.

Oates, Stephen B. *Abraham Lincoln: The Man Behind the Myths.* Harper & Row, 1984.

Weinberg, Larry. *The Story of Abraham Lincoln: President for the People.* Gareth Stevens, 1997.

Wills, Garry. *Lincoln at Gettysburg.* Simon & Schuster, 1992.

Web sites

Lincoln, Abraham. *The Emancipation Proclamation: January 1, 1863.* Washington, D.C.: [Online] National Archives Records Administration. http://www.nara.gov/exhall/featured-document/eman/emanproc.html/ (accessed on September 16, 1999).

Edmund Dene Morel

Born c. 1873
Paris, France
Died November 12, 1924
Devonshire, England

Journalist, author, public speaker, government lobbyist, anti-war activist

Edmund Dene Morel was a twenty-eight-year-old, French-born shipping clerk and freelance writer working in Liverpool, England, when he discovered evidence of horrendous crimes being committed against the people of Africa by the king of Belgium, Leopold II (1865–1909). Instead of looking the other way, as he was encouraged to do by his employers, Morel spent the next ten years exposing the crimes of King Leopold. In pursuit of his goal, Morel founded and ran a weekly newspaper and an international human rights organization. His efforts stand as a great example of what a single person can do—even against the greatest of odds—to fight injustice in the world.

Founder of the Congo Reform Association, the first international human rights organization created in the twentieth century, and leader of a movement to end slave labor in the Congo region of Africa.

Early life of a writer

Edmund Morel was born in a suburb of Paris. Morel's father was French and his mother was English. Morel's father, a civil servant, died when Edmund was four years old, leaving the family without a pension. Morel's mother went to work as a music teacher in Paris. Morel was sent to England to attend Bedford Modern, a public school with a good reputation and

Edmund Dene Morel.

modest fees. When he was fifteen Morel was forced to return to Paris to work and support his ailing mother.

In 1890, when Morel was seventeen, he landed a job in England, as a clerk at Elder Dempster, a shipping company based in Liverpool. Morel found it hard to support himself and his mother on his meager wages so in his spare time he gave French lessons. He also began to write freelance articles on African trade issues for publications such as the *Shipping Telegraph* and the *Liverpool Journal of Commerce*. Morel wrote his articles from a businessman's point of view, praising the great boom in trade that was apparently taking place between the Europeans and the Africans.

Morel dismisses reports of abuse

For ten years Morel worked in the day as a shipping clerk and at night as a freelance writer. By 1899 he was considered the leading British authority on West Africa. Morel, like most of the rest of the world, believed that the European colonization of Africa that was taking place at the time was good for both Europeans and Africans. In his articles Morel consistently dismissed reports of atrocities (extreme cruelty) being done to African natives by Europeans as false, and if true, a small price to pay for the "civilizing" influences of the West on that "dark" continent.

In the late 1890s, part of Morel's job was to travel across the English Channel to Antwerp, Belgium, to supervise the arrival and departure of Elder Dempster ships on what was called the Congo run. The steamers of Elder Dempster had for years worked the west coast of Africa, hauling goods from Europe to Africa and back. At the time of Morel's employment, Elder Dempster had an exclusive contract for carrying all cargo to and from the Congo Free State (now the Democratic Republic of Congo, formerly Zaire, and before that, the Belgian Congo). The Congo Free State was created in 1885 by King Leopold of Belgium.

Leopold's reality

King Leopold told the world that he wanted to save the people of the Congo from enslavement by Arabs. The re-

The Scramble for Africa

At the end of the nineteenth century, most of Africa was under direct European control. In 1884, at the Conference of Berlin, the countries of Germany, France, England, Portugal, and Belgium each staked out territories in Africa that they wished to occupy and colonize. The map of Africa changed almost overnight as the Europeans divided the lands of the vast continent among themselves.

The Berlin Conference, with pressure from the United States, granted King Leopold of Belgium the right to rule over the Congo Basin, an area of central Africa seventy-five times the size of Belgium. King Leopold named his personal kingdom the Congo Free State, and told the world he wanted to rescue the African people from

King Leopold of Belgium.

Arab slave traders, and bring them education and "civilization."

ality was that King Leopold replaced the Arab slave trade with an even more brutal system of slavery. Leopold's strategy was to plunder (drain) the area of its natural resources using the forced labor of the native African population. Without ever setting foot in the Congo, Leopold directed Belgian troops to round up whole communities of Africans and put them to work harvesting ivory and wild rubber.

The native Congolese were also forced to build the facilities needed for trade such as railroads and ports. Leopold, and the private companies he worked with, imposed a quota (a set amount of work to be completed each day) system on the natives, and when they failed to meet it, amputated the hands of the workers. Sometimes they kidnapped the women and children of a village and held them as hostages until the quota was met.

A Belgian government commission investigated Leopold's reign of terror and found that from the late 1870s to 1919 (the year of the report), the population of the Congo Basin had been reduced from twenty million to ten million, making it, as one historian later called it, "a death toll of Holocaust proportions." Most of the people died from starvation and disease, a direct result of being driven from their homes and food sources. Other African natives died from the horrible conditions of their enslavement. Many of the dead had been murdered by Leopold's forces.

Morel's discovery

Public reports of atrocities in the Congo were made by individuals in the 1890s but for one reason or another they were not given widespread credibility in Europe or abroad. Even Morel, an "expert" on West Africa, was inclined to believe that King Leopold's intentions in the Congo were good and that reports of Africans being mistreated were exaggerated. By 1900, however, Morel came to believe otherwise.

At dockside in Antwerp, Morel noticed that Elder Dempster ships from the Congo came in loaded with ivory and rubber, but ships going back to the Congo were full of army officers, arms, and ammunition. Morel also discovered that the records he compiled for his employer did not match the records released to the public by the Congo Free State. Leopold's books showed a balanced and fair trade taking place. The reality was that thousands of tons of rubber and other tropical products were reaching Belgium without an equal flow of goods in trade back to the Congo. The imbalance could only be explained one way, Morel figured: The rubber and ivory of the Congo were being obtained with slave labor. And, if that were so, then the reports of brutalities inflicted on the Congolese by Leopold's forces were also probably true.

Morel exposes the "Congo scandal"

In the summer of 1900 Morel went to his supervisor at Elder Dempster and informed him of his discovery. Morel was advised to overlook the whole affair as the king of Belgium was one of the company's best customers. Morel instead

A SLAVE-SHED.

anonymously wrote a series of expert articles in *The Speaker* on the "Congo scandal." Elder Dempster attempted to silence Morel by offering him a raise and a transfer to another country. Morel refused and in 1901, at twenty-eight years of age, quit his job to work full-time to expose the truth about King Leopold's Congo.

Morel was filled with moral outrage over Leopold's blatant disregard for human life in the pursuit of personal profits. But unlike the people who had tried to expose Leopold before him by appealing to the public on solely humanitarian grounds, Morel's strategy was to show how Leopold's monopoly on trade in the Congo was bad business for England. Morel argued that Leopold had abolished the rights of free trade in the Congo that were guaranteed to the international community by the Berlin Act of 1885. In other words, the Congo Free State was not only robbing African peasants but British merchants as well. Morel had hoped to

Drawing of Congolese slaves being held in a "slave shed." *(The Granger Collection, New York. Reproduced by permission.)*

arouse Britain's business community to act in its own self-interest and break up Leopold's grip on the Congo in the name of free trade.

Morel the crusader

Morel was determined to find out everything possible about the workings of Leopold's Congo empire and reveal it to the world. Before he was through Morel produced a huge body of work on the subject: three full books and portions of two others; hundreds of articles and letters to the editor for British, French, and Belgian newspapers; and several dozen pamphlets. He did all this while writing for—and editing—his own newspaper, the *West African Mail*, a weekly publication he started in 1903 to expose injustice in the Congo. Somewhere along the way, although the record isn't clear on this, Morel married Mary Richardson Morel, who raised their five children and supported her husband in his cause.

Initially, Morel's campaign for reform attracted support in England from some members of Parliament as well as humanitarian groups such as the Anti-Slavery Society and the Aborigines Protection Society. Through his newspaper, books, speeches, articles, and pamphlets, Morel became well known as the most outspoken critic of the Congo state. As such many people came to him with eyewitness accounts or smuggled insider documents.

Missionaries provided some of the most gruesome accounts of human rights violations, including descriptions of Belgian soldiers cutting off hands of natives, and Africans being tied naked to a stake for days without food or water for stealing rubber. Missionaries also provided what turned out to be one of the most powerful public relations tools for Morel's campaign—photographs of severed hands and heads, children without hands or feet, and destroyed villages. Morel published it all in the *West African Mail*.

Birth of Congo Reform Association

In May 1903, Morel and his allies forced a major debate on the Congo question in the British House of Commons, where a resolution was unanimously passed urging that Congo "natives should be governed with humanity." Further, the Foreign Office was instructed to investigate conditions in the Congo and to report back to Parliament. The job fell to Roger Casement, Britain's roving consul (government representative) in Africa. After several months in the Congo Free State, Casement returned to Europe in late 1903 to prepare his report.

Casement, who had visited the Congo before the rubber terror days of Leopold, was very upset by what he witnessed during his investigation. His report confirmed that a slave labor system was in place in the Congo and that Leopold's forces systematically abused the native Africans with torture, forced amputations, hostage-taking, and murder. The report was published in early 1904 and gave a great boost to the credibility of Morel's writings and opinions on the subject.

Casement had read Morel's writings while in the Congo and sought him out when he returned to England. After several meetings between the two men, Casement persuaded Morel to found the Congo Reform Association (C.R.A.), an organization devoted solely to campaigning for justice in the Congo. The C.R.A. attracted more than one thousand people to its first meeting in Liverpool on March 24, 1904.

Leopold's downfall

Morel and his allies in the Congo Reform Association spent the next few years trying to convince the world that King Leopold's reign of terror in the Congo should come to an end. Morel traveled to the United States and personally lobbied President Theodore Roosevelt (1858–1919) at the White House. The C.R.A. opened a branch in the United States and more than two hundred mass meetings to protest slave labor in the Congo were held.

At the peak of the crusade in England, more than three hundred mass meetings were held in a year, some drawing as many as five thousand people at a time. With thousands of members, and branches in Europe and the United States, the C.R.A. and its government supporters in 1908 forced Leopold to surrender personal control of the Congo Free State to the government of Belgium.

Morel and his followers in the C.R.A. were pleased that control of the Congo was transferred to the hands of the Belgian government. Leopold died in 1909, and Belgium's new king, Albert I (1875–1934), was publicly opposed to forced labor and promised reforms. In 1913 the Congo Free State officially became the Belgian Congo. On June 6, 1913, the C.R.A. held its last meeting in London.

Morel's passion continues

For years Morel was well known and well respected in England for his Congo reform campaign. World War I (1914–18) would change all that. Morel was one of a tiny minority of people in Europe who opposed the war from the very beginning. In 1914 Morel formed the Union of Democratic Control, which quickly became the main anti-war organization in the country. Morel, targeted by pro-war opponents in the government, was arrested in 1917 and sentenced to six months hard labor for the crime of sending anti-war literature to a neutral country.

Morel was released from prison in early 1918. His hair had turned completely white while incarcerated. Once a burly man (his nickname was "Bulldog"), Morel was now very thin. Yet Morel resumed his speaking and writing, and in a matter of a few years, was again accepted and respected by the public. With hindsight, the public came around to Morel's negative viewpoint of World War I, which resulted in 8.5 million casualties (deaths) and 21 million wounded. In 1922 Morel was elected to the House of Commons on the Labor Party ticket from his home district in Dundee, Scotland. He was re-elected in 1923 and 1924, but did not live to serve his last term in full; Morel died on November 12, 1924.

Further Reading

Books
Hochschild, Adam. *King Leopold's Ghost*. New York: Houghton Mifflin Co., 1998.

Pakenham, Thomas. *The Scramble for Africa*. New York: Random House, 1991.

Periodicals
Ascherson, Neal. "Touch of Evil." *Los Angeles Times,* January 10, 1999: BR7.

Harding, Jeremy. "Into Africa." *The New York Times,* September 20, 1998: G8.

Moses

Born c. fourteenth century B.C.
Egypt
Died c. thirteenth century B.C.
Egypt

Hebrew leader, prophet

M oses was the great Hebrew leader who delivered the Hebrew people (also called the Israelites) out of slavery
from Egypt during the thirteenth century B.C. According to
the Bible, Moses gave the Hebrews the laws (Torah) that
formed the basis of Judaism, the Jewish religion. He is also
considered a prophet (one whose words are inspired by God)
by Christians and Muslims. Christians are followers of the religion founded by Jesus of Nazareth (also called Jesus Christ;
c. 6 B.C.–c. A.D. 30). Muslims are followers of Islam, the religion founded by the Prophet Muhammad (c. 570–632).
Scholars are uncertain about the dates of Moses' birth and
death because the Bible gives conflicting accounts of his
achievements. Many of the events in the story of Moses,
however, are based on facts that have been verified by other
historical accounts.

"And there arose not a
prophet since in Israel
like unto Moses, whom
the Lord knew face to
face."

Deuteronomy 34:10

Adopted by Egyptian royalty

According to the Bible, Moses ("Moshe" in the Hebrew language) was born in Egypt to Amram and Jochebed, a

Moses. *(Corbis-Bettmann.*
Reproduced by permission.)

slave couple in the Hebrew tribe of Levi. They also had another son, Aaron, and a daughter, Miriam. Although the Hebrews had been in Egypt for hundreds of years, they were ultimately enslaved by the Egyptians. In particular, the Egyptians needed many slaves to work the extremely rich land along the Nile River (the longest river in the world, beginning in Africa and emptying into the Mediterranean Sea). Stretching from the Mediterranean to the Persian Gulf, this region was called the Fertile Crescent because it enabled ancient peoples to create advanced civilizations.

At the time of Moses' birth, the pharaoh (Egyptian king) was trying to restrict the Hebrew population, so he ordered that all newborn Hebrew males be drowned in the Nile. Determined to save Moses, Jochebed kept him hidden until he was three months old. Then she put him in a basket and set it in the river at a spot where she knew the pharaoh's daughter came to bathe every day. Upon finding the baby, the princess adopted him, but she told Jochebed to nurse (breast feed) him until he was old enough to be brought up in the Egyptian court. And so Moses became the foster son of the pharaoh.

Forced to flee

Nothing is known about Moses' life as a child and young adult, but scholars speculate that he received an education in religion, law, and military arts. He probably learned about the culture of the ancient Near East because Egypt controlled Canaan (present–day Palestine) and part of Syria, and the Egyptians had contacts with other nations along the Fertile Crescent.

At some point Moses learned he was a Hebrew. He may have been around twenty–five years old when he made his first visit among his people, witnessing firsthand their terrible living conditions. One day he saw an Egyptian beating a Hebrew slave to death, so he stepped in and killed the Egyptian. When the pharaoh found out, he tried to have his foster son executed. Moses then fled to Midian, an ancient region south of the present–day country of Jordan.

Speaks directly to God

Upon reaching Midian, Moses stopped to rest at a well. While he was there the seven daughters of Jethro, the priest of the Midianites, brought their father's sheep to drink from the well. Soon they were chased away by other shepherds who wanted the water for their own sheep. Witnessing this incident, Moses stepped in and drove the shepherds off. He then went to live with Jethro's family, eventually marrying Zipporah, one of the priest's daughters.

Now in charge of his father–in–law's flocks, Moses wandered the wilderness in search of pasture land. According to the Bible, one day he came upon a bush that was burning but was not being consumed. Drawing closer, he heard a voice speaking to him from the flames. The voice told Moses to take off his sandals because he was standing on holy ground. Moses obeyed, realizing he was in the presence of a divine being (deity or god). Much to his surprise, the voice told him to return to Egypt and lead the Hebrews out of slavery. Moses protested that he could not take on this responsibility because he was unworthy. Another reason why he may not have wanted to return to Egypt was because he had committed a murder and he feared Ramses II (fourteenth––thirteenth century B.C.), the current pharaoh.

Next Moses asked the name of this deity. The voice from the bush responded that he was Yahweh (the great "I Am"), the God of the Hebrews, who ruled over nature and all the nations of the world. Moses continued to resist delivering the Hebrews from slavery, claiming that he could not speak well and was therefore not a good choice as a prophet. Yahweh was becoming angry, yet he would not give in to Moses' excuses. Finally they agreed that Moses would be Yahweh's representative and Moses' brother Aaron, who was a persuasive public speaker, would be the spokesman. Moses went to Jethro and received permission to return to Egypt, but he did not reveal that he was being sent by Yahweh.

"Let my people go."

Upon reaching Egypt Moses and Aaron told Ramses II to release the Hebrews, announcing: "Thus says the Lord, the God of Israel, 'Let my people go.' " Ramses refused. The

Ramses II

Ramses was the name shared by several kings, or pharaohs, of Egypt during the nineteenth and twentieth dynasties. Ramses II ruled Egypt for sixty-seven years (c. 1304–1237 B.C.), expanding the empire into southern Syria and around the Nile River. In the early years of his reign he achieved fame as the victor in a battle with the Hittites, a people who also occupied parts of Syria. After a nearly twenty-year-long conflict with the Hittites, Ramses negotiated a treaty of friendship in 1283. He then married a Hittite princess.

During Ramses's reign Egypt attained great wealth and political power. He increased the use of slaves, including the Hebrews, and built up a large army. Ramses built many monuments to himself throughout Egypt, including the temple at Karnak, Ramses's tomb at Thebes, the temple of Luxor, and the rock temple at Abu Simbel. Ramses's appetite for luxury and the accumulation of slaves led to the downfall of Egypt. Other kings were unable

Ramses II.

to maintain the level of wealth and power, and the Egyptian social system ultimately collapsed when the twentieth dynasty ended in 1090 B.C. Historians are fairly certain that Ramses II was the pharaoh mentioned in the Bible, who was forced by Moses to free the Hebrews from slavery.

pharoah was considered to be a god in human form, so he did not take orders from any other gods, including this unknown Yahweh. "Who is the Lord, that I should heed his voice and let Israel go?" Ramses demanded. "I do not know the Lord, and moreover I will not let Israel go."

Instead of freeing the Hebrews, Ramses made their lives even more difficult. For instance, he gave them the added task of carrying straw for making bricks on top of the work they were already required to do each day. Many Hebrews blamed Moses for their increased hardship. In despair Moses turned to Yahweh, pleading "Why didst thou ever send me?" But Yahweh promised revenge against Ramses in the form of ten plagues.

Throughout the summer and the following spring Egypt was devastated by the plagues. First the Nile turned to "blood" in a tremendous flood. (Modern scientists have concluded that this flood was caused by extremely heavy rains that washed red clay from nearby hills into the river.) Then the kingdom was attacked by hordes of frogs, gnats (tiny flying insects), and mosquitos. The Egyptian people were afflicted with boils (body sores), their cattle became sick, and the land was overwhelmed by hail (icy rain), locusts (large insects that eat vegetation), and darkness. (Scientists confirm that all of these events occurred and were caused by unusual weather patterns.) The tenth plague resulted in the death of the firstborn sons of the Egyptians. Finally, Ramses agreed to Moses' demands.

Hebrews flee Egypt

The biblical story of the Hebrews' flight from Egypt is complicated and sometimes conflicting. For instance, one version claims that 600,000 people fled from Egypt, while another says 2,000,000. Historians have determined that the number was probably around 15,000. Yet it is known that Ramses changed his mind and sent his troops to recapture the Hebrews.

Moses and his people—including his own family—had reached the Red Sea when the Egyptian army began to surround them. According to the Bible, at that moment Moses raised his staff (a long stick used by shepherds to herd sheep) and parted the waters, thus letting the Hebrews cross safely. The Egyptians surged forward, but just as they entered the river the waters engulfed them and they drowned. Moses' sister Miriam then led the Hebrews in a song of victory.

In an attempt to explain this dramatic event, scholars have concluded that the Red Sea was actually the Sea of Reeds, a shallow lake where papyrus (tall, woody plants) grew. The "parting" of the waters probably was the result of a high wind that created a dry corridor through the papyrus and permitted

Moses, on Mt. Sinai, receives the Ten Commandments.
(Archive Photos, Inc. Reproduced by permission.)

the Hebrews to get to the other side. The Egyptians were drowned when the wind died down and the waters returned.

Receives the Ten Commandments

Although they were now freed from the Egyptians, the Hebrews faced many difficulties as they roamed through the deserted lands of the present–day Sinai Peninsula (in northeastern Egypt). Food and water were always in short supply, and the Hebrews were in constant danger of being attacked by other tribes.

After three months of wandering, the Hebrews came upon Mount Sinai (also called Horeb) in the southern part of the peninsula. While the people waited below, Moses climbed the mountain. According to the Bible, God gave Moses the Ten Commandments, a moral code the Hebrews were to live by. Among the acts forbidden by the Commandments were murder, adultery (having sexual relations outside marriage), and stealing.

Most laws at that time had been established to keep order in society, but they were written by rulers who themselves did not have to live by the laws. (One of the earliest systems of laws was created by the Babylonian ruler Hammurabi, who died in 1750 B.C.) The Ten Commandments were different because they affected everyone equally and they applied to all aspects of social and religious life. The religious laws of Judaism, Christianity, and Islam are based on the principles of the Commandants.

Dies on Mount Pisgah

Led by Moses, the Hebrews wandered for forty years in the wilderness of the Sinai Peninsula. Their destination was Canaan, a land that had been promised to them by Yahweh. During this time Moses served as leader, priest, and prophet, compiling the written record of the Hebrew laws. He had to face many more battles with tribes whose lands the Hebrews crossed, however, and he had to calm rebellions among his own people.

Finally, the Hebrews reached the Jordan River, which separated them from Canaan. Climbing to the top of Mount Pisgah (also called Nebo; in present–day northeast Jordan), Moses saw the "promised land." He never achieved his goal of leading the Hebrews into Canaan because he died on the mountain. According to some accounts, Moses was buried at Moab (in present–day southwest Jordan), but other versions of the story state that the Hebrews did not see him again.

Moses was succeeded by the prophet Joshua, who had proven himself in battle in the wilderness, and later by the priest Eleazar, the son of Aaron. Yet no one ascended to the greatness of Moses, who is still revered as one of the most outstanding figures in human history.

Further Reading
Auerbach, Elias. *Moses*. Detroit, Mich.: Wayne State University Press, 1975.

Daiches, David. *Moses: The Man and His Vision.* Westport, Conn.: Praeger, 1975.

Kirsch, Jonathan. *Moses: A Life.* New York: Ballantine, 1998.

Klagsbrun, Francine. *The Story of Moses.* Danbury, Conn.: Franklin Watts, 1968.

Petersham, Maud Fuller. *Moses, from the Story Told in the Old Testament.* New York: Macmillan, 1958.

Tenney, Merrill C., ed. *The Pictorial Bible Dictionary.* Nashville, Tenn.: Southwestern Co., 1975.

Solomon Northrup

Born July 1808
Essex County, New York
Died 1863
Warren County, New York

Freeborn black, slave, slave narrative author

The story of Solomon Northrup's life as a free black man in the North who was abducted into slavery in the Deep South gained widespread notoriety in the early 1850s. This was due in part to the vast popularity of Harriet Beecher Stowe's 1852 novel, *Uncle Tom's Cabin,* in which the horrors of slavery in the American South were vividly portrayed. Solomon Northrup, with the help of an editor, told of his incredible misfortune in a book called *Twelve Years a Slave,* which was published in 1853. Northrup's autobiography of life as a plantation slave, an account that was hailed as entirely believable even by slavery's allies in the South, added credibility to Stowe's fictionalized depiction of the same subject.

Historians today view Northrup's book with great interest. It is the only slave narrative written from the point of view of a black person who was free for many years and then subjected to the cruelties of slavery. Northrup's story sheds light on many aspects of the institution of slavery including the intrastate slave trade, slave auctions, the separation of slave families through sale, the role of slave drivers, and the extent of slave resistance. *Twelve Years* is considered one of

Kidnapped from the North into slavery for twelve years in the Deep South, Northrup regained his freedom and wrote one of the most widely read slave narratives of his time.

the most valuable descriptions of the life of a slave on a southern plantation in the mid-1840s and early 1850s.

Born free

Solomon Northrup was born to free black parents in the northern state of New York. Northrup's father, Mintus, had grown up a slave in Rhode Island, owned by a family named Northrup. Mintus moved to New York with his owner at the beginning of the nineteenth century. A few years before Northrup's birth, Mintus's owner died and in his will directed that his slave be set free.

Mintus Northrup became a landowning farmer who was able to meet the $250 property qualification required of black voters in the state of New York. Northrup was born the second of two sons to Mintus and his wife, and grew up working with his family on their farm. He learned to read and write and in his leisure time read books or played his violin.

Mintus Northrup died on November 22, 1829. On Christmas day of that same year, Solomon Northrup married Anne Hampton, a woman of mixed ancestry—African, Native American, and European. Northrup and Anne had three children: Elizabeth, Margaret, and Alonzo. From the time of his father's death until he was abducted in 1841, Northrup lived an uneventful life, farming and working at various semi-skilled jobs in and around the small towns of upstate New York. In the winter season Northrup often made money playing the fiddle at dances.

Tricked

In 1834 the Northrup family moved to Saratoga Springs, New York, where Northrup continued to work at odd jobs and earn money from his violin playing. In March 1841 Northrup was in the village of Saratoga Springs looking for work when he met two strangers who claimed to be looking for musicians to join their traveling circus. They offered Northrup immediate wages and future long-term employment. Northrup accepted and accompanied the men to New

York City, and then to Washington, D.C., where they planned to meet up with the circus company.

At no time was Northrup suspicious of the two men. They did little things to earn his trust such as giving him cash up front, and helping him obtain his freedom papers from the New York authorities before he left the state and entered the South, where slavery was still legal. Once in Washington the three of them went sightseeing and in the course of the day stopped at taverns for food and drink. The two men made a habit of pouring Northrup's drinks for him. Although he did not consume much alcohol, that night at his hotel room Northrup became very ill and lost consciousness.

Captured

When Northrup woke up he found himself in total darkness, in chains, and robbed of his money and his free papers. What he didn't know at the time was that he had been drugged and was now a prisoner of Price, Burch, and Company—one of Washington's major slave traders. What happened next is best described in an 1853 *New York Times* article based on an interview with Northrup shortly after he had gained his freedom:

> In the course of a few hours, James H. Burch, a slave dealer, came in, and the colored man [Northrup] asked him to take the irons off of him, and wanted to know why they were put on. Burch told him it was none of his business. The colored man said he was free and told where he was born. Burch called in a man by the name of Ebenezer Rodbury, and the two stripped the man and laid him across a bench, Rodbury holding him down by the wrists. Burch whipped him with a paddle until he broke that, and then with a cat-o'-nine tails, giving him a hundred lashes, and he swore he would kill him if he ever stated to any one that he was a free man. From that time forward the man says he did not communicate the fact from fear, either that he was a free man, or what his name was, until the last summer.

Sold into slavery

Northrup remained in the slave pen for about two weeks before being put on a ship to New Orleans. There he was purchased off the auction block by a planter in the Red

Depiction of slaves being sold on an auction block. Solomon Northrup was illegally kidnapped and sold by auction in 1841. *(Archive Photos, Inc. Reproduced by permission.)*

River region of Louisiana, where for the next twelve years he would serve several masters as a slave. Even though Northrup had been illegally kidnapped, the sale of slaves between states was entirely legal; importing slaves from Africa was made illegal in 1808 although the trade continued until the outbreak of the Civil War (1861–65).

Northrup worked as a carpenter for his first master and was owned for a short period by another master before being sold in 1843 to Edwin Epps, the owner of a cotton plantation in Bayou Beauf, Louisiana. Epps was a mean master; when he drank too much he took delight in forcing his slaves to dance to the crack of his whip just to hear them scream and shriek. When sober, Northrup recalls in *Twelve Years,* Epps had very good aim with his whip and applied it frequently to slaves that he thought were not working hard enough or who had somehow disobeyed him.

Worked like a dog

Northrup spent ten years as a field slave on the Epps plantation. During that time he worked at many different jobs, described in great detail in *Twelve Years*. Northrup and the other field slaves worked six days a week from dawn to dusk throughout the year. They planted corn in February and cotton in March and April; hoed and weeded the crops as they grew in May, June and July; and at the end of August they started the harvest season. Northrup describes a typical work day during cotton-picking time, which on some plantations lasted through January:

> The hands are required in the cotton field as soon as it is light in the morning, and with the exception of ten or fifteen minutes, which is given them at noon to swallow their allowance of cold bacon, they are not permitted to be a moment idle until it is too dark to see and when the moon is full they often times labor till the middle of the night. They do not dare to stop even at dinner time, nor return to their quarters, however late it be, until the order to halt is given by the driver.

Plantation punishment

Northrup witnessed the brutal punishments handed out to slaves who did not meet their daily work requirements or who misbehaved. Slaves who were expected to pick two hundred pounds of cotton, for example, were punished for weighing in with less at the end of the day. Northrup describes in *Twelve Years* the process that occurred at the time the cotton was weighed:

> The delinquent, whose weight had fallen short, was taken out, stripped, made to lie upon the ground, face downwards, when he received a punishment proportioned to his offense. It is the literal, unvarnished truth, that the crack of the lash, and the shrieking of the slaves, can be heard from dark till bedtime, on Epps' plantation, any day almost during the entire period of the cotton-picking season.

Rescued

Solomon Northrup, from the very beginning of his enslavement, sought a way to escape or to communicate his predicament by letter to his family and friends in New York. He managed to post a letter from New Orleans in June 1841,

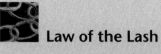

Law of the Lash

The Black Codes of the South, laws made to govern the behavior and punishment of slaves, were extremely harsh. Slaves, according to the law, were property, not people, and therefore had no human rights. Slave owners, such as the one who owned Solomon Northrup, were entitled to punish their slaves as they saw fit. The law, in effect, gave Master Epps the power to act independently as judge, jury, and executioner. In *Twelve Years a Slave,* Northrup describes the laws on the Epps plantation and consequences for breaking them:

The number of lashes is graduated according to the nature of the case. Twenty-five are deemed a mere brush, inflicted, for instance, when a dry leaf or piece of boll is found in the cotton, or when a branch is broken in the field; fifty is the ordinary penalty following all delinquencies of the next higher grade; one hundred is called severe: it is inflicted for the most serious offense of standing idle in the field; from one hundred and fifty to two hundred is bestowed upon him who quarrels with his cabin-mates, and five hundred, well laid on, besides the mangling of the dogs, perhaps, is certain to consign the poor, unpitied runaway to weeks of pain and agony.

to Henry P. Northrup (a member of the family that used to own his father), asking for help regarding his kidnapping. At the time that he wrote the letter to Henry P. Northrup, however, Northrup was unable to state his final destination, thus leaving no way of finding him.

All the time Northrup was living on the Epps plantation he was under orders from his master to not be caught with a book, or pen and ink, or he would receive one hundred lashes. At one point, Northrup made his own ink and managed to write a letter. However, he could find no one he could trust enough to post it. If not for the chance meeting by Northrup with Samuel Bass, a traveling carpenter from Canada, Northrup might have died a slave in Louisiana.

In 1852 Bass was employed by Epps to build a house, and since Northrup had carpentry experience, he was assigned to work with him. The two became friends and conspired to arrange Northrup's escape. Bass posted letters on Northrup's behalf, which brought Henry P. Northrup to the rescue as an official agent of the governor of the state of New York.

Returned from exile

After much legal wrangling, and over the strong objections of Master Epps, Solomon Northrup was freed from bondage and returned to his family in Glenn Falls, New York, in January 1853. He immediately began writing the narrative of his enslavement. Within months a manuscript was ready for publication and by July 1853, copies of *Twelve Years a Slave* were in the hands of reviewers.

The book was immediately successful; the first printing of 8,000 copies sold out in one month. In the course of Northrup's lifetime the book sold over 30,000 copies. Northrup received $3,000 for the copyright of his narrative, money he used to buy a house, where he lived with his wife and the family of his oldest daughter until he died in 1863.

The publication of Northrup's autobiography led to the identification and arrest of his kidnappers in 1854. One of the book's readers remembered a chance encounter with the kidnappers and Northrup in Washington in 1841. Charges were pressed by New York authorities against the two men, and although their guilt was never in doubt, they were eventually set free after several complicated trials and appeals based on legal technicalities.

Further Reading

Blassingame, John W. *The Slave Community.* New York: Oxford University Press, 1972.

Blassingame, John W., ed. *Slave Testimony: Two Centuries of Letters, Speeches, Interviews, and Autobiographies.* Baton Rouge, LA.: Louisiana State University Press, 1977.

Logan, Rayford W., and Michael R. Winston, eds. *Dictionary of American Negro Biography.* New York: W. W. Norton & Co., 1982.

Meltzer, Milton. *Slavery: A World History,* updated edition. New York: De Capo Press, 1993.

Northrup, Solomon. *Twelve Years a Slave.* Baton Rouge, LA.: Louisiana State University Press, 1968.

Saint Patrick

Born c. 385
Britain
Died c. 461
Ireland

Christian missionary, patron saint of Ireland

Throughout the world Catholics and non–Catholics alike celebrate March 17 as St. Patrick's Day with parades, festivals, and other special events. The patron saint (holy protector) of Ireland, Patrick has become a legendary figure, yet the real–life Patrick had little in common with the mythical St. Patrick. Born in the late fourth century, he was actually a simple man who was sold into slavery as a teenager. He then served as a Catholic missionary in Ireland during the fifth century, spreading Christianity outside the Roman Empire (the Romans did not occupy Ireland). Nevertheless, he did perform the near–superhuman feat of converting virtually the entire Irish population. The most reliable source of information about Patrick is his *Confession,* which he wrote in Latin when he was an old man. He composed this work to justify his career to church leaders who criticized his lack of education and questioned his commitment to Christianity.

> "A young man, almost a beardless boy, I was taken captive before I knew what I should desire and what I should shun."
>
> *St. Patrick,* Confession

Sold into slavery by pirates

According to his *Confession,* Patrick was born to Calpurnius, a deacon (a church official), whose own father,

145

Potitus, was a priest. The family lived in a small country estate near the settlement of Bannavem Taburniae. The exact location of Bannavem Taberniae is not known, but it was part of the Roman Empire in Britain, possibly near the Servern River in present–day Pembroke, Wales. Patrick's family were Roman citizens and Calpurnius was a nobleman.

The date of Patrick's birth is uncertain, although it was probably sometime during the last years of Roman domination (the empire began to decline in Britain in A.D. 409). Historians believe that Patrick may have been born around A.D. 385, or even as late as 415. His original name was Maewyn Succat (he became known as Patrick or Patricius when he entered the Christian priesthood). Despite coming from a noble family, Patrick received hardly any formal education. In fact, in the *Confession* he repeatedly apologizes for his poor command of Latin (the official language of the Catholic church) and his inferior writing skills. Most significantly, he showed little interest in Christianity while he was growing up.

When he was sixteen years old, Patrick was captured by pirates and carried across the Irish Sea (the body of water between Britain and Ireland) to be sold as a slave in Ireland (known as Scottus by the Romans). Patrick wrote in the *Confession* that he felt he had been taken captive because he had not been faithful to God.

Enters priesthood in France

Patrick was bought by Milchu, a chieftain–king. He worked as a shepherd on Slemish Mountain, and possibly on another mountain (now called Croaghpatrick in his honor), near present–day Ballymena in County Antrim, Northern Ireland. While tending his sheep he began to feel "the love of God," and experienced a spiritual conversion. Sorry for his earlier failure to obey God, he began to pray both day and night. He recalled that he "used to stay out in the forests and on the mountain" and would "wake up before daylight to pray in the snow, in icy coldness, in rain. . . ."

After six years, Patrick had a dream urging him to escape from Milchu and return home. He later wrote in the

Confession that he traveled two hundred miles to reach the coast of Ireland. He then had to convince a group of sailors to take him on board their ship. After a three–day voyage they reached France, where Patrick roamed for several years.

Patrick possibly visited the Monastery of St. Martin at Marmoutier before entering the monastery (a place for a community of men who have taken religious vows) at Lérin, where he was admitted to the Catholic priesthood. Around 413 he returned to Britain and lived with his family for several years. Although they begged him to stay home, his dreams once again forced him to act.

This time Patrick had a vision in which he was "visited by a man named Victoricus," who told him to return to Ireland and convert the people to Christianity. Around 419 he left his homeland to prepare himself as a missionary (a person who tries to convert others to different religious beliefs) with the famous bishop Germanus (later St. Germanus) at Auxerre, France. Patrick remained at Auxerre for the next twelve years before heading to Ireland.

The Legends of St. Patrick

Over the centuries storytellers have exaggerated the facts of St. Patrick's life with miraculous tales. According to one legend, Patrick used the three–leaf clover (called the shamrock) to explain the Holy Trinity (the Christian concept of God the Father, Christ the Son, and the Holy Spirit) to an Irish king. Thus the shamrock has become the symbol for St. Patrick—and for Ireland. Another legend credits Patrick with driving all the snakes out of Ireland. He also supposedly brought on earthquakes, sudden darkness, and general confusion in places where people refused to convert to Christianity. And in one wild tale, a wizard mocked both God and Patrick, so Patrick had the wizard lifted high into the air and then dropped to the ground, where he was smashed into pieces.

Sent as missionary to Ireland

Patrick was not the first Christian to preach in Ireland. The missionary bishop Palladius (later St. Palladius) went there in 431, but he failed to gain any converts. After a year Palladius left the country and died on the way home. In 432 Germanus sent Patrick to take Palladius's place as bishop (the official representative of the pope, the head of the Catholic church). At that time the Irish believed in their own gods and were highly suspicious of Christianity. They had a tradition of myths and legends, dating to prehistoric times, that had been passed down through the generations by poets and druids (priests or teachers).

Because the Irish worshiped several gods, they were considered to be pagans (derogatory word for non-christians) by the Christians, who believed in the "one true God" revealed by Jesus of Nazareth (founder of Christianity, known as the Christ). Since Palladius had been unable to spread his message, Patrick knew he had to take another approach. In the Roman Empire, Christianity was practiced mainly in the cities, but the Irish were nomads (people who do not settle in one place) and lived in tribal villages. So Patrick would have to travel throughout the countryside, going from tribe to tribe.

Wins pagans to Christianity

Patrick had reached Ireland in the winter and started his first church at Saul (present–day Strangford Lough on the east coast of Northern Ireland) in 432. His first major attempt at conversion took place the following spring near the Hill of Tara (in County Meath, northwest of present–day Dublin), the seat of the high kings of Ireland (chiefs of all the tribes).

It was a dramatic confrontation. Patrick had deliberately chosen to preach at Beltaine (the feast of the sun god Bel, the giver of life), a Celtic ritual held on May 1 to celebrate the beginning of summer. (The Celts were peoples who lived in the British Isles, Spain, and Asia Minor.) It was the custom to light bonfires in honor of Bel throughout Ireland, but only after the high kings and druids lit the first fires at Tara. That year Beltaine coincided with the Christian Easter (a holiday commemorating the death and resurrection of Jesus Christ). As the kings and druids gathered at Tara on May Eve (the night of April 30), Patrick camped on Slane, a nearby hill. Before the Beltaine celebrants had a chance to light their bonfires, Patrick started the first fire—in celebration of Easter.

Patrick's act initially caused extreme outrage, but gradually he gained the respect of the kings. Finally he even set up his headquarters at Tara. With a band of followers he began converting and baptizing hundreds of people in northern and western Ireland. His mission, though, was not without danger. Many non–Christians, especially kings and other

St. Patrick's *Letter to the Soldiers of Coroticus*

The following excerpt appears in Seamus Deane's *The Field Day Anthology of Irish Writing* (pp. 70–71):

> With my own hand I have written and composed these words, to be given, delivered, and sent to the soldiers of Coroticus. . . .

> . . . I do not know what to lament more: those who have been slain, or those whom they have taken captive, or those whom the devil has mightily ensnared. Together with him they will be slaves in Hell in an eternal punishment; for those who committeth sin is a slave and will be called a son of the devil. . . .

> . . . Hence the Church mourns and laments her sons and daughters whom the sword has not yet slain, but who are re-moved and carried off to faraway lands, where sin abounds openly, grossly, impudently. There people who are freeborn have been sold, Christians made slaves, and that, too, in the service of the abominable, wicked, and apostate Picts [inhabitants of Scotland]!...

> I ask earnestly that whoever is a willing servant of God be a carrier of this letter, so that on no account it be suppressed or hidden by anyone, but rather be read before all people, and in the presence of Coroticus himself. May God inspire them sometime to recover their senses for God, repenting, however late, their heinous deeds . . . and set free the baptised women whom they took captive, in order that they may deserve to live to God, and be made whole, here and in eternity!

tribal leaders, were hostile to Patrick's teachings. His life was frequently threatened, and once he was jailed for two weeks.

Many senior church officials also despised him because of his lack of education. In 444 or 445, with the permission of Pope St. Leo I, Patrick founded a cathedral (main church) at Armagh (now a city in the southern part of Northern Ireland), which continues to be a religious center in Ireland.

Demands return of slaves

Patrick devoted his career to saving pagans. Yet on at least one occasion, several years before he wrote the *Confession,* he turned his attention to the atrocities (extreme cruelty) of slavery. A British–Roman prince named Coroticus, who was supposedly a Christian, headed a kingdom in southwest Scotland and northwest England, not far from Patrick's boyhood home. Coroticus staged a raid on Ireland and captured newly converted Christians. Several captives were killed and the survivors were sold into slavery in Scotland and Ireland.

Appalled by this event, Patrick sent a letter to Coroticus, requesting the return of the slaves. He was ignored. He wrote a second appeal, the *Letter to the Soldiers of Coroticus*, which was addressed to Coroticus's men and was intended to be read aloud in public. This remarkable document, which still exists, vividly conveys Patrick's anger and feelings of betrayal at the violence committed against Christians by other Christians.

Makes lasting contributions

Little is known about Patrick's work beyond the facts provided in the *Confession,* but he made lasting contributions that are still in evidence today. Historians note that he was successful in his mission because he understood the Irish people. As bishop of Ireland he initiated a system of church organization, with bishops overseeing monasteries headed by abbots, that was based on the tribal units he found when he arrived in the country. He also helped change and soften Irish laws, especially those pertaining to slaves and taxation of the poor, and he introduced the Roman alphabet to Ireland. Patrick retired in 457 and went to live at Saul. When he died four years later, Ireland was almost entirely Christian. This achievement transformed a barely educated former slave into one of the most successful missionaries in history.

Further Reading

Books

Hanson, R. P. C. *The Life and Writings of the Historical Saint Patrick.* Seabury Press, 1983.

Hopkin, Alannah. *The Living Legend of St. Patrick.* St. Martin's Press, 1989.

Reynolds, Quentin James. *The Life of Saint Patrick.* Random House, 1955.

Thompson, E. A. *Who Was Saint Patrick?* St. Martin's Press, 1985.

Web sites

The Ultimate St. Patrick. [Online] http://www.toad.net/~sticker/patrick. html/ (accessed on September 9, 1999).

Mary Prince

Born c.1788
Brackish Pond, Bermuda (British Colony)
Death date unknown

West Indian slave of African descent

The publication in England in 1831 of *The History of Mary Prince, a West Indian Slave, Related by Herself* caused quite a stir. The story of Mary Prince's life as a slave in the West Indian colony of Bermuda was widely read by the general public and lawmakers alike at a time when the country was fiercely debating the abolition of slavery in the British colonies. Mary Prince's *History* was especially shocking as it was the first time that a British female slave's life story was published, complete with tales of murder, torture, sexual abuse, and general mistreatment of slaves.

"This is slavery," Mary Prince declared at the end of *History.* "I tell it to let English people know the truth; and I hope they will never leave off to pray God, and call loud to the great King of England, till all the poor blacks be given free, and slavery done up for evermore."

Oh happy days?

Mary Prince was born a slave on a small farm in Brackish Pond, Devonshire Parish, Bermuda. Unlike many of

The first African British female ex-slave to have her life story published; her story greatly influenced public debate on the abolition of slavery in the British colonies.

Europe's New World island colonies at the time, the major industries of Bermuda were shipbuilding and salting, not plantation farming. In 1788 the population of Bermuda, a collection of seven major islands and over a hundred smaller ones, was around eleven thousand people. Almost half of the people were slaves of African descent, some of whose ancestors had arrived in Bermuda as early as 1616.

Mary Prince's mother was a house slave and her father was a sawyer (a person who saws wood for a living). Her father was owned by Mr. Trimmingham, a shipbuilder, and Mary and her mother were owned by Mr. Myners. When Mary Prince was just an infant, Mr. Myners died, and she was sold along with her mother to Captain Darrel. The captain bought Mary Prince as a present for his grandchild, Miss Betsey Williams. Mary Prince's mother became the house slave for Mrs. Williams—Betsey's mother, and the wife of the captain's son.

In *History,* Mary Prince called her childhood "the happiest period of my life." Looking back on those first years with the wisdom of a forty-year-old woman telling her life story, she added, "for I was too young to understand rightly my condition as a slave." For her first twelve years, Mary Prince and her brothers and sisters were raised by her mother. Given only light tasks to do, Mary Prince and her siblings played with Miss Betsey like a sister. Mrs. Williams, who ran the house in her husband's absence (which was most of the time), was a kind mistress to her slaves. "I was truly attached to her," Mary Prince recalled in *History,* "and, next to my own mother, loved her better than any creature in the world."

Early education

Mary Prince had just turned twelve years old when she was forced to confront the cold realities of her enslavement. Two years after the sudden death of Mrs. Williams in 1798, Mary Prince and her sisters, Hannah and Dinah, were sold in the local slave market to raise money for Mr. Williams's upcoming wedding. Mary was sold first. "I then saw my sisters led forth," she wrote in *History,* "and sold to different owners; so that we had not the sad satisfaction of being partners in bondage. . . . It was a sad parting; one went one way, one another, and our poor mammy went home with nothing."

Mary Prince's new masters were Captain John Ingham and his wife, who lived at Spanish Point, about five miles from the Williams estate. Under the Inghams, Mary Prince learned how to milk cows, herd sheep and cattle, rub down horses, feed animals, take care of children, cook for a family, and do all the household chores. In *History* Mary Prince describes other things she learned, such as "the exact difference between the smart [pain] of the rope, the cart-whip, and the cow-skin."

First rage

Slaves under the Inghams were punished for the most minor mistakes or disobedience. And none was worked harder, or beaten more, than the Inghams' household slave, Hetty. Hetty, who was pregnant at the time, was flogged so hard after letting a cow escape that she and her unborn baby died from the injuries. Hetty's work—and her beatings—then fell on Mary Prince.

After being beaten nearly to death herself for breaking a jar, and another time for letting a cow escape, Mary Prince ran away to where her mother lived. She was soon returned to the Ingham household by her father, who pleaded with her master to treat her better. With her father at her side, Mary Prince verbally took a stand against her master, as she recalls in *History*: "I then took courage and said that I could stand the floggings no longer; that I was weary of my life, and therefore I had run away to my mother; but mothers could only weep and mourn over their children, they could not save them from their cruel masters." Mary Prince won a small victory: she was not flogged by her master that day.

Salt slave on Turk's Island

Mary Prince endured five more years of daily abuse from the Inghams before being sold in 1805 to her new master, identified only as "Mr. D—" in her story. At first Mary Prince was glad to make the 750-mile sea voyage to Turk's Island, if only to get away from her cruel masters. She soon learned, however, that her new master was no better. Mr. D—

was a cold-blooded taskmaster whose business was extracting salt from sea water with the use of slave labor.

The work on Turk's Island was very hard and involved hours of standing knee-deep in saltwater, which caused the skin on Mary Prince's legs to break out in great boils that never had a chance to heal properly. Except for short meal breaks, Mary Prince and her fellow slaves stood in saltwater from four in the morning until dark. They were given daily rations of boiled corn in the morning, corn soup for lunch, and raw corn at quitting time, which they pounded into mortar and boiled in water for supper. "We slept in a long shed, divided into narrow slips, like the stalls for cattle," Mary Prince wrote in *History.* "Boards fixed upon stakes driven into the ground, without mat or covering, were our only beds."

Mary Prince and her fellow slaves sometimes worked around the clock—if salt had to be prepared for a waiting ship, for example. Being tired or sick made no difference to Mr. D—. Mary Prince developed boils on her feet that kept her from working as fast as the others, and like other slaves who could not keep up, she was beaten mercilessly by her master. Mary also witnessed the torture of an ill slave named Daniel, the beating and stabbing of another slave, Ben, and the brutal murder of an old and sick slave named Sarah.

A turning point

Around 1810, after five years in the salt ponds at Turk's Island, Mary Prince was forced to return to Bermuda with her master. She was assigned to work in the house as a servant to Mr. D—'s daughters and in the fields raising such crops as sweet potatoes, Indian corn, bananas, cabbages, pumpkins, and onions. She did all the household work and attended the cow and horse as well. The work was better than on Turk's Island but the cruelty of Mr. D— was still a force that Mary Prince had to reckon with.

"He [Mr. D—] had an ugly fashion of stripping himself quite naked and ordering me to wash him in a hot tub of water," Mary Prince wrote in *History.* "This was worse to me than all the licks [hits from beatings]." After some time, Mary Prince refused her master's advances and demanded to be sold.

Freedom's first steps

Mary Prince's wish was soon met, when around 1816 she was bought for $300 by Mr. John Wood, a Bermudian merchant who was in the process of moving his family to the island of Antigua (pronounced ann-TEE-gwa). Most slaves had one or two owners in their lifetimes. Mary Prince had five. The Woods turned out to be her last as Mary Prince, slowly, over a period of more than ten years, gained her freedom from them, one small step at a time.

Mary Prince and Mrs. Woods did not get along well from the very beginning. Suffering from rheumatism (pronounced ROO-meh-tiz-em; swelling and pain in muscles and joints) and St. Anthony's Fire (a disease of the skin), Mary Prince was seldom able to keep up with the loads of washing that were heaped upon her by her mistress. Mrs. Woods did not hesitate to use the whip on Mary Prince either, which strengthened her resolve to seek freedom, however she could attain it.

One way Mary Prince was able to assert herself was by earning and saving money she hoped would purchase her freedom. When the Woods vacationed in the country, Mary Prince stayed at home and took in washing; sold yams, coffee, and other supplies to the captains of ships; and bought and sold livestock in the local market. Mary Prince, independent of her masters' knowledge or permission, also converted to the Methodist religion and learned how to read and write. Her greatest act of rebellion was her marriage in 1826 to James Daniels, a free black widower who worked as a carpenter, like her father. For this act, Mary Prince was flogged by Mr. Woods. Mary Prince begged the Woods to sell her or allow her to buy her own freedom. They refused time after time.

Fed up

The last phase of Mary Prince's life as a slave began in 1828, when she accompanied the Woods on a trip to London, England, to pick up their daughters from school. Leaving her husband behind in Antigua, Mary Prince hoped the change of climate would improve her health. She also believed that the Woods would grant her manumission (a formal release from bondage) in England, where slavery had been abolished since 1772, and allow her to return to her husband in Antigua a free woman.

History makes History

It was Mary Prince's association with the Anti-Slavery Society of England that led to the publication of her life story, *The History of Mary Prince, a West Indian Slave, Related by Herself,* in pamphlet form in 1831. In 1829 Mary Prince was hired as a house servant by Thomas Pringle, the secretary of the society and editor and publisher of her narrative. Sometime during 1829 or 1830, Mary Prince told her story to a house guest of the Pringles, Susanna Strickland, who wrote it down word for word. There is no way of telling how much of Mary Prince's story was edited before publication to fit the needs of the Anti-Slavery Society and their abolition campaign.

What is known is that what was printed and distributed, in three editions in 1831, caused a great uproar in England as the country was debating the emancipation of all slaves in the British colonies.

Mary Prince's autobiography, the first ever published of an African British female slave, was called a fraud by proslavery advocates. Antislavery readers, on the other hand, had little trouble believing the horrors of colonial slavery. The debate over the book's authenticity ended on July 31, 1833, when Parliament (governing body of the United Kingdom) passed a bill that abolished slavery throughout the British colonies.

The Woods, it turned out, had no intention of ever selling Mary Prince or setting her free. They knew Mary Prince would be legally free once on English soil but they thought that she would be unable to leave them due to her poor health and the fact that she was a stranger in a strange land. Indeed, Mary Prince's rheumatism worsened in England, swelling her body and crippling her limbs. Fed up with increased work loads in the face of her illness, Mary Prince, in November 1828, left the Woods and sought help from the Moravian (Methodist) Missionaries and the Anti-Slavery Society.

Bittersweet freedom

The Anti-Slavery Society went to great lengths to help Mary Prince establish herself as a free person in London. They helped her find work, and made repeated, but unsuccessful, attempts to purchase her unconditional freedom from the

Woods, who returned to Antigua without Mary Prince sometime in 1829.

Did Mary Prince ever return to her husband in Antigua or her family in Bermuda, a free woman, to live her life out in peace and liberty? There is no evidence to suggest that her life ended so happily. On the contrary, the last information that is known about Mary Prince's condition is from a note in the second edition of *History,* which suggests a bleak future: "Mary Prince has been afflicted with a disease of the eyes, which, it is feared, may terminate in total blindness." Mary Prince's life story, a tale as bleak as it is full of strength and hope, opened the eyes of the British to the horrors of slavery in their colonies in a way that had never been done before.

Further Reading

Ferguson, Moira., ed. *The History of Mary Prince, a West Indian Slave, Related by Herself,* revised edition. Ann Arbor, Mich.: University of Michigan Press, 1997.

Rodriguez, Junius P., ed. *The Historical Encyclopedia of World Slavery.* Santa Barbara, Calif.: ABC-CLIO, Inc., 1993.

Sacagawea

Born c.1784
near present-day Lemhi, Idaho
Died 1812
South Dakota (not determined)

Interpreter, guide

Sacagawea (pronounced sak-uh-juh-WEE-uh) was a Shoshone (pronounced sho-SHO-nee) interpreter and guide for the Corps of Discovery, one of the most famous expeditions in American history. She was also the only woman member of the party. Most of the information about her life comes from the journals of Meriwether Lewis and William Clark, leaders of the exploring party. Her skills as an interpreter and as contact between the Shoshone and the explorers, her knowledge of the plants and wildlife along the route, and her common sense and good humor contributed to the journey's success. Nevertheless, there is much controversy surrounding the story of Sacagewea's life.

Captured by Hidatsa war party

Sacagawea was born into the Native American tribe known as the Shoshone. Her name at birth was Boinaiv, which means "Grass Maiden." She was born sometime between 1784 and 1788 into the Lehmi band of the Shoshone, who lived in the eastern part of the Salmon River area of present-day central Idaho. Her father was chief of the village. In 1800, when Boinaiv

> "[She] reconciles all the Indians as to our friendly intentions—a woman with a party of men is a token of peace."
>
> *William Clark*

Sacagawea. *(Corbis-Bettmann. Reproduced by permission.)*

159

was about twelve years old, her band was camped at the Three Forks of the Missouri River in Montana. There they were attacked by Hidatsa warriors. Several girls and boys, including Boinaiv, were captured and taken back to the Hidatsa village.

Boinaiv was given the name *Sacagawea,* which means "Bird Woman," by her captors. Historians disagree about the origin and spelling of her name. It is often written as *Sacajawea,* a name meaning "Boat Launcher" in Shoshone. Sometime between 1800 and 1804, Sacagawea and another girl were sold to (or won in a gambling match by) a French-Canadian trader, Toussaint Charbonneau, who lived among the Hidatsa. He eventually married both women.

Joins Corps of Discovery

In 1803 U.S. president Thomas Jefferson (1743–1826) and the U.S. Congress authorized a Corps of Discovery for the purpose of exploring the territory between the Mississippi and Columbia Rivers and attempting to find a water route to the Pacific Ocean. Meriwether Lewis (1774–1809), who was Jefferson's secretary, and his friend William Clark (1770–1838) were assigned to lead the expedition. The party of about forty-five men left St. Louis, Missouri, on May 14, 1804. They arrived at the Mandan and Hidatsa villages near the mouth of the Knife River in North Dakota on October 26, 1804. There, they built cabins in a clearing below the villages and settled in for the winter.

Lewis and Clark realized that they would need someone to help communicate with the Shoshone in order to obtain supplies. In November they met Charbonneau and hired both him and his wife, Sacagawea, as interpreters. The process turned out to be quite complicated, however. Sacagawea talked with her husband in the language of the Gros Ventre people. Charbonneau then passed on Sacagawea's words in French to a member of the party who spoke French and English; that person then relayed the information to Lewis and Clark in English. Sacagawea also used sign language, which many in the party could understand.

River named for Sacagawea

By the time the party had arrived in the Mandan villages, Sacagawea was pregnant. In February 1805 she gave birth to a boy named Jean Baptiste Charbonneau. On April 7, 1805, Sacagawea—carrying her infant in a cradleboard on her back—accompanied the expedition out of the Mandan villages for the trek west. Sacagawea showed Lewis and Clark important passageways through the wilderness. She also quickly demonstrated her knowledge of edible plants along the trail. Lewis wrote on April 9 that when the expedition stopped for dinner Sacagawea "busied herself in search for the wild artichokes. . . . This operation she performed by penetrating the earth with a sharp stick about some collection of driftwood. Her labors soon proved successful and she procured a good quantity of these roots."

On May 14 the party encountered heavy winds near the Yellowstone River. Charbonneau was at the helm of the *pirogue* (canoe), which held supplies and valuables gathered during the expedition. Lewis and Clark were onshore at the time. Knowing Charbonneau was not comfortable in the water, they could only watch in horror as the boat overturned. Sacagawea, however, quickly handled the situation. Lewis wrote, "The Indian woman, to whom I ascribe equal fortitude and resolution with any person on board at the time of the accident, caught and preserved most of the light articles which were washed overboard." The articles included the records of the trip. About a week later, Lewis recorded that he and Clark had named a recently discovered river in Sacagawea's honor.

Reunited with Shoshone

On June 10 Sacagawea became ill. Lewis and Clark were concerned for her welfare, and they took turns tend-

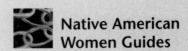

Native American Women Guides

Sacagawea was part of a long tradition of Native American women who guided Europeans through the frontier wilderness. After arriving in North America in the early 1500s, white fur traders discovered that native women were excellent interpreters and diplomatic agents. The women carried messages to tribal leaders, familiarized Europeans with native customs, resolved differences and misunderstandings, and taught native languages to the white men. They also provided services such as carrying supplies, mending tents, cooking meals, and making clothing. Since there were few white women on the frontier, native women—like Sacagawea—frequently married European explorers and traders. Too often, however, Native American women were forced into these roles. Like Sacagewea, many were captured by enemy warriors and thrust into the white world.

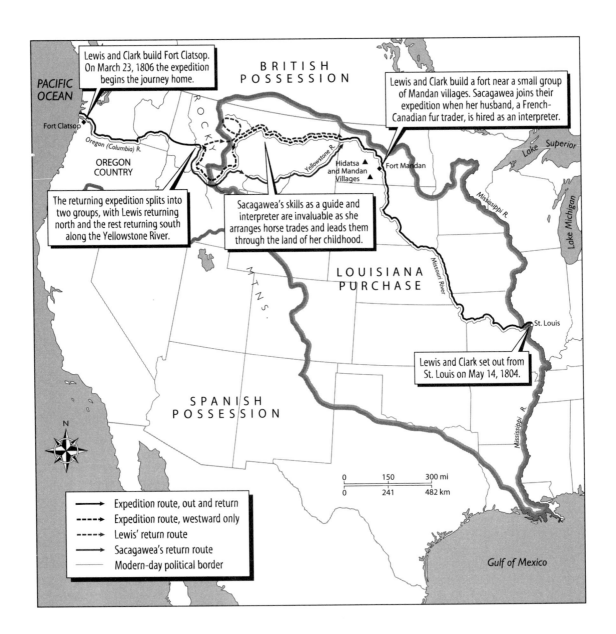

Map showing the routes taken by Lewis, Clark, and Sacagawea during their exploration of the American West. *(Reproduced by permission of the Gale Group)*

The map contains the following labels:

PACIFIC OCEAN

BRITISH POSSESSION

Lewis and Clark build Fort Clatsop. On March 23, 1806 the expedition begins the journey home.

Lewis and Clark build a fort near a small group of Mandan villages. Sacagawea joins their expedition when her husband, a French-Canadian fur trader, is hired as an interpreter.

Fort Clatsop

Oregon (Columbia) R.

OREGON COUNTRY

Yellowstone R.

Hidatsa and Mandan Villages

Fort Mandan

Lake Superior

The returning expedition splits into two groups, with Lewis returning north and the rest returning south along the Yellowstone River.

Sacagawea's skills as a guide and interpreter are invaluable as she arranges horse trades and leads them through the land of her childhood.

Mississippi R.

Lake Michigan

R O C K Y

M T N S.

LOUISIANA PURCHASE

Missouri River

St. Louis

SPANISH POSSESSION

Lewis and Clark set out from St. Louis on May 14, 1804.

Mississippi R.

N

| 0 | 150 | 300 mi |
| 0 | 241 | 482 km |

→ Expedition route, out and return
- - - → Expedition route, westward only
- - - - Lewis' return route
→ Sacagawea's return route
—— Modern-day political border

Gulf of Mexico

ing to her for several days. Her condition worsened until Charbonneau convinced her to take medicine. The explorers noted privately that if she died, it would be his fault. Lewis wrote that Sacagawea's illness "gave me some concern as well for the poor object herself, then with a young child in her arms, as from the consideration of her being our only dependence for a friendly negotiation with the Snake [Shoshone] Indians on whom we depend for horses to assist us in our portage from the Missouri to the Columbia River."

On July 30, 1805, the party passed the spot on the Three Forks of the Missouri where Sacagawea had been taken from the Shoshones five years earlier. A little over a week later, at Beaverhead Rock, Sacagawea recognized her homeland. On August 13 Lewis took an advance party to find the Shoshone while Clark remained behind with Sacagawea and the rest of the group. The next day Clark saw Charbonneau hit his wife and spoke angrily to him about his behavior. On August 17 Clark, Sacagawea, and the others found Lewis, who had met the Lehmi-Shoshone chief Cameahwait. They sent Sacagawea to interpret between Lewis and Clark and Cameahwait:

> She came into the tent, sat down, and was beginning to interpret, when in the person of Cameahwait she recognized her brother; she instantly jumped up and ran and embraced him, throwing over him her blanket and weeping profusely . . . after some conversation between them she resumed her seat, and attempted to interpret for us, but her new situation seemed to overpower her, and she was frequently interrupted by tears.

Sacagawea learned that her only surviving family were two brothers and a son of her eldest sister, whom she immediately adopted. She also met the Shoshone man to whom she had been promised in marriage when she was a child. He was no longer interested in marrying her, however, because she had borne a child with another man.

"A token of peace"

Leaving her adopted son in the care of Cameahwait, Sacagawea continued on the journey. Eventually the party followed the Snake River to its junction with the Columbia, then headed toward the Pacific Ocean. On October 13, 1805, Clark again commented on Sacagawea's value to the expedition, saying she "reconciles all the Indians as to our friendly intentions—a woman with a party of men is a token of peace." In November, a lead party reached the ocean. Upon hearing the men had discovered a beached whale, Sacagewea insisted that Lewis and Clark take her to see it.

When the party separated on the return trip in order to explore various routes, Sacagawea joined Clark, directing

One of several memorials erected to honor Sacagawea. *(Library of Congress)*

him through Shoshone territory. She also suggested that he take the Bozeman Pass—a mountain pathway that runs between what are now the states of Colorado and Montana—to rejoin the other members at the junction of the Yellowstone and Missouri Rivers.

On August 14, 1806, the expedition arrived back at the Mandan villages. Charbonneau and Sacagawea decided to stay there. Clark arranged to adopt their infant son, whom he had affectionately nicknamed "Pomp." On the return trip to St. Louis, Clark wrote a letter to Charbonneau, inviting him to work in St. Louis and telling him that Sacagawea deserved a "great reward" for her help on the journey. Yet only Charbonneau was paid for his services.

Controversy over Sacagawea's later years

There is reason to believe that Sacagawea lived only a few years after leaving the expedition. Charbonneau possibly accepted Clark's invitation to go to Missouri. On April 2, 1811, a lawyer and traveler named Henry Brackenridge was on a boat going from St. Louis to Native American villages in North and South Dakota. In his journal he mentioned meeting the Frenchman and his Snake Indian wife. Brackenridge admired Sacagawea's gentle personality and added that she tried to imitate European styles of clothing and manners. He also expressed regret that she looked ill and that she wanted to visit her people again but her husband wanted to live in a city.

Many historians believe that Charbonneau and Sacagawea left their son, eventually called Jean Baptiste, with Clark in St. Louis. The boy grew up to become a respected interpreter and mountain man. Then they took their infant daughter, Lizette, and traveled to the Missouri Fur Company of Manuel Lisa in South Dakota. An employee of the fur company, John C. Luttig, recorded in his journal on December 20, 1812: "This Evening the Wife of Charbonneau, a Snake Squaw died of a putrid fever she was a good and the best Woman in the fort aged abt 25 years she left a fine infant girl." Sacagawea was buried on the grounds of the fort. William Clark later published an account book for the period 1825 to 1828, in which he listed the members of the expedition and whether they were then either living or dead. He noted that Sacagawea was deceased.

According to another theory, Sacagawea left her husband, took Jean Baptiste and her adopted son, Bazil, and went to live with a tribe of plains Indians known as the Comanche (kuh-MAN-chee). There she married a man named Jerk Meat and bore five more children. She later returned to live with the Shoshone at the Wind River Reservation in Fort Washakie, Wyoming. She was called *porivo* (chief) and became an active tribal leader. Some Shoshones, Indian agents, and missionaries reported that she died at the age of about 100 in 1884 and was buried at Fort Washakie. Critics argue that this "Sacagawea" was actually a different Shoshone woman.

Honored with numerous memorials

The Shoshones of Fort Washakie started a project to document the descendants of Sacagawea. Many among them believe that she indeed lived a long and full life. Sacagawea has become one of the most memorialized women in U.S. history. A bronze statue of her was exhibited during the centennial (hundred-year) observance of the Lewis and Clark expedition in St. Louis in 1904. Another statue was commissioned by a women's suffrage group in Oregon, with the unveiling set to coincide with the Lewis and Clark Centennial Exposition in Portland, Oregon, in 1905. Statues were also erected in Idaho, Montana, North Dakota, Oklahoma, and Virginia. In addition to the river in Montana named for Sacagawea, other memorials include three mountains, two lakes, and numerous markers, paintings, musical compositions, schools, and a museum.

Further Reading

Books

Brown, Marion Marsh. *Sacagawea: Indian Interpreter to Lewis and Clark.* Children's Press, 1988.

Clark, Ella E., and Margot Edmonds. *Sacagawea of the Lewis and Clark Expedition.* Berkeley, Calif.: University of California Press, 1979.

Hebard, Grace Raymond. *Sacajawea: A Guide and Interpreter of the Lewis and Clark Expedition, with an Account of the Travels of Toussaint Charbonneau, and of Jean Baptiste, the Expedition Papoose.* Glendale, Calif.: Arthur H. Clark Company, 1933.

Howard, Harold P. *Sacajawea.* Norman, Okla.: University of Oklahoma Press, 1971.

Reid, Russell. *Sakagawea: The Bird Woman.* Bismarck, N.D.: State Historical Society of North Dakota, 1986.

Remley, David, "Sacajawea of Myth and History," in *Women and Western American Literature,* edited by Helen Winter Stauffer and Susan J. Rosowski. Troy, N.Y.: 1982, pp. 70–89.

St. George, Judith. *Sacagawea.* Putnam, 1997.

White, Alana J. *Sacagawea: Westward with Lewis and Clark.* Enslow, 1997.

Periodicals

Dawson, Jan C., "Sacagawea: Pilot or Pioneer Mother?" *Pacific Northwest Quarterly,* 83, January 1992, pp. 22–28.

Aleksandr Isayevich Solzhenitsyn

**Born December 11, 1918
Kislovodsk, Soviet Union**

**Slave in Soviet labor camps,
world-renowned author**

From 1927 to 1953, the Union of Soviet Socialist Republics (USSR) was ruled by the dictator Joseph Stalin (1879-1953). During Stalin's rule, the government of the USSR enslaved millions of Soviet citizens in labor camps in central Russia, Siberia, central Asia, and above the Arctic Circle. Russian-born novelist, dramatist, and poet Aleksandr Solzhenitsyn was one of those victims, accused of political crimes and forced as punishment into the Soviet corrective labor camp system known as the gulag (pronounced GOO-lahg) from 1945 to 1953.

First as a critic of Stalin's government, and then as a critic of the Soviet system in general for its abuse of human rights and its censorship of writers, for over thirty years Solzhenitsyn waged a one-man war against the powerful communist government of the USSR. Although very few of Solzhenitsyn's extensive writings have ever been published in the former Soviet Union, his novels, short stories, and plays about his experiences in Stalin's slave labor camps have been widely read throughout the world. Solzhenitsyn won the Nobel Prize for literature in 1970.

A survivor of an eight-year sentence in the Soviet Union's corrective labor camps, Solzhenitsyn emerged to become one of the great literary figures of the twentieth century.

Aleksandr Solzhenitsyn.
*(AP/Wide World Photos.
Reproduced by permission.)*

The young writer

Aleksandr Solzhenitsyn (pronounced sohl-zuh-NEET-sin) was born in Kislovodsk (pronounced KEES-luh-votsk), a health resort in the northern Caucasus (KAH-kuh-suhs) between the Black and Caspian seas. His father, Isaaki, survived four years on the German front as a Russian artillery officer in World War I (1914–18) only to die in a hunting accident six months before his son's birth. When Solzhenitsyn was six years old he and his mother, Taisiya, moved to the city of Rostov-on-Don, in the northern Caucasus, where she worked as a typist when she was not ill.

Despite their impoverished conditions, Solzhenitsyn was able to indulge in his love of reading, and according to his own account, by the age of ten had read most of the Russian literary classics including Leo Tolstoy's (1828–1910) *War and Peace* in its entirety. Solzhenitsyn admits that he wanted to be a writer from the time he was nine years old and when he was growing up he longed to go to Moscow to pursue literary studies. He excelled as a student and graduated in 1936 from the best high school in the city. During that time Solzhenitsyn was an active member of Komsomol, the Communist youth organization.

Soviet citizen

Not wanting to move away from his ailing mother, Solzhenitsyn enrolled at the University of Rostov in 1938. Although his passion was for literature, Solzhenitsyn was not impressed with the university's literary studies faculty and enrolled instead in the mathematics department. In 1940 Solzhenitsyn married Natalya Reshetovskaya, a fellow Rostov University student who later became a professor and research chemist. In 1941 Solzhenitsyn graduated with honors, with the help of a Stalin scholarship along the way. In the same year Solzhenitsyn began his formal literary studies through correspondence courses with the Moscow Institute of History, Philosophy, and Literature.

Solzhenitsyn briefly taught mathematics at a Rostov secondary school before being drafted into the Red Army after Germany's invasion of the Soviet Union in 1941. Solzhenitsyn served as a driver of an army wagon train, with the rank of private until November 1942, when he completed training as an artillery officer. Solzhenitsyn was sent to the front as a commander of an artillery battery. There he served with distinction, earning two wartime decorations for bravery and attaining the rank of captain by 1945.

Imprisoned

In February 1945 Solzhenitsyn was called into the headquarters of his commanding officer where he was put under arrest by the Soviet secret police. He was immediately transported to Lubyanka Prison in Moscow. The charge: criticizing Russian leader, Joseph Stalin, in letters to a school friend between 1944 and 1945. Stripped of his captain's rank, Solzhenitsyn was sentenced in the summer of 1945 by a three-man court, without a hearing, to eight years in a labor camp.

Solzhenitsyn was transferred to another prison in Moscow for about a year. There he worked as a laborer on a building project. Due to his skills in mathematics Solzhenitsyn was sent to Marfino, a specialized prison on the outskirts of Moscow that forced mathematicians and scientists to do research for the state. In 1950 Solzhenitsyn was sent to a hard labor camp at Ekibastuz, Kazakhstan (pronounced eh-kee-BOS-tus, kuh-zok-STON), in central Asia, perhaps because of his refusal to cooperate fully in research projects for the government.

Conditions at Ekibastuz, a special camp created for political prisoners only, were much harsher. It was bitter cold without warm clothing and proper shelter, the discipline was strict, and

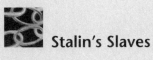

Stalin's Slaves

Under Joseph Stalin's rule (1927-53), as many as five to eight million people were in "corrective labor camps" in the USSR at any one time. Stalin used his huge prison work force in a variety of ways to bolster the Soviet economy without having to pay for labor. Prisoners built and maintained roads, canals, and rail lines, and constructed housing and hydroelectric plants. They labored in the coal, gold, chrome, and ore mines, and in the oil fields. Prisoners also worked in agriculture, fishing, lumbering, and manufacturing. The prisoners were paid in food, not wages. Their clothing and shelter were minimal. Living conditions were so poor that the death rate for inmates at many labor camps was thirty percent a year.

The use of prison labor does not always constitute a form of slavery. The conditions of Soviet-style forced labor, however, were nothing short of slavery. People were arrested without reasonable causes, shipped on trains like animals to faraway places, forced to do unbearable work without compensation, and frozen and starved to death.

hunger was a fact of life. The work was hard. In his three years at the camp Solzhenitsyn provided slave labor as a bricklayer, a foundry worker, and a general laborer. While in Ekibastuz, Solzhenitsyn developed a cancerous growth in his stomach that was operated on in a prison hospital. He was not expected to live.

Exiled

Having served his full term in prison, Solzhenitsyn was released on March 5, 1953, the same day that Stalin's death was announced. Solzhenitsyn walked out of the labor camp without guards for the first time in eight years but he was not free. Soviet authorities instead sent him into permanent exile (forced removal from one's native country) in Kokterek, in southern Kazakhstan. At the end of 1953, on the verge of death, Solzhenitsyn was allowed to go to Tashkent, Uzbekistan, for treatment in a cancer clinic. There he underwent successful radiation therapy and then returned to Kazakhstan where he taught mathematics and physics in a rural school, always under surveillance by the Soviet secret police.

In the hard labor camp, Solzhenitsyn was able to write only bits of poetry on scraps of paper, which he destroyed once he committed them to memory. In exile, even though he was constantly monitored, Solzhenitsyn spent great amounts of time secretly writing prose despite being convinced that Soviet authorities would never allow its publication.

With the death of Stalin the political atmosphere of the Soviet Union changed and the country began to move away from some of its harsher institutions and policies. In June 1956 Solzhenitsyn was released from forced exile, and in 1957, Solzhenitsyn's 1945 conviction was officially recognized as invalid, which allowed him to return to central Russia. He settled in the city of Ryazan (pronounced ri-ZON), southeast of Moscow, where he found work as a secondary school teacher. His wife, who had remarried while he was in the labor camp, divorced her second husband to remarry Solzhenitsyn.

Begins to publish

The rise to power of Nikita S. Kruschev (1894–1971; pronounced kroosh-CHAWF) in the mid-1950s, and his policy of de-Stalinization of the USSR, led Solzhenitsyn in 1961 to believe that it was finally safe for him to try to publish some of his writings. His first attempt was successful. In 1962 the Soviet Union's leading literary journal, *Novy Mir* (New World), published Solzhenitsyn's novel, *One Day in the Life of Ivan Denisovich*. The story describes a single day in the life of Ivan Denisovich Shukhov, a labor camp inmate sentenced to ten years corrective labor because he had been taken prisoner by the Germans during the war. Publication of the short novel was approved by Krushchev himself as part of an official anti-Stalin campaign.

The reaction to *Ivan Denisovich* was instant worldwide acclaim for Solzhenitsyn as an important Russian author. In the USSR, he was admitted to the Union of Soviet Writers and the book received high praise from critics in the official newspapers, *Pravda* and *Izvestia*. In 1963 Solzhenitsyn published three more short stories in *Novy Mir* and was nominated for, but did not win, a Lenin Prize for literature in 1964. Solzhenitsyn, however, had accumulated enough royalties (money from sales of his book) at this point to quit his teaching job to devote all of his time to writing.

Final showdown

After Krushchev was removed from power in December 1964, Solzhenitsyn found it increasingly difficult to get his work published in the Soviet Union. The USSR's new leadership viewed Krushchev's policies—and Solzhenitsyn's writings—as having gone too far in their criticism of established Soviet policies. In 1965 Soviet authorities confiscated Solzhenitsyn's manuscript of *The First Circle,* a novel about his forced labor at the Marfino penal research facility, as well as other manuscripts that Solzhenitsyn considered as unfinished works in progress. Manuscripts of *The First Circle* and *Cancer Ward* found their way to the West, however, where they were published in 1968.

In May 1967 Solzhenitsyn wrote a famous letter to the Fourth National Congress of Soviet writers, criticizing the Soviet system of censorship of its writers. Eighty-two writers petitioned the Communist Party's Central Committee on Solzhenitsyn's behalf but in November 1969 he was expelled from the Writer's Union. When he won the Nobel Prize for literature in 1970 Solzhenitsyn did not travel to Stockholm,

Sweden, to receive the award for fear that he would not be permitted to return home by Soviet authorities.

Solzhenitsyn's next major novel, *August 1914* (the first in The Red Wheel series of books on World War I and the Russian Revolution), was rejected by seven Soviet publishers before Solzhenitsyn allowed it to be published abroad in 1971. In 1973 when Soviet authorities seized the manuscript of Solzhenitsyn's major work about the Soviet penal system, *The Gulag Archipelago,* Solzhenitsyn immediately authorized its publication in Paris, France, where a copy had earlier been smuggled. Parts one and two of the seven-part work appeared in print in December 1973.

Later years

On February 12, 1974, Solzhenitsyn was arrested and charged with treason (betrayal of one's country). He was stripped of his citizenship and deported (banished) to West Germany. Solzhenitsyn's second wife, Natalya Svetlova (they were married in 1973 after Solzhenitsyn divorced his first wife), and her three sons were permitted to join him. The Solzhenitsyn family lived for two years in Zurich, Switzerland, before moving to the United States where they settled in rural Vermont.

Solzhenitsyn continued to write novels in exile and had books published in 1984 and 1986. In 1989 *Novy Mir* published the first officially sanctioned excerpts from *The Gulag Archipelago,* and in 1990, Solzhenitsyn's Soviet citizenship was officially restored. Solzhenitsyn returned to Russia in 1994, three years after the collapse of the Soviet Union.

In May 1997 Solzhenitsyn was hospitalized for a heart ailment. In 1999, Solzhenitsyn's latest installment in The Red Wheel series, *November 1916,* was released in English translation (the Russian-language edition was issued in 1993).

Further Reading

Books

Meltzer, Milton. *Slavery: A World History,* updated edition. New York: De Capo Press, 1993.

Pohl, J. Otto. *The Stalinist Penal System*. Jefferson, N.C.: McFarland & Co., Inc., Publishers, 1997.

Solzhenitsyn, Aleksandr I. *One Day in the Life of Ivan Denisovich*. New York: Farrar, Straus and Giroux, 1991.

Solzhenitsyn, Aleksandr I. *Solzhenitsyn: A Pictorial Autobiography*. New York: Farrar, Straus and Giroux, 1974.

Sylvester, Theodore L. *Slavery Throughout History: Almanac*. Detroit: Gale Group, 1999.

Periodicals
Steiner, George. "Books: And the reds go marching in . . .," *The Observer*, June 14, 1999.

Web sites
Solzhenitsyn, Aleksandr. [Online] Available http://vweb.hwwilsonweb. com/ggi-bin/webspirs.cgi (Accessed September 2, 1999)

Spartacus

Birth date unknown
Thrace (a region in southeast Europe near Italy)
Died 71 B.C.E.

Roman slave and gladiator, rebellion leader

The slave war started by Spartacus in 73 B.C.E. was the largest slave outbreak in Roman history. In the two years of armed revolt tens of thousands of slaves ran away from their owners to join the original rebels. Not long before the Spartacan war, the Romans had already brutally crushed two previous slave wars in Sicily (a large island off the southern tip of Italy), the First Servile War (135–133 B.C.E.), and the Second Servile War (104–100 B.C.E.). Spartacus and his followers for two years battled one of the world's greatest armies and in the process occupied and controlled at one time or another large parts of central and southern Italy. Spartacus and his followers were eventually defeated but it took a military force as great as Caesar would later require to conquer all of Gaul (France) to do it.

Unknown origins

What little information there is about the personal life of Spartacus (pronounced SPART-uh-kuhs) comes to us from accounts of the "War of the Gladiators" by ancient writ-

Taken from his native Thrace and sold into slavery in Rome, Spartacus led the greatest slave rebellion in ancient history.

Spartacus. *(Library of Congress)*

ers such as Plutarch (c. 46–119; Greek biographer), Sallust (c.86–35 B.C.E.; Roman historian), and Appian (second century A.D.; Greek historian). Spartacus was a man from Thrace, a region of southeast Europe composed of northeast Greece, south Bulgaria, and European Turkey. Some ancients claimed he was of noble birth; others that he was born to a slave mother. Spartacus served for a while in the Roman army, but deserted and turned brigand (outlaw; bandit). The Romans recaptured him and took Spartacus and his wife to Rome where they were sold into slavery to the highest bidder.

The legend of Spartacus that developed after his death includes the following story about his character, as told by Plutarch: "The story goes that when he was first brought to Rome to be sold, a snake appeared and wound itself round his face as he was asleep, and his wife, who came from the same tribe as Spartacus and was a prophetess . . . stated that it signified that a great and fearful power would accompany him to a lucky conclusion." The story may be untrue but it does show that Spartacus was regarded as an almost supernatural being.

Life as a gladiator

Spartacus and his wife were bought in Rome by Lentulus Batiatus, a slave trader who ran a training school for gladiators (men trained for fighting) in the city of Capua. Gladiators in ancient Rome, as early as 400 B.C.E., fought each other—and sometimes wild beasts—to the death in public arenas as a form of mass entertainment. One of the larger arenas, the Colosseum in Rome, could hold fifty thousand spectators. Gladiators were chosen among slaves, war captives, and criminals for their fighting potential. Death in the arena was the sentence for crimes such as murder, treason, and robbery.

While it is impossible for historians to know exactly what life was like for Spartacus and the other gladiators in the training school or in first-century B.C.E. Capua, some generalizations can be made. Most of the gladiators at Batiatus's training school were probably first-generation slaves, having been captured in war or obtained through the slave trade. Like slaves used for agriculture or industry, gladiators were acquired from all over the Roman empire—from Gaul (France), Germany, Thrace, Greece, Egypt, and Arabia.

Slaves in Roman Society

Slaves under the Roman Republic (509–27 B.C.E.) had no legal rights. They were not allowed to own property or marry without their owner's permission. A slave owner could whip, beat, maim, torture, and even kill a slave without being prosecuted. If a slave, however, killed his or her master, all the slaves of the household were, by law, condemned to death. If caught, runaway slaves faced crucifixion (being nailed or bound to a cross until death). If not killed, runaway slaves were branded or made to wear a slave collar with their master's name inscribed on it. Roman law did not protect slaves, male or female, from sexual assault by their masters. Slaves could also be left to starve or sent to die in the arena fighting gladiators if they disobeyed their masters.

Slaves under the Roman Empire (27 B.C.E.–A.D. 180) slowly acquired some legal rights. The first emperor, Augustus (27 B.C.E.–A.D.14), restricted the practice of taking legal testimony from slaves under torture (a common practice in ancient times). The emperor Claudius (A.D. 41–54) made it a crime to murder a slave or to turn a sick slave out to die. Other emperors continued the trend: the selling of female slaves into prostitution was banned (c. A.D. 75); mutilation of slaves was prohibited (c. A.D. 88); and killing of slaves except by judicial authority (with the court's permission) was outlawed (c. A.D. 127).

It should be noted that the more humane laws of the empire did not necessarily mean that slaves were treated well. The most important factor in that regard was still the character of the slave owner, for a master still had tremendous power in the day-to-day life of a slave.

Gladiators were chosen from the general population of slaves because of their size and strength. Men from Gaul, Germany, and Thrace were considered the best suited for the fighting profession and it was these three groups that made up most of the trainees at Batiatus's school. That Spartacus had a wife with him when sold into slavery was not unusual. Gladiators, like other categories of slaves, were sometimes allowed to marry and have families. However, their family lives were controlled by their owners and could be broken up at any time through the sale of one or more family members to different owners.

Revolt

Slaves in Rome could obtain their freedom in a limited number of ways. If they were very fortunate their owner might grant them manumission (formal release from bondage) in their will. Some slaves were able to earn wages and save enough money to eventually buy their freedom. Most slaves, however, were left with the harsher options of running away, killing their master or themselves, or revolting.

While Spartacus and his fellow gladiators may have lived long enough to have been manumitted as a reward for their prowess (skills) in the fighting arena, they apparently chose not to wait for that opportunity. In the spring of 73 B.C.E., Spartacus led a breakout of about seventy gladiators from their training school. The rebels set up a base camp near Mount Vesuvius (pronounced veh-SOO-vee-us), and attacked nearby towns, freeing slaves, and killing slave owners, sometimes forcing them to fight each other to the death. As word spread, the gladiator-led revolt attracted thousands of runaway slaves to the rebel camp. By the time Rome sent a small military force to Vesuvius to end the rebellion, they faced thousands of liberated and runaway slaves. The Romans were soundly defeated.

War and defeat

For two years the rebels led by Spartacus roamed Italy, first to the Alps, a mountain range in the north, and then to the very southern tip of the country. They fought and defeated the Romans in battle after battle, gaining wealth from looting cities and country estates along the way. In 72 B.C.E., disagreements among the rebel leadership (Spartacus was only one of three leaders) led to a split of rebel forces, and the defeat of one faction of twenty thousand slaves by the Romans.

In the winter of 72–71 B.C.E., Spartacus and his followers found themselves trapped on the southern Italian peninsula by the Roman army. Having been betrayed by pirates who were supposed to supply a fleet of ships for their escape off the mainland, the rebels were forced into a decisive battle with the Romans. By the spring of 71 B.C.E., Spartacus and most of his seventy thousand followers were killed by a massive Roman force—ten legions under the command of Marcus

Spartacus: The Movie

In 1960, the story of Spartacus came to the big screen. Compare how the movie version lives up to the facts.

- Spartacus is originally from Thrace. Roman slaves came from all over the empire. Make a list of the places that slaves came from in the movie.

- Slaves in the Roman Empire had many different jobs and skills. Make a list of the jobs and skills that slaves had in the movie.

- The story of Spartacus in the movie is different from the actual history. Make a list of how the movie is true to—or different from—the historical facts.

Spartacus as portrayed by Kirk Douglas in the 1960 film. *(The Kobal Collection. Reproduced by permission.)*

Crassus (115?–53 B.C.E.), and the armies of Pompey (106–48 B.C.) and Lucullus (c. 117–58? B.C.E.; recalled from foreign wars to fight Spartacus). The six thousand surviving rebel slaves were crucified alongside the road that led from Capua (where the revolt began) to Rome.

Spartacus's legacy

Since Spartacus left no writings, nor did any of the participants of the revolt, historians are left with many unanswered questions as to the motivations of the rebels. Did Spartacus ever intend to mount a widespread slave insurrection that would challenge the authority of Rome and possibly lead to the freedom of all slaves in the empire? If so, why didn't Spartacus attack Rome itself when his army was at full strength and he had the strategic advantage? If Spartacus and his fellow gladiators were only looking to obtain their personal freedom why didn't they escape to their native countries of Gaul, Germany, and Thrace when the Spartacan army reached the Alps and their passage was clear?

While the historical record may never provide adequate answers to these questions, Spartacus remains a powerful and influential figure, a bold leader who paid with his life for the cause of freedom. In the modern era Spartacus has been idolized by revolutionaries such as the German socialists, who from 1916 to 1919 called themselves "Spartacists" when they tried to lead a worker-based revolution after World War I (1914–18). Spartacus made his entry into Western popular culture in 1960 when American filmmaker Stanley Kubrick (1928–99) directed what was at the time the most expensive movie ever made. *Spartacus,* the movie, is a fact-based dramatization of the cruelty and violence of Rome's slave-based society.

Further Reading

Bradley, Keith. *Slavery and Rebellion in the Roman World.* Bloomington, Ind.: University Press, 1989.

Bradley, Keith. *Slavery and Society at Rome.* Cambridge, England: Cambridge University Press, 1994.

Meltzer, Milton. *Slavery: A World History,* updated edition. New York: De Capo Press, 1993.

Sylvester, Theodore L. *Slavery Throughout History: Almanac.* Detroit: Gale Group, 1999.

Harriet Beecher Stowe

**Born June 14, 1811
Litchfield, Connecticut
Died July 1, 1896
Hartford, Connecticut**

Author, abolitionist, teacher

Harriet Beecher Stowe.
(Corbis-Bettmann. Reproduced by permission.)

During the course of her long literary career, Harriet Beecher Stowe published sixteen books, hundreds of short stories, and countless articles, children's tales, and religious poems, but nothing ever equaled the success of her 1852 novel, known by its shortened name, *Uncle Tom's Cabin*. Almost overnight, the book ended her family's financial problems and made her an international celebrity. More important, historians give the popularity of Stowe's book credit for unifying public opinion in the North against slavery, a sentiment that ultimately led to the Civil War (1861–65) and the end of slavery in the United States.

> Writer of one of the most important books in U.S. history, *Uncle Tom's Cabin; or Life Among the Lowly.*

The preacher family

Harriet Beecher was born the sixth child of Roxana and Lyman Beecher in Litchfield, a little town in western Connecticut. Her mother died when she was just four years old and her father remarried a year later to Harriet Porter. Harriet Beecher was born into a large family; Lyman fathered seven children with his first wife and four with his second wife. If

Harriet had been born a boy she most likely would have ended up a preacher, like her seven brothers and her father.

Lyman Beecher was one of the most popular and prominent ministers of his time. He was a leader in the community as well as a strong influence on his children. Reverend Beecher was a Calvinist who practiced and preached a strict brand of Christianity. He was known for his fiery sermons in which he told his congregation of an angry God waiting to punish people for their sins if they did not repent and ask for forgiveness.

Stowe's education

Stowe was a very intelligent child. By the time she was four she had learned dozens of hymns and whole chapters of the Bible by heart. By the time she was six she was reading books from her father's library—mostly religious sermons and tracts—but she occasionally found a novel that took her to faraway places in her imagination. When Stowe was eight she was enrolled in Miss Sally Pierce's Litchfield Female Academy, an unusual school for girls in that it taught science, languages, and the classics (classic works of literature) in addition to needlework, drawing, and music.

In 1824 thirteen-year-old Stowe left her family and friends in Litchfield to attend the Hartford Female Academy, a school founded by her sister Catharine a year earlier. Stowe was shy and had few friends in Hartford so she spent much of her time studying grammar, French, Italian, and Latin, as well as painting and drawing. At sixteen she became a part-time teacher at her sister's school, a position that turned into a full-time job when she was eighteen.

Transitions

In 1826 Reverend Beecher found a new job at a bigger church with more pay. He moved his family to Boston, Massachusetts, to become the minister of the Hanover Street Church. Stowe spent her summer vacations in Boston and from 1827 to 1830 her favorite brother, Edward, was a minister at the city's Park Street Church.

In 1829 Stowe was in her brother's church to hear a speech marking the Fourth of July holiday. The speaker was newspaper editor and abolitionist William Lloyd Garrison (1805–79), a member of Lyman Beecher's congregation who was about to leave Boston and become the editor of an anti-slavery newspaper in Baltimore. The Fourth of July could not be properly celebrated as a day of freedom and independence, Garrison told his audience, as long as there were two million slaves in bondage in the South. The slaves must be set free immediately, he said, and he challenged his audience, as Christians, to work for the abolition of slavery.

On the border

In the fall of 1832 most of the Beecher family, including Harriet and Catharine, moved to Cincinnati, Ohio, where Reverend Beecher became the president of Lane Seminary and the pastor of the Second Presbyterian Church. In the spring of 1833 Catharine opened the Western Female Institute in downtown Cincinnati with herself and Harriet as the school's associate principals. The sisters moved into the city to be near their school.

Stowe spent the next seventeen years in Cincinnati, a city in the free state of Ohio, just across the Ohio River from the slaveholding state of Kentucky. Cincinnati in 1833 had about twenty-five thousand residents and was one of the larger cities in the United States. One in ten residents was black. When Ohio became a state in 1803 a law was passed forbidding black people to enter the state. The law was ignored and many blacks migrated into the state from the South; most were ex-slaves. Cincinnati's location made it a magnet for runaway slaves, and the city's newspapers were full of advertisements offering rewards for missing slaves.

Cincinnati life

Stowe spent most of her time teaching at the institute, writing articles for local magazines and newspapers, and working on a book, *A New Geography for Children,* which was published in May 1833. In the summer, Stowe and a friend visited a plantation in the Kentucky countryside. They stayed in a large, elegant house and could see the slaves laboring in the fields of corn, hemp, and tobacco. After dinner they sat in the parlor where the slaves were forced to sing and dance for their masters' entertainment. Although she did not write about it upon her return, much of what she saw on that trip would be used almost twenty years later as material for her famous novel, *Uncle Tom's Cabin*.

On January 6, 1836, Harriet married Calvin Stowe and became Harriet Beecher Stowe. Calvin was a professor at Lane Seminary, a preacher like her father and brothers, and one of the country's leading biblical scholars. On September 29, 1836, Stowe gave birth to twins, Eliza and Harriet. The Stowe family moved into their own house in Walnut Hills, near Lane Seminary, and hired a black woman as a housekeeper. It turned out that the woman was a runaway slave whose owner was looking for her. Calvin Stowe and Harriet's brother, Henry Ward, smuggled the fugitive slave out of the city at night to a farm that served as a stop on the Underground Railroad, a secret network of people who helped slaves find their way to freedom in the North.

Hard times

Stowe had no doubts that slavery was wrong and that it was her Christian duty to try to abolish it, but her mounting duties as a mother, housekeeper, and wife left her little time for political concerns. While living in Cincinnati she gave birth to Henry in 1838, Frederick in 1840, Georgiana in 1843, and Samuel in 1848. Calvin's salary at the college was never enough to support the ever-growing family and Stowe began churning out more articles and stories for magazines and newspapers to earn income for her family.

As it turned out the time Stowe spent in Cincinnati provided her with many stories and ideas that she would use later in *Uncle Tom's Cabin*. In 1842, for example, the Stowes, along with some students from Lane, helped shelter nine runaway slaves from Kentucky until they were picked up by an antislavery worker. Stowe also learned how slavery operated and the kind of impact it had on the lives of ordinary people by listening to the stories of the many black women who worked in the Stowe household over the years, helping with the cooking, cleaning, and washing. Most of them were from the South and many of them were ex-slaves.

Stowe's years in Cincinnati were spent in virtual poverty and ended in tragedy. In the summer of 1849 a cholera (severe diarrheal disease) epidemic swept Cincinnati, and claimed the life of Stowe's eighteen-month-old baby, Charles. Stowe was deeply affected by the death. Because of her religious upbringing she saw it as punishment from God for not acting more forcefully against slavery—something she knew was wrong but neglected to do anything about. Stowe was happy when she learned that Calvin had been offered a job at a college in Brunswick, Maine, and she could return to her native New England.

With pen in hand

After Congress passed a new Fugitive Slave law in 1850, making it easier for slave owners to pursue and apprehend their runaway slaves in the North, Stowe decided that she must take up her pen and write about slavery. Then one Sunday in February 1851 Stowe was with her children in church, daydreaming, when she envisioned a scene of a black man being brutally beaten and dying because he would not deny the existence of his true master, Jesus Christ. Stowe wrote down what she had seen as soon as she returned home, and with that first step, she began what turned out to be *Uncle Tom's Cabin; or Life Among the Lowly,* a full-length novel about slavery in the United States.

Stowe never actually intended to write a whole novel. She started publishing her story in weekly installments in June 1851, in *The National Era,* a Washington, D.C.-based antislavery newspaper. She expected it to run for maybe five or six weeks but her series was so popular that it continued until March 1852, when it was published in book form. The first printing of *Uncle Tom's Cabin* was only 5,000 copies but it sold out in two days. In its first year, *Uncle Tom's Cabin* sold 300,000 copies. By the time of the Civil War (1861–65) millions of copies of *Uncle Tom's Cabin* had been sold in the United States and Britain. The book was also translated into over forty different languages and read by people all over the world.

135,000 SETS, 270,000 VOLUMES SOLD.

UNCLE TOM'S CABIN

FOR SALE HERE.

AN EDITION FOR THE MILLION, COMPLETE IN 1 Vol., PRICE 37 1-2 CENTS.
" " IN GERMAN, IN 1 Vol., PRICE 50 CENTS.
" . " IN 2 Vols., CLOTH, 6 PLATES, PRICE $1.50.
SUPERB ILLUSTRATED EDITION, IN 1 Vol., WITH 153 ENGRAVINGS,
PRICES FROM $2.50 TO $5.00.

The Greatest Book of the Age.

Poster advertising Harriet Beecher Stowe's *Uncle Tom's Cabin.*

A simple but powerful message

The impact of the book on the country was nothing short of explosive. Never before had anyone touched the hearts and minds of the American public with such effect. The reason for her success, especially on the controversial subject of slavery, is that she did not lecture or condemn. Instead, Stowe painted with words a series of pictures of the operation of slavery that was so vivid and compelling that people finally understood just how cruel and unjust slavery really was in the United States.

The people of the South, however, responded to *Uncle Tom's Cabin* by attacking Stowe in the press and from the pulpit. They realized that her book was an assault on their way of life and many of the myths they used to perpetuate the system of slavery. *Uncle Tom's Cabin* was the first American novel that was peopled by black heroes of dignity, strength, intelligence, and religious conviction. Anyone who read the book knew that slaves were not happy to be slaves even under the best of conditions. The message of the book was simple: the problem was not with the *abuses* of slavery but with slavery *itself.*

Life after *Uncle Tom's Cabin*

Stowe's success as the author of *Uncle Tom's Cabin* made her one of the world's most admired women and finally ended the Stowe family's financial troubles, enabling them to live for the rest of their lives in relative comfort. Stowe traveled to Europe twice and was hailed as a great author by everyone from the person on the street to the Queen of England.

At home, Stowe was invited to the White House by President Abraham Lincoln (1809–65) in November 1862, in

The Stereotyping of "Uncle Tom"

Unfortunately for Harriet Beecher Stowe and the true character of her 1852 novel, *Uncle Tom's Cabin,* the term "Uncle Tom" has over the years become a name that black people are called when they are viewed as being too eager to please white people. The characterization of Uncle Tom as cowardly and stupid came from the racist minstrel shows (musical skits and plays) that were based on Stowe's novel, not the novel itself. The book's Uncle Tom was powerful and intelligent, a strong healthy man in the prime of his life, but on stage he was portrayed as just the opposite.

The productions of *Uncle Tom's Cabin* that played in cities across the United States from the Civil War (1861–65) to the outbreak of World War I in 1914 regularly featured white actors with darkened faces playing the black characters in the story. They sang songs such as "Happy Are We, Darkies So Gay," and "Uncle Breve Tells About The Good Times He Had On The Plantation." In addition to the plays, there were toys, games, and figurines based on the book, none of which Stowe had any control over or made any money from.

the middle of the Civil War, just a few months before the Emancipation Proclamation freed most of the slaves. He greeted her with, "So you're the little woman who wrote the book that started this great war!" Lincoln was only half jesting as most historians agree that *Uncle Tom's Cabin* was extremely influential in waking up the North to the realities of slavery and in doing so convinced the public that the practice must end, even if the cost was war and bloodshed.

Stowe continued to write books, children's stories, religious poetry, and countless articles until her death of natural causes at eighty-five years old. She outlived her husband Calvin by ten years but the two were able to spend many of their later years happily together, living in Florida in the winter and New England in the summer, looked after by their unmarried twin daughters, Eliza and Harriet.

Further Reading

Bland, Celia. *Harriet Beecher Stowe.* New York: Chelsea House Publishers, 1993.

Fritz, Jean. *Harriet Beecher Stowe and the Beecher Preachers.* New York: G. P. Putnam's Sons, 1994.

Garraty, John A., and Marc C. Carnes, eds. *American National Biography.* New York: Oxford University Press, 1999.

Scott, John Anthony. *Woman Against Slavery: The Story of Harriet Beecher Stowe.* New York: Thomas Y. Crowell Co., 1978.

Stowe, Harriet Beecher. *Uncle Tom's Cabin; or Life Among the Lowly.* New York: Macmillan College Publishing Co., 1994 (reprint of the 1852 edition).

Tippu Tib

Born c. 1837
Zanzibar
Died 1905
Zanzibar

Slave trader

Tippu Tib (pronounced TEE-poo tib) was a brave and daring adventurer, a good administrator, and a great leader of men. Much of his financial success, however, came at the expense of other human beings. His exploits can hardly be called heroic by today's standards, yet Tippu Tib played an important role in the history of East and Central Africa in the late nineteenth century. The opening of Africa's interior to European explorers and missionaries with help from Tippu Tib led to great changes in that part of the continent. European exploration led to European colonization and the end of Arab domination of the African interior. For Tippu Tib, it led to his own destruction in the very countries that he conquered and held for almost thirty years.

One of the last great slavers of the nineteenth century, Tippu Tib's name was known and feared in most of East and Central Africa.

Heritage

Tippu Tib was born Muhammed bin Hamid on the island of Zanzibar off the east coast of Africa in the 1830s. He later acquired the nickname Tippu Tib, meaning "the one who blinks," because of a tick or nervous twitch in one eye.

Tippu Tib. *(Brecelj/Corbis-Bettmann. Reproduced by permission.)*

Tippu Tib was of mixed racial heritage. His mother, Bint Habib bin Bushir, was an Arab woman whose family came from Muscat; his father and grandfather were Swahili (members of the Bantu-speaking people of Zanzibar and its adjacent coast) traders from the African coast, and his father's great-grandmother was the daughter of an African chief of the Nyamwezi. Tippu Tib claimed that he was a full-blooded Arab, but he was born with his great-great-grandmother's African features including an undeniably dark complexion.

Tippu Tib was born into the upper class of Zanzibar. His family could afford plantations, town houses, and a great number of slaves. Tippu Tib's father, Muhammed bin Juma, was an established and wealthy trader of slaves and ivory. He made his fortunes by traveling to the interior of East and Central Africa and trading goods for ivory and slaves, which he then brought back to sell in Zanzibar, the most important slave market in the Indian Ocean. Slaves were bought for the local plantations but most slaves were sold for export to the markets of Arabia, Muscat, Persia, Turkey, or Egypt.

Early years

Tippu Tib was one of many children fathered by Muhammed bin Juma. Tippu Tib's mother was just one of Muhammed's many wives. However, Tippu Tib was his father's first son by an Arab wife and thus heir to his father's business and fortunes. When he was six years old Tippu Tib was sent to a teacher of the Koran (the sacred text of Islam) to learn to read and write. In his early years he also spent time helping his mother with her garden, but more than anything he longed to join one of his father's trading caravans.

When Tippu Tib was twelve he was allowed to join his uncle's trading expedition to the mainland. Tippu Tib sailed in a small *dhow* (boat) back and forth from the island, hauling gum-copal (a byproduct of tropical trees), and an occasional slave or two.

When he was fifteen, Tippu Tib was finally allowed to join his father in the slave and ivory trade. His first trip was to Tabora, his father's base of operations on mainland Africa, a 500-mile, three-month journey. From there he joined his father in a trade caravan to Ugangi, northeast of Lake Nyasa, a 300-mile, two-month trip south into eastern Africa. Tippu Tib and his father traded such items as colored beads, coils of copper and wire, bales of cotton, cowry shells, and various types of cloth for ivory and slaves.

Not only was the trip peaceful but it was also very profitable. On their return they found the demand for slaves in Zanzibar's markets higher than ever as were the prices they got for their human cargo. One visitor to the area estimated that about forty thousand slaves were bought and sold in Zanzibar in 1859 alone.

Amasses a fortune

As a young man Tippu Tib represented his father's interest in the interior of the continent. He traveled with Nyamwezi trading caravans around the southern end of Lake Tanganyika, south to Katanga in what is today called the Democratic Republic of the Congo (known as Zaire from 1971 to 1997). Nyamwezi were African traders who lived between Lake Tanganyika and the coast. They were known as exceptionally good porters or bearers, and by the early 1800s they had developed a trading network across the region. The Nyamwezi traders dealt in ivory, slaves, and copper well before Arab traders ventured into Africa's interior.

Tippu Tib stayed in Katanga for about two years. Around 1869 Tippu Tib went northwest looking for ivory. In a daring raid against Nsama, a chief reputed to have killed Arabs, Tippu Tib captured his capital and took his ivory. Tippu Tib's victory over this much-feared chief gained him the reputation of a powerful and dangerous man. Other chiefs paid him tribute in elephant tusks. So great was his store of ivory that he had special storage places built to house it.

"Big Man of Nyangwe"

About the time Tippu Tib was establishing himself in trade independent of his father's business, several Arab merchants from Zanzibar reached the Lualaba River and founded a settlement called Nyangwe. There they established a major market center. In 1874 the Arabs recognized Tippu Tib as the overlord of the area. His personal empire was huge: it stretched from Lake Tanganyika as far as the Lomami River and north to the Congo forest. Although Tippu Tib held this territory in the name of the sultan (ruler of a Muslim state) of Zanzibar, he actually served as an independent ruler. Tippu Tib became known as the "Big Man of Nyangwe" and made his capital, Kasonga, into a showpiece on the Lualaba River.

Although not officially a sultan, Tippu Tib ruled like one. With his monopoly on the sale of ivory, he controlled the political structure of his kingdom. He selected local leaders as chiefs and appointed his own officials to supervise the chiefs, to collect tribute, to enforce the laws, and to recruit soldiers. From his base west of Lake Tanganyika, Tippu Tib maintained good relations with the Nyamwezi to the east of the lake. These relations were important because the Nyamwezi lay between Tippu Tib and his outlet to the markets of Zanzibar.

The slave trade

Tippu Tib kept a steady flow of ivory and slaves from his empire to the markets on the Indian Ocean coast. In usual practice, Tippu Tib's men would pay a casual visit to a village to see if the chief had hidden away any ivory. If so, they would return later with sufficient men and firepower to take the ivory from the chief. Or when they raided the villages, they would take captives, usually women and children, and then ransom them to the village chief for his ivory. If the village did not have sufficient ivory, they would take the remaining captives along with them as they traveled, then trade them in another place.

Sometimes Tippu Tib's men would form an alliance with a local chief, and together they would raid a neighboring village. The raiders would set fire to the huts, wait for villagers to run out, and then capture the women and children. Later they would take them to market and either trade them locally for food and supplies or take them to the east coast for sale at the slave market in Zanzibar.

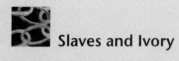

Slaves and Ivory

African slaves were important to the Muslim nations because, according to Muhammad the Prophet (the father of Islam; c. 570–632), Muslims could not be enslaved. Slave trade along Africa's Indian Ocean coast also grew in response to restrictions placed on slave trade along the Atlantic coast, including the presence of British and American naval patrols stationed there to prevent slave export to the West.

While slaves from Zanzibar's markets were exported mostly to the Arab world and the east, most of the ivory ended up in the Western world, especially in the United States. By the late 1890s the U.S. was importing eighty percent of the ivory exported from Zanzibar. It was used for such household items as knife handles, snuff boxes, and ladies' fans. Religious statues and crucifixes were often made of ivory as well.

The slave and ivory trade in East Africa seemed to go hand in hand through much of the nineteenth century. In the beginning ivory was the prized commodity. Acquiring slaves, by comparison, was not as profitable and considered a sideline. As the slaughter of elephants moved further and further into the interior of Africa, however, caravans had to travel more miles inland from the coast to obtain ivory. And that meant there was a greater need to take captives and enslave them as porters or sell them to offset the greater costs.

Into the heart of Africa

Over the years, Tippu Tib welcomed European explorers to his capital and provided aid and protection for their expeditions into the deepest parts of the African interior. In 1867, while working for his father, he guided the caravan of Scottish missionary and explorer Dr. David Livingstone (1813–73) south toward Lake Merwu. From 1872 to 1874 he escorted British explorer Verney Lovett Cameron (1844–94) part of the way on his trek to the Atlantic coast from Lualaba. And in 1876 Tippu Tib assisted the British explorer and journalist Sir Henry Morton Stanley (1841–1904) in his search for the upper reaches of the Congo River, known as the Lualaba River.

Stanley is said to have given $5,000 to Tippu Tib for his guidance to Nyangwe. Tippu Tib also supplied 140 men with guns, another 140 men with spears and traditional weapons, and about 20 women from his harem (group of women living with one man). Later, for another $2,600, Tippu Tib agreed to accompany Stanley for sixty days beyond Nyangwe and then return. Eventually Tippu Tib did turn back but Stanley continued to travel along the Lualaba River.

Two months after Tippu Tib left him, Stanley came out of the dense rain forest onto a lake 15 miles across surrounded by white cliffs. He named the lake Stanley Pool after himself. (It is now known as Malebo Pool.) From there, Stanley and his men followed the raging river 220 miles to Matadi, where the river became navigable again, and went the final 100 miles to the river's mouth. In all it had taken Stanley 999 days to cross the African continent from the Indian Ocean to the Atlantic Ocean.

Explorers and slavers

The explorers and slave traders needed each other: European explorers needed the help of men like Tippu Tib because of their intimate knowledge of the African terrain. The slavers and ivory hunters benefitted from the explorers because they helped open new paths to Africa's interior. Stanley's successful trip down the Lualaba encouraged travel by the once-skeptical Arab traders. In fact, Tippu Tib was one of the first traders to follow. The traders created chaos along the river. They burned and looted entire villages and took people captive.

According to Peter Forbath in *The River Congo,* Stanley was shocked at what he saw six years later when he revisited the area. As they traveled down the river, Stanley described a village where the slave traders held their captives: "There rows and rows of dark nakedness, relieved here and there by the white dresses of their captors. . . . observe that mostly all are fettered [chained]; youth with iron rings around their necks, through which a chain . . . is drove [driven], securing the captives by the twenties. The children over ten are secured by three copper rings. . . . The mothers are secured by shorter chains . . ." Later Stanley learned that this camp held 2,300 captives taken in raids on 118 villages. The slavers had killed at least another 4,000 Africans.

Later years

In 1885 Stanley returned to the Congo to head a relief expedition. He went to Zanzibar in 1887 to ask Tippu Tib to help him. In exchange, Stanley appointed Tippu Tib the Belgian governor of Stanley Falls (Kisangani), an area he already controlled. One condition of the arrangement was that Tippu Tib had to agree to try and stop the slave trading. Although he could not succeed in doing this, he was able to stop the Arabs from coming into contact with the Europeans.

Tippu Tib left the interior in 1890 and retired to Zanzibar. He died there in 1905. His son, Sef, represented his interests at Stanley Pool. When the Belgians settled in the area and tried to restrict the Arabs by force from trading slaves, the Arabs rose against them. Sef was killed in 1892, and within eighteen months the Belgians had completely crushed the Arabs.

Further Reading

Farrant, Leda. *Tippu Tib and the East African Slave Trade.* London: Hamish Hamilton, 1975.

Forbath, Peter. *The River Congo.* New York: Harper, 1977.

Hallet, Robin. *Africa Since 1875.* Ann Arbor: University of Michigan Press, 1974.

Hibbert, Christopher. *Africa Explored: Europeans in the Dark Continent, 1769–1889.* New York: Norton, 1982.

McLynn, Frank. *Hearts of Darkness: The European Explorations of Africa.* Carroll & Graf, 1994.

Moorehead, Alan. *The White Nile.* New York: Harper, 1971.

Oliver, Roland, and Anthony Atmore. *Africa Since 1800.* New York/UK: Cambridge University Press, 1972.

Pakenham, Thomas. *The Scramble for Africa.* New York: Random House, 1991.

Toussaint L'Ouverture

Born May 20, 1743
Cap Francais, Saint Domingue
Died April 7, 1803
Fort de Joux, France

Former slave, Haitian general, revolutionary

As leader of Saint Domingue's slave revolution, Toussaint L'Ouverture oversaw the expulsion of the French from their New World colony and the establishment of Haiti as the Western Hemisphere's second independent republic in 1804 (the first was the United States).

Former West Indian slave of African descent who became the most important black leader in the Americas.

Royal beginnings

François-Dominique Toussaint (pronounced too-SAHN) was born a slave in 1743 on a sugarcane plantation two miles outside of Cap Francais, a city in Saint Domingue (a French colony occupying the western third of the Caribbean island, Hispaniola; the eastern two-thirds was a Spanish colony known as Santo Domingo). Toussaint was the grandson of a West African king whose son—Gaou-Guinou—had been captured in a war in Africa and sold to Count de Breda, a French colonist who grew sugarcane on the island and manufactured it into sugar for export to Europe.

Toussaint's father was given special privileges on the Breda estate due to his family's former high status in Africa.

Toussaint L'Ouverture *(The Granger Collection, New York. Reproduced by permission.)*

197

This was very unusual for the times as plantation slaves in the West Indies were treated very harshly. Typically, they were forced to work in the fields very long hours in the tropical heat, fed minimum rations of food, and beaten for the most minor offenses. Of the twenty thousand slaves who arrived on the island yearly in the mid-eighteenth century, one out of nine died before the end of their first year. Toussaint's father, however, enjoyed full liberty on the Breda estate and was given five slaves to cultivate a plot of land. He became a member of the Catholic church, married, and had five children (Toussaint was the youngest of four sons).

Childhood

Toussaint's home was larger than most slave cabins, but it was still made of mud and branches with a thatched palm roof. Toussaint's mother grew flowers and herbs and his father taught him about their healing powers, a skill he learned in his homeland. Toussaint helped his mother feed the chickens, sweep the yard, and haul water from a stream for the family's prized possession, a pig. At home the family spoke their native African language, and Toussaint listened to stories of his ancestors and their strategies and prowess (skills) in fighting and war.

As a young slave, Toussaint was given the work of a shepherd. Tending to the flocks and herds, Toussaint had a job that gave him the opportunity to locate and study the many medicinal herbs and flowers that grew in the wild. A shepherd's life also allowed Toussaint the time and opportunity to think and dream. Toussaint dreamed of being a warrior like his father and of being wise and respected like his grandfather, the king. Despite being small for his age, at twelve years old Toussaint became known as a fearless swimmer, and for his daring and skilled horsemanship.

Education

During his formative years Toussaint was greatly influenced by Pierre Baptiste, an old and respected slave who lived on the Breda estate. Baptiste became Toussaint's godfather, a very important position in the culture of the West Indies (a group of islands in the Caribbean, of which Hispaniola was one). Baptiste passed on to Toussaint the religious instructions and teachings he had learned from Catholic missionaries and laid the foundations of Toussaint's lifelong religious faith.

Baptiste also taught the young Toussaint the French language, Latin, and the basics of geometry (which Baptiste had learned from a Catholic priest, despite unwritten laws that forbade educating slaves). After reading every book—mostly religious in nature—that Baptiste could supply him with from the priest's library, Toussaint turned to the collection of the Breda estate. The plantation's manager, impressed by Toussaint's intelligence, loaned many history and philosophy books to his young slave.

Plantation life

Toussaint's self-education and interest in animals earned him a promotion by age eighteen to husbandman (manager) of all the animals of the estate. He was especially protective of animals and was known to exhibit rage and anger at anyone who mistreated them, including his white overseer, whom he struck in a dispute over a horse. Despite the Black Codes, laws that made it a crime punishable by death for a black to hit a white, Toussaint's value as a skilled slave saved him from punishment. Toussaint, in fact, was never beaten or treated poorly on the Breda estate. But he was never far away from the suffering and cries of less fortunate slaves, always well aware of their mistreatment by their white masters.

When Toussaint was in his late twenties, a new owner took over the estate. Toussaint became a favorite of his new master's family and was made their personal coachman. Toussaint would drive his master and family in a horse-drawn carriage to balls and assemblies, on social visits to neighboring plantations, and into the city to the clubs and shops.

After years of resisting pressure to marry a slave of his master's choice, Toussaint, at forty years old, chose Suzanne Baptiste, the daughter of his godfather. Suzanne was pregnant at the time of their marriage from a previous relationship with a mulatto (a person of mixed black and white ancestry).

Saint Domingue's Slave Revolution

In 1789 there were nearly 500,000 slaves in Saint Domingue, 30,000 colonists, and 30,000 free blacks and mulattos. There had been slave uprisings in Saint Domingue before, four in the 1500s and two in the 1600s, but nothing like what happened on August 22, 1791. The rebellion had been brewing for some time. In September 1789 the National Assembly of France granted independence to the whites of Saint Domingue, giving them control of their own government and taxes. In 1791, the rights granted to the whites were also given to Saint Domingue's mulattos and free blacks, but not to the slaves.

Hundreds of years of pent-up hatred for their colonial masters exploded among the field slaves near the city of Le Cap on that hot August night in 1791. Rebellious slaves torched everything: the cane fields, the sugar mills, and the properties and homes of the planters. Armed with machetes and knives, they killed white men, women, and children by the hundreds. The next day the rebels attacked the city, and after suffering heavy losses, were forced to retreat and set up camp on an abandoned plantation. The number of rebel slaves grew from 1,500 to 40,000 within a month.

She eventually gave birth to a boy named Placide, whom Toussaint adopted and treated as well as his own children—Isaac, who was born a year later, and Jean-Paul, who was born ten years later.

Toussaint joins the rebels

There is no evidence that Toussaint participated in the planning or initial stages of Saint Domingue's slave revolt of 1791. The Breda plantation owners, at first protected by Toussaint, in a matter of weeks fled for their lives. Toussaint sent his wife and children to safety in Spanish-ruled Santo Domingo (the eastern part of the island). Two months after the beginning of the revolt, Toussaint rode off to join the rebels, taking horses and the most reliable slaves of Breda with him.

When Toussaint reached the rebel camp he found great disorder and suffering. The slave army was nothing

Slavery Throughout History: Biographies

more than an unsheltered, weary mob, with many dying from festering wounds and tropical fevers. Toussaint's first reaction was to use his knowledge of herbs and medicines to treat the sick and the wounded. His healing skills earned him the title of chief physician to the army, and his fighting skills led to his promotion to commander of a section of the army. Toussaint instilled strict discipline among his troops, making it a crime punishable by death to rape a woman. He also put an end to the abuse of prisoners in rebel hands. He trained his troops to fight the French using guerrilla warfare tactics— a hit-and-run strategy that resulted in great military successes for the rebel army.

Shifting alliances

In September 1792 the French sent six thousand troops to Saint Domingue to try to restore order. Toussaint responded by making an alliance with the Spanish in Santo Domingo, believing that the Spanish were truly interested in the emancipation (freedom) of the island's slaves. Toussaint was made a colonel and his army, freshly supplied by their new allies, captured much of Saint Domingue's northern province. In a matter of months, Toussaint's army grew from six hundred to almost five thousand.

On August 29, 1793, the French commissioner of Saint Domingue declared the emancipation of the colony's slaves. Four days earlier, Toussaint had sent out a written appeal to his people to join him in his fight for "Liberty and Equality." He signed the statement Toussaint L'Ouverture (pronounced LOO-ver-chur; an opening), explaining later that he thought "it was a good name for bravery."

On September 20, 1793, British troops landed on the southern tip of the island and in a short time captured the capital of the southern province, Port au Prince, and major ports and towns in the west. Within a year, thanks to Toussaint, two-thirds of the French colony was occupied by either the British or the Spanish. On February 4, 1794, the French National Convention in Paris confirmed the emancipation of all slaves in Saint Domingue. No longer trusting the Spanish to do the same, Toussaint in May 1794 sent his family out of Spanish Santo Domingo and declared his loyalty to France.

Taking control

In a matter of months, Toussaint's army regained control of northern Saint Domingue from the Spanish. After successfully battling the British in a two-year campaign (1795–96), Toussaint was made a brigadier general, then commander in chief of the armed forces by the colony's head commissioner. Toussaint was treated as a god—their liberator from the degradation of slavery—by the people of Saint Domingue, ninety percent of whom were ex-slaves. The French authorities treated Toussaint as a potential threat to their rule. He controlled two-thirds of their colony—the north and west provinces. The south province was in the hands of the army led by Toussaint's rival, a mulatto general named André Rigaud (1761–1811). After Toussaint drove the British off the island in 1798, he engaged and defeated Rigaud in a civil war in 1799.

As a general and unelected leader of the colony, Toussaint still needed to accomplish two more goals: expel the French and liberate the slaves still held in Spanish-controlled Santo Domingo. In 1801 when the French commissioner of the colony refused Toussaint's request to invade Santo Domingo, Toussaint put him and his family on a ship back to France. He easily defeated the Spanish forces, freed the slaves, and installed his brother Paul as governor of the new province. The entire island of Hispaniola was now under Toussaint's control.

King of Saint Domingue

Toussaint declared his main goal to be "freedom for all—be they black, white, or red." Throughout his career as a military leader Toussaint enforced strict discipline among his troops: no looting, burning, or raping was allowed; prisoners of war and civilians, including whites and mulattos, were treated with respect. In 1801 and 1802, as a leader in peace, Toussaint tried to instill that same sense of responsibility among Saint Domingue's civilians.

After many years of war, the country was in ruins. The once-profitable sugar industry was at a standstill. Toussaint's generals took over sections of the island and forced the people back to work (for wages). Blacks, whites, and mulattos were all to be treated without prejudice. Estates were still managed by whites but they were run on a cooperative basis.

Toussaint reorganized the courts of law and made justice more accessible to everyone. Severe laws were imposed against such crimes as corruption and smuggling. With help from the Roman Catholic Church, Toussaint opened high schools throughout the country. Toussaint personally oversaw the rebuilding of many of the war-damaged towns, including his favorite, Le Cap. He also built for himself a palace—complete with marble floors, French furniture, a painted ceiling, and garden.

Birth of a nation

During Toussaint's short rule he rebuilt the island's roads, ports, the export trade, education, the arts, and justice system. With stability came economic growth and the attention of France's new ruler, Napoleon Bonaparte (1769–1821). When Toussaint wrote a new constitution for the island, with himself as governor for life, Catholicism as the state religion, and slavery abolished forever, Napoleon decided to invade Saint Domingue and restore French rule. In early 1802 Napoleon sent his brother-in-law, Captain General LeClerc, and twenty thousand veteran troops to take over the island and restore white rule and slavery.

The French began their assault on February 2, 1802. Superior weaponry and numbers forced Toussaint's army to retreat from the coastal towns to the interior, burning everything as they fled to the hills. In the next few months both sides suffered heavy losses in battles and skirmishes. The French also lost fourteen thousand troops to yellow fever, leaving LeClerc with only five thousand soldiers. In May 1802, in a move to prolong the conflict into the rainy season (the end of April) when many more French troops would die of the fever, Toussaint offered peace.

Arrest and exile

Still fearing his power to rouse the people against the French, LeClerc, on orders from Napoleon, arrested Toussaint in early June and put him, his wife, and family on a ship to France. On August 25, 1802, Toussaint arrived at his prison, Fort de Joux, near the Swiss border. It did not take long for the cold and damp of the mountain fortress, with its twelve-foot-thick stone walls and eight months of snow-cover, to take its toll on a sixty-year-old man who had lived his whole life in a tropical climate. In less than eight months, on April 7, 1803, Toussaint died of pneumonia.

Inspired by his death, Toussaint's generals in Saint Domingue waged a fierce war against the French. The French, having lost almost forty-five thousand troops to disease alone, decided to surrender the island. On November 19, 1803, Saint Domingue's top three generals proclaimed Hispaniola's independence from France, effective January 1, 1804. The island's first ruler promptly changed the name from Saint Domingue to Haiti (meaning mountainous country).

Further Reading

Beard, John R. *The Life of Toussaint L'Ouverture*. Westport, Conn.: Negro Universities Press, 1853.

Parkinson, Wenda. *This Gilded African: Toussaint L'Ouverture*. London: Quartet Books, 1978.

Sojourner Truth

Born c. 1797
Ulster County, New York
Died 1883
Battle Creek, Michigan

Abolitionist, women's rights advocate, preacher

S ojourner Truth was born a slave. After gaining her freedom, she began a quest to end slavery and to assist former slaves. Truth was an early civil rights advocate—she fought the segregation policy of Washington, D.C., streetcars shortly after the end of the Civil War (1861–65). She was also a noted speaker who lectured frequently on the ills of racism and sexism, and the injustice of denying women the right to vote. A deeply religious woman, Truth rose to prominence at a time when African Americans and women were expected to live in the shadows of society.

One of the most persuasive speakers in the antislavery, African American rights, and women's rights movements.

Childhood as a slave

Sojourner Truth was born Isabella Baumfree in Ulster County, New York, sometime in 1797 (the exact birth and death dates of slaves were not typically recorded). Her father's name was James Baumfree, after his original Dutch owner, and her mother's name was Elizabeth, although she was better known as Mau Mau Bett. Like both her parents, Truth was a slave of wealthy landowner Charles Hardenbergh. Prior to

Sojourner Truth. *(Archive Photos, Inc. Reproduced by permission.)*

Truth's birth, her mother had given birth to eleven other children—all but one had been sold away from the plantation. The name "Isabella" had been selected by Master Hardenbergh; Truth's parents called her "Belle."

In 1806 Truth's family was shattered when Truth and her brother were taken away and sold at an auction. Truth was purchased, along with a flock of sheep, for one hundred dollars. Her new masters were an English immigrant couple named the Neelys. Both Mr. and Mrs. Neely beat Truth mercilessly. One day Truth's father, who was old and crippled but had been freed, came to see her. When he saw her back, bloodied and scarred from beatings, he sought to help her.

Baumfree convinced a tavern owner named Martin Schryver to purchase his daughter. During her three years with Schryver, Truth was not mistreated and had adequate food, clothing, and shelter. Truth was unaware, however, of the terrible conditions in which her parents were living. She later learned that they had run out of food and firewood, and died.

The escape to freedom

In 1810 Truth was again sold, this time to a wealthy landowner in New Paltz, New York, named John Dumont. Dumont arranged for Truth to be married to an older slave named Thomas, so that the couple would bear children (children born to slaves became the master's property). Over a period of ten years, Truth gave birth to five children.

In 1817 Truth was heartened by a new law that required all slaves in New York to be freed on July 4, 1827, (slaves over forty years old were freed immediately). In 1825 Dumont told Truth that if she worked exceptionally hard for the next year, he would grant her and her husband their freedom one year early. He would also give them a log cabin that they could call home. Truth held up her end of the bargain, but on the agreed-upon date Dumont went back on his word. Truth had her mind so set on freedom that she could not continue to live as a slave.

Three months later—only nine months before the law would set her free—Truth took her infant daughter, Sophia, and escaped in the early morning hours. She went down the road to a farmhouse, where she had heard Quaker abolitionists lived. (An abolitionist is someone who actively opposes slavery.) The Quaker couple, named the Van Wageners, took her in. When Dumont came to the house looking for Truth, the Van Wageners purchased Truth and her daughter. The Van Wageners then granted the mother and daughter their freedom, and allowed them to stay on in their house.

Truth soon learned that her son, Peter, had been sold to a wealthy farmer in Alabama. Determined to get her son back, Truth enlisted the help of the Van Wageners and their Quaker-abolitionist friends. They informed Truth that Peter's sale had been illegal—that New York law prohibited the sale of slaves out of state. With the aid of a lawyer, whom the Quakers hired and paid, Truth filed suit and won back her son. Truth's victory in the courts was exceptionally unusual—in the 1820s the legal system rarely worked in favor of former slaves or women.

Truth lets religion be her guide

In 1829 Truth moved to New York City with Peter, leaving Sophia with her older daughters. Truth hoped to find a job that would pay enough for her to start a home and provide for all her children (her husband had died a year earlier). In the city, Truth found housing in a growing community of free blacks. She was hired to work as a servant and enrolled Peter in a navigational school.

Truth, who had been deeply religious her whole life, began attending services at the Mother Zion African Methodist Episcopal (A.M.E.) Church. In church Truth met two of her siblings who had been sold to different masters before she was born. Truth then learned that another woman with whom she had been friendly in church, and who had recently died, was also her sister.

Before long, Truth became acquainted with a religious and charitable couple, the Piersons, who operated a shelter for homeless women. She went to work for them part-time. In 1932 a man named Robert Matthews, who called himself Matthias and claimed he was God, arrived at the shelter. Matthews was really a con artist, but Truth believed his story.

What's In a Name?

One of the first rights exercised by slaves who gained their freedom was to legally acquire a new name. As slaves, their names had been given to them by their masters, who often chose names that seemed to mock their slaves' degraded position in life—such as Caesar (a great Roman general), or Cato (a great Roman orator). Most masters recognized their slaves by their first name only, although many slaves took their master's surname (last name) as their own. When freed, many blacks saw advantages to being associated with their former white masters and kept their master's surname but changed their first and second names.

When finally given a choice, most free blacks chose English, not African, names. It was one way of trying to blend in and gain acceptance into their new homeland of America. Some blacks chose surnames based on the complexion of their skin, which explains why a great number of freed blacks had the last names of Brown and Black. Other blacks chose names that reflected their occupations. A bricklayer might take Mason as a surname; gardeners perhaps chose Green; and blacksmiths and silversmiths found the name Smith appropriate. Some blacks, inspired by their newly found liberty, chose surnames like Justice and Freeman. Other blacks chose names from the Bible, such as Moses and Gabriel. Sojourner Truth took the literal approach when she chose her name (sojourner means "a temporary resident," or a "traveler").

Matthews enlisted Elijah Pierson in a scheme and the two men established a commune called "The Kingdom." The commune drew many believers, among them Truth, who had to donate all their worldly possessions to the organization. Truth went to work at the commune as an unpaid cook and maid. Eventually, Truth caught on to the deceit of the two men and left.

Truth's experience with the con artists, however, did not dampen her religious convictions. She resumed her membership in the Zion A.M.E. Church. In June 1843, Truth had a dream in which God told her, "Go East." Truth packed her bags the next morning and headed east into farm country. Along the way, she decided to change her name from Isabella Baumfree to Sojourner Truth. She took this new name because she believed it was God's will that she "walk in truth."

That day in June 1843 was the beginning of Truth's life as a traveling preacher. She gave sermons and sang in churches, on street corners, at religious revivals, and in homes. She found food and shelter wherever she could. Sometimes Truth spoke about her life as a slave. Truth rapidly gained a reputation as a provocative and inspirational speaker. She was often met with large crowds waiting to hear her speak.

Introduction to abolitionism and women's rights

In late 1843 Truth arrived at a cooperative farm called the Northhampton Association of Education and Industry. There she met several noted abolitionists, among them William Lloyd Garrison (1805–79) and Frederick Douglass (1817–95). The cooperative's residents also taught Truth about the antislavery movement and the budding women's rights movement.

Olive Gilbert, a feminist and member of the Northhampton cooperative, convinced Truth of the need to record her life story. Since Truth was illiterate, she dictated her memoirs to Gilbert. The year 1850 saw the publication of *Narrative of Sojourner Truth: A Northern Slave.*

Blossoms as an antislavery lecturer

Truth made her first major appearance on the antislavery lecture circuit in late 1850. Her friend Garrison, who spotted Truth while he was speaking at the podium, invited her to speak. Although Truth had not prepared a speech, she headed to the front of the room.

Standing nearly six feet tall, Truth had a commanding presence. She started her address by singing a hymn of her own composition. It began: "I am pleading for my people, A poor downtrodden race, Who dwell in freedom's boasted land, With no abiding place." She then told the story of her life as a slave, the separation of her family, and the selling of her son Peter, and how she got Peter back. The audience was moved to tears and many people bought copies of Truth's book.

Truth then embarked on a national speaking tour. She addressed women's rights conventions and antislavery groups, and often traveled with Garrison and other noted abolitionists. In 1854 Truth gave one of her most famous and often-quoted speeches at the Women's Rights Convention in Akron, Ohio. After listening to clergymen claim that women were inferior to men and had no God-given rights, Truth launched into her well-known "Ain't I a Woman?" speech:

> That man over there says that women need to be helped into carriages, and lifted over ditches, and to have the best place everywhere. Nobody ever helps me into carriages, or over mud puddles, or gives me any best place, and ain't I a woman? . . . I have plowed, and planted, and gathered into barns, and no man could head me—and ain't I a woman? I could work as much and eat as much as a man (when I could get it), and bear the lash as well—and ain't I a woman? I have borne five children and seen most all sold off into slavery and when I cried out with a mother's grief, none but Jesus heard—and ain't I a woman?

Audiences were not always sympathetic to her message. In some places, her opponents burned a figure that looked like her in front of the hall where she was to speak; in other places, they disrupted meetings. Truth was clubbed by a crowd in Kansas and was at the center of mob violence in Missouri. Truth refused to let such people stand in her way.

Retirement and return to action

In 1857, Truth, then sixty years old, decided it was time to retire. She moved to a spiritual community in Harmonia, Michigan, just outside of the city of Battle Creek. Within three years, two of her daughters and their families joined Truth in Harmonia. Truth made her home in a converted barn and one of her grandchildren, Sammy, moved in with her. For a time, Truth was content sitting on her porch and telling stories to her grandchildren. That time did not last long

The Dred Scott decision of 1857 made Truth come out of retirement. Dred Scott (1795?–1858) was a slave from Missouri who had traveled with his owner into Illinois, where slavery had been outlawed. On his return to Missouri, Scott sued for his freedom. *Dred Scott v. Sanford* ended up before the Supreme Court, where Scott's claim was rejected. The court wrote that slaves were not citizens of the United States and had no right to file lawsuits. Chief Justice Roger B. Taney

(1777–1864) added insult to injury by claiming that blacks "had no rights which the white man was bound to respect." Truth decided that retirement could wait. In 1859, accompanied by Sammy, she returned to the antislavery lecture circuit.

Aids black soldiers and freed slaves during Civil War

When the Civil War began in 1861, many blacks enthusiastically supported the Union (Northern) cause. When the Union army began accepting black soldiers in 1862, nearly 180,000 blacks signed up (including Truth's grandson, James Caldwell). Truth supported black soldiers by collecting food and clothing for them and by caring for the wounded. She also advocated that black soldiers receive pay equal to white soldiers.

Truth was named "counsellor to freed people" by the National Freedmen's Relief Association in 1864, and began a two-year stay in Washington, D.C. Truth's job was to assist newly freed slaves who had poured into Washington, D.C., many of whom were living in squalid refugee camps and slums.

On October 29, 1864, Truth was granted her wish to meet President Abraham Lincoln (1809-65). At the White House, Lincoln told Truth he had known of her for many years before he thought about running for president. Lincoln signed Truth's scrapbook, which she called her "Book of Life."

During her tenure in Washington, Truth challenged the city's segregation (separation of people along racial lines) policy on streetcars. In 1867 Truth was ordered by a driver to sit in the rear of the car. Truth refused; the driver slammed her against the door and dislocated her shoulder. Truth sued the driver for assault and battery and won. Thereafter, until the passage of Jim Crow laws, blacks received courteous treatment on Washington streetcars. (The Jim Crow system, which began in 1887 and lasted until the 1960s, dictated the segregation of the races at every level of society.)

In the late 1860s Truth resumed speaking and selling copies of her book. In her lectures she combined aspects of Christian religion, mysticism, women's rights, and African American rights.

Final years in Harmonia, Michigan

Truth returned to Harmonia in 1875 to take care of Sammy, who had fallen ill. Later that year Sammy died, just shy of his twenty-fifth birthday. Sammy's death sent Truth into a long period of grief and mourning. Truth believed she would follow Sammy in death; however, she survived another nine years.

In 1878 Truth set off on a speaking tour of thirty-six cities in Michigan and served as a delegate to a women's rights convention. In early 1883 Truth returned to Battle Creek in poor health. She died on November 26, 1883, at the age of eighty-six. Just before her death, Truth told her family and friends, "I'm going home like a shooting star."

Further Reading

Altman, Susan. *The Encyclopedia of African-American Heritage*. New York: Facts on File, Inc.,1997, pp. 250–51.

Giddings, Paula. *When and Where I Enter: The Impact of Black Women on Race and Sex in America*. New York: Bantam Books, 1984.

Mabee, Carleton. *Sojourner Truth: Slave, Prophet, Legend*. New York: New York University Press, 1993.

McKissack, Patricia C., and Fredrick McKissack. *Sojourner Truth: Ain't I a Woman?* New York: Scholastic, Inc., 1992.

Plowden, Martha Ward. *Famous Firsts of Black Women*. Gretna, La: Pelican Publishing Co., 1993, 107–28.

Smallwood, David, et. al. *Profiles of Great African Americans*. Lincolnwood, Ill.: Publications International, Ltd., 1996, pp. 176–79.

Memorial for Sojourner Truth.

Harriet Tubman

Born c. 1820
Dorchester County, Maryland
Died March 10, 1913
Auburn, New York

Fugitive slave, abolitionist, Underground Railroad conductor, Union Army scout, spy, nurse, cook, social reformer

More than probably any single individual of her times, Harriet Tubman successfully rebelled against the slave system of the United States, devoting enormous amounts of time and energy for most of her life to fight for liberty and equality for her fellow African Americans.

Araminta, the young slave

Harriet Tubman was born a slave, one of eleven children of plantation slaves Benjamin Ross and Harriet Green. From the day she was born, according to the laws of the times, Harriet was the "property" of Edward Brodas, who also owned her parents and siblings. Brodas originally named the newborn child Araminta Ross; her mother called her Minty. As an infant, Araminta was fortunate to be able to live with her mother Rit, as she was called, in a slave cabin on the Brodas plantation. Often, slave owners separated a slave mother from her child, selling or hiring out the mother to live and work on another farm soon after the child's birth.

One of the most famous conductors on the Underground Railroad, Tubman made at least nineteen trips from the North into the South within a ten-year period, and led over three hundred slaves into freedom.

Harriet Tubman (Corbis-Bettmann. Reproduced by permission.)

213

Araminta stayed with her mother at night. In the day, while her mother was working in the field, Araminta and the other slave children were watched over by one of the grandmothers—women who were too old to work in the fields any longer. When Araminta was six years old she was sent off the plantation to work for Mr. and Mrs. Cook. Mrs. Cook tried to teach Araminta how to weave. When Araminta showed little interest, Mr. Cook put her to work checking his muskrat traps in the river. Araminta returned to the Brodas plantation a year later, sick from the measles and her constant exposure to the cold water of the river.

After Rit nursed the seven-year-old Araminta back to health, she was again hired out, this time to Miss Susan. Araminta's job was to clean Miss Susan's house and take care of her baby—holding the child during the day and rocking its cradle at night if the child cried. If the child's crying woke up Miss Susan in the night, or if Araminta somehow failed in her daytime duties, Miss Susan lashed her with a cowhide whip. One day, caught in the act of stealing from the sugar bowl, Araminta ran away from Miss Susan's to escape a whipping. She hid for several days in a pigsty before returning. Shortly after the incident, Miss Susan returned Araminta—worn down from lack of food and sleep, and scarred from the whippings—to the Brodas plantation.

Harriet, the field slave

As soon as Rit nursed her back to health, Araminta was hired out again by her master. This time it was to do odd jobs in the field, as she was deemed untrainable as a house slave. Araminta was still very small but she was expected to chop wood and haul heavy loads like an adult. And when she failed in her tasks, she was whipped like an adult. When Araminta was eleven years old, she started wearing a bright colored bandanna wrapped around her head, a custom among slaves that meant she was no longer a child. From that time on, Araminta would be known as Harriet, the name of her mother. Years of hard work in the fields made Harriet, in spite of her small size, as strong as any man. She could work long hours and lift heavy loads.

As a young teenager, Harriet was again hired out by her master to a neighbor at harvest time. One evening, as the slaves were working in the fields, Harriet noticed a slave sneaking away, followed by the plantation's overseer (the boss of the slaves in the field). In the course of trying to catch the runaway, Harriet was hit in the head with a two-pound iron weight. The wound scarred Harriet's forehead and caused her to have seizures for the rest of her life. Brodas tried to sell Harriet while she was still sick, but no one wanted her, even at the lowest price possible.

Tickets to freedom

In 1836 Harriet went back to work in the fields of the Brodas plantation. She soon gained permission from her master to hire her time out. Under this arrangement Harriet was free to work for other people for whatever wages they would pay; she was also required to pay Brodas $75 per year. In 1844 Harriet married John Tubman, one of sixty-two thousand free blacks in the state of Maryland (there were ninety-two thousand slaves in the state at the time). John had his own cabin, but due to competition from hired-out slaves, he earned meager wages for his work. Harriet lived with John in his cabin but was not happy. She longed for freedom and dreamed of escaping to the North.

Harriet Tubman's master died in 1849. Fearing that she would be sold to the Deep South to pick cotton, Tubman and two of her brothers decided to escape to the North. Shortly after they set out, her two brothers tried to convince Tubman to return. Two days later Tubman, without her brothers, sought help from a local Quaker woman who was known for aiding fugitive slaves. The woman gave Tubman two slips of paper, each containing the name of a family that lived on the road north. These people, she explained, would feed and shelter her, and then tell her how to get to the next house. Tubman had heard talk of an "underground railroad" that slaves could take to freedom in the North. She was now a passenger.

Tubman traveled by night, using the North Star as her guide, and hid during the day. After traveling through ninety miles of swamp and woodland she finally reached the Mason-Dixon line, the boundary between Maryland and Pennsylva-

Harriet Tubman (left) with a group of slaves she helped escape via the Underground Railroad. *(Library of Congress)*

nia—between the slave South and the free North. Tubman headed to Philadelphia, home to a large population of free blacks. She found work there washing dishes in a hotel kitchen.

Underground Railroad conductor

In 1850, Congress passed the Fugitive Slave Act. Under this federal law, any black person could be accused of being a runaway slave and brought before a federal judge. Accused runaways were denied a jury trial and could not testify on their own behalf. The law also made it a federal crime to aid or harbor a fugitive slave, with strict penalties for helping a slave escape. The law gave a boost to the professional slave catchers, who for a fee captured runaway slaves and returned them to their owners. Always a grave threat to blacks—free or slave—in the South, they now operated boldly in the North, in states where slavery had been abolished for some time.

THE ROUTES OF THE UNDERGROUND RAILROAD

Free state
Slave state

Harriet Tubman and other fugitive slaves and free blacks were no longer very safe in the free North. At that time, many chose to head even further north, into Canada, where slavery had been abolished since 1833. From 1852 through 1857, Tubman lived in St. Catharines, Ontario, Canada, a small town with a population of six thousand people, seven hundred of whom were African Americans. Tubman, however, chose to head south, back over the Mason-Dixon line, intent

Map of the eastern United States showing the routes of the Underground Railroad. *(Reproduced by permission of the Gale Group)*

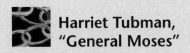

Harriet Tubman, "General Moses"

Although they were not legally allowed to learn to read or write, many slaves were familiar with the stories of the Bible. In particular, they were well acquainted with the story of how Moses led the enslaved Hebrews out of captivity in Egypt to the promised land of Israel and freedom. Among both black and white abolitionists, Harriet Tubman's daring rescues as an Underground Railroad conductor earned her the name of "Moses." The slave owners of the South, on the other hand, detested Tubman and offered a $40,000 reward for her, dead or alive.

Abolitionist John Brown (1800–1859), who led a raid on a federal arsenal at Harpers Ferry, Virginia, in October 1859—in what many historians refer to as the "first shots" of the Civil War (1861–65)—called her "General Tubman." Brown knew of Tubman's courageous accomplishments and sought her help for the raid. Tubman encouraged Brown but illness prevented her from directly participating in the revolt.

on helping other slaves escape to freedom. During that time she made eleven trips into Maryland.

From 1850 to 1860, Tubman made at least nineteen trips into the South and escorted over three hundred slaves on their northern journey to freedom in Canada, including her brother and her parents (her husband did not want to leave the South). Tubman resettled her parents in Auburn, New York, in a house that her friend, U.S. Senator and former New York governor William Seward (1801–72), helped her buy.

Civil War spy and scout

When war between the Confederacy (the South) and the Union (the North) broke out in April 1861, Tubman went back into action. With a letter in hand from the governor of Massachusetts, she reported to the Union Army camp in Beaufort, South Carolina. There she went to work in a field hospital for war refugees, caring for injured and wounded contraband, which is a word meaning "property of war." In this case, the contraband were slaves who had fled their plantations for refuge behind Union lines and soldiers.

On January 1, 1863, U.S. president Abraham Lincoln (1809–65) issued the Emancipation Proclamation that freed all slaves in the Confederacy, urging them to join the Union Army. That summer Tubman worked in the Charleston, South Carolina, area as a scout and a spy for an all-black Union regiment led by Colonel James Montgomery. Their mission was to carry out raids on the rebels—releasing slaves and terrorizing the enemy. As a spy, Tubman was known for her cleverness and courage in gathering information from behind enemy lines, skills that she had sharpened for years as a conductor on the Underground Railroad.

Life after the war

In 1864 Tubman returned to her home and parents in Auburn, New York, without money and exhausted from the war. Despite serving the Union Army in many useful capacities, Tubman was never paid for her services as were other scouts, spies, and cooks (Civil War nurses were unorganized, unpaid volunteers). After the war ended on April 9, 1865, Tubman traveled to Washington, D.C., to try to secure a position as a paid nurse at a freedman's hospital in Virginia, and to see if she could collect her back pay from the army. She again went home empty-handed.

Fortunately for Tubman, her friends came to her aid. Abolitionist friends placed ads seeking donations of money and clothing for Tubman, who supported her parents and fed and sheltered many poor ex-slaves who showed up at her front door. In 1869 Tubman's friend Sarah Bradford wrote a short biography of her life, *Scenes in the Life of Harriet Tubman*. Sales of the book raised enough money for Tubman to pay off the mortgage on her Auburn home.

In 1869 Tubman married Nelson Davis, a black Civil War veteran. Davis was younger than Tubman but suffered from tuberculosis. Their marriage lasted nineteen years, until 1888 when Nelson died from his disease. Tubman never got her back pay (she calculated that the army owed her around $1,800) but she did finally collect a pension of $8 a month for her late husband's service. Ten years later, an Act of Congress increased Tubman's widow's pension to $20—still the government refused to officially reward Tubman for her own services.

Fighting to the end

In 1896, at seventy-five years old, Tubman began yet another project to improve the quality of life for the poor and aged. With help from a bank, and royalties from a second edition of Bradford's book, she purchased twenty-five acres of land that were located next to her property and started a co-operative farm. Tubman wanted to create a place where able-bodied people could work together to help support those who were too old or ill to work. Using her nursing and cooking skills, Tubman managed the farm until 1903.

Now in her eighties, Tubman could no longer run the place by herself so she donated the land to her church, the African Methodist Episcopal Zion Church (she also attended the white Central Church in Auburn every Sunday morning). The A.M.E. church formally opened the Harriet Tubman Home for Aged and Indigent Negroes in 1908. Tubman wanted it to be called the John Brown Home. The church had only people of color on its board of directors. Tubman wanted both black and white board members. The church charged $100 a year to live there. Tubman wanted it to be free. Tubman lost these last battles but spent her remaining years peacefully at the home she had founded. When she died in 1913 at age ninety-two, Tubman was given a full military service for her funeral.

Further Reading

Bentley, Judith. *Harriet Tubman.* New York: Franklin Watts, Inc., 1990.

Bradford, Sarah. *Harriet Tubman: The Moses of Her People.* New York: Corinth Press, 1961 (reprint of 1886 edition).

Burns, Bree. *Harriet Tubman and the Fight Against Slavery.* New York: Chelsea House Publishers, 1992.

Logan, Rayford W., and Michael R. Winston, eds. *Dictionary of American Negro Biography.* New York: W. W. Norton & Co., 1982.

McClard, Megan. *Harriet Tubman: Slavery and the Underground Railroad.* Englewood, N.J.: Silver Burdett Press, 1991.

Sterling, Dorothy, ed. *We Are Your Sisters: Black Women in the Nineteenth Century.* New York: W. W. Norton & Co., 1984.

Nat Turner

Born October 2, 1800
Southampton County, Virginia
Died November 11, 1831
Southampton County, Virginia

Slave, slave preacher, revolt leader

The South was never the same after Nat Turner's revolt of 1831. Turner and approximately seventy slaves killed about sixty white men, women, and children in Southampton County, Virginia—some even as they slept. The myth of the happy slave was forcefully exploded and slaveholders throughout the South no longer slept peacefully. Every little sound in the night reminded them of Nat Turner's reign of terror and the possibility that their slaves might do the same.

Organizer and leader of the most violent—and successful—slave revolt in U.S. history.

Marked at birth

On October 2, 1800, Nat Turner was born into slavery on a plantation in Southampton County, Virginia, about seventy miles southeast of Richmond. The plantation's owner, Benjamin Turner, had bought Turner's mother a year earlier from the slave market in Norfolk, a port on Virginia's Atlantic coast. She had been taken a few years earlier from her African homeland, the ancient land of the Upper Nile (in Sudan), and brought to the Americas by slave traders. Benjamin Turner gave his newly acquired human property the Christian name of "Nancy."

Nat Turner. *(Library of Congress)*

Very little is known about Turner's father, not even his name. When Turner was just a child his father fled from the plantation to escape to freedom in the North. No one is sure if he ever made it as he was never heard from again. Turner's grandmother (his father's mother), "Old Bridget," along with Nancy, raised Turner and had a very strong influence on his early and formative years.

When Nat Turner was born, he had strange bumps and marks on his skin. In the part of Africa where his mother was from, these marks meant that he would grow up to be a great prophet (a religious leader with special, almost magical powers). In his published *The Confessions of Nat Turner* (1831), Turner describes his earliest memory of being considered special: "Being at play with other children, when three or four years old, I was telling them something, which my mother overhearing, said it had happened before I was born. . . . I surely would be a prophet, as the Lord had shewn me things that had happened before my birth. And my father and mother strengthened me in this my first impression, saying in my presence, I was intended for some great purpose."

Early childhood

The Turner plantation was a large farm, spread over several hundred acres. The labor of more than thirty slaves produced yearly crops of tobacco, corn, apples, and cotton. As a child, Turner probably spent his years playing games, fishing, swimming, and trapping with the other children—black and white—of the plantation, watched over by slave women who were too old to work in the fields. Turner, like the other black children, grew up listening to his grandmother's folktales—the stories, myths, and legends of her African homeland. Turner's grandmother, Bridget, was also a Christian, and taught him about Christianity as well.

Somehow, Turner learned to read at a very early age. Some historians think that his grandmother may have taught him; others think that he learned from a member of Benjamin Turner's family (although it was against the law to teach a slave how to read or write). In *Confessions,* Turner recalls: "The manner in which I learned to read and write, not only had great influence on my own mind, as I acquired it with the most perfect ease, so much so, that I have no recollection whatever of learning the alphabet—but to the astonishment of the family, one day, when a book was shewn to me to keep me from crying, I began spelling the names of different objects—this was a source of wonder to all in the neighborhood."

Turner's intelligence and abilities did not go unnoticed by his master, Benjamin Turner. He took Turner with him to Bible meetings and even gave him his own Bible to read. Although he was forbidden by his master to read anything but the Bible, in *Confessions* Turner tells how he secretly read the books of the plantation's white schoolchildren at every opportunity. Nat Turner *was* special and he knew it. He truly felt that someday he would be a leader of his people and even as a child planned for it to happen. "Having soon discovered to be great," he says in *Confessions,* "I must appear so, and therefore studiously avoided mixing in society, and wrapped myself in mystery, devoting myself to fasting and prayer."

Field slave

When Benjamin Turner died in 1810, his land and slaves were divided among his three surviving children. Nat Turner, his mother, and his grandmother became the legal property of Samuel Turner. When Turner reached the age of twelve he was forced to work in the fields with the other slaves on Samuel Turner's small farm. Although he was considered special by both blacks and whites, he could not escape the reality of being a slave.

For six days a week Turner and his fellow slaves worked from dawn to dusk plowing, planting, hoeing, weeding, building and mending fences, feeding animals, and harvesting crops. On Sunday Master Turner allowed his slaves to attend a prayer meeting led by a white preacher. Afterwards, the slaves were allowed to hold their own, separate prayer groups, dances, and picnics.

At one Sunday prayer meeting, Turner recalls in *Confessions,* he was struck by a passage from the Bible: "Seek ye the kingdom of Heaven and all things shall be added unto you." He prayed daily for God to help him understand the meaning of this directive. "As I was praying one day at my plough," he recalls in *Confessions,* "the spirit spoke to me, saying 'Seek ye the kingdom of Heaven and all things shall be added unto you.'" Two years later, he again heard a voice repeating those same words. The experience, Turner explains in *Confessions,* "fully confirmed me in the impression that I was ordained for some great purpose in the hands of the Almighty."

Plantation life

Despite his obvious intelligence, and possible better use to his master as a house slave, Nat Turner labored in the fields of Samuel Turner for the better part of ten years. During that time, Turner tried to lead a life that he thought would please God and prepare him for the role of leader of his people: he didn't drink, gamble, smoke, or steal. He married another slave on the Turner plantation, Cherry, and together they had three children.

When an economic depression hit Virginia in 1820, the price of cotton dropped dramatically and Samuel Turner hired an overseer to manage his farm and get more work from his slaves. In 1821, perhaps because he was beaten or overworked, Turner ran away. He hid in the nearby woods and swamps and somehow escaped detection from the patrols and their hunting dogs. Everyone thought that he had run off for good like his father had done years earlier, and the search was called off after two weeks.

Surprising both his master and his fellow slaves, Turner returned to the Turner farm exactly thirty days after he had escaped. Samuel Turner was so pleased that he did not even have Turner punished. The slaves, on the other hand, were astonished that anyone who had escaped to freedom would voluntarily return to slavery. In his mysterious way, as Turner relates in *Confessions,* he told them: "the reason of my return was, that the Spirit appeared to me and said I had my wishes directed to things in this world, and not to the kingdom of Heaven, and that I should return to the service of my earthly master."

Waiting for a sign

When Samuel Turner died in 1822, his widow put the farm's slaves on the auction block to be sold to the highest bidders. The Turner widow kept his mother but Turner was sold to Thomas Moore, and Cherry and their children were sold to Giles Reese, whose place was not far from the Moore farm. Turner was only one of three slaves on Moore's seven hundred-acre farm and he was forced to work harder than ever.

During his time as a slave for Moore, Turner gained a reputation among the local whites for being a trusted servant. Among the local blacks, Turner was seen as a powerful slave preacher who talked about divine visions and voices, and the coming of what he called "the Great Day of Judgment." On Sundays, when he was not visiting Cherry and his children at the Reese farm, Turner traveled from farm to farm preaching to mostly black audiences. As a result Turner came to know almost every slave, back-road, woods, swamp, and town in the county.

The years passed as Turner waited for a sign from God that would provide for him some direction. Finally on May 12, 1828, as he relates in *Confessions*: "I heard a loud noise in the heavens, and the Spirit instantly appeared to me and said the Serpent was loosened, and Christ laid down the yoke he had borne for the sins of men, and that I should take it on and fight against the Serpent, for the time was fast approaching when the first should be last and the last should be first." The spirit, Turner says, instructed him to wait for another sign before he began the battle to free his people.

When Thomas Moore died at the end of 1828, his widow remarried a man named Joseph Travis, a local wheelwright (maker and repairer of wheeled vehicles) who assumed control of the farm and slaves. In *Confessions*, Turner recalls that Travis was "a kind master, and placed the greatest confidence in me; in fact I had no cause to complain of his treatment to me."

The Great Day of Judgment

On February 12, 1831, when the sky went totally black as a result of a solar eclipse, Turner was sure it was the sign the spirit had promised him. He began to make plans for a revolt of slaves in the area. They would rise up and kill their white masters who had held them in bondage for so long. Age or sex would not matter; no one was to be spared. As the slaves did what Turner called in *Confessions* their "work of

Violence, Repression, and Freedom

Nat Turner's revolt, like earlier uprisings led by Jemmy (1739), Gabriel Prosser (1800), and Denmark Vesey (1822), was a local event, yet it affected the entire nation, especially the slaveholding South. For slave owners, the revolts were reasons to fear their slaves all the more, and to pass even more restrictive laws to control them. With each uprising, blacks in the South, free and slave, lost more of their rights. Shortly after the Turner revolt Virginia, for example, banned night-time religious meetings for slaves. Slaves could go to church only in the day, with their masters, to hear only white preachers. By 1835 the right for blacks, free or slave, to assemble in groups for any purpose without a white person present was denied throughout the states of the Deep South.

For the antislavery movement, the slave rebellions focused the attention of the nation on the brutality of the slave system. And, as examples of the price slaves were willing to pay in pursuit of freedom, the slave revolts and conspiracies inspired, and helped to unify, the abolitionists and eventually brought an end to slavery in the United States.

death," they would gather arms and supporters, march on the nearby town of Jerusalem, Virginia, and seize more arms and ammunition. Turner hoped that his revolt in Southampton County would spark slave rebellions throughout the South and that slavery would end as a result.

Turner told his plan to his most trusted friends. They selected the Fourth of July as the date to strike. Turner was ill on that day, however, and the plot was postponed until another sign appeared, this time, the "greenish blue color" of the sun on August 13. Six slaves, led by Turner, began the rebellion at two o'clock in the morning on Monday, August 22. Turner and the rebels began the massacre by killing Turner's master, Joseph Travis, and his family. The rebels then took some arms and horses, and began going from farm to farm killing whites.

Within twenty-four hours about seventy slaves had joined the revolt. By the morning of August 23, fifty-seven whites—men, women, and children—had been slaughtered. The rebels had covered about twenty miles and were slowly making their way, worn from their task, toward Jerusalem, where there was a warehouse of weapons. About three miles outside the town, the slaves were drawn into battle with bands of armed white men and forced to scatter.

Hung in Jerusalem

Word of the bloody revolt spread quickly, and a massacre of blacks by whites immediately followed. Hundreds of

The building where Nat Turner was held during his trial and until his execution.

soldiers and militiamen (an army made up of citizens) hunted down and executed anyone they thought was connected to the uprising. At least two hundred blacks were killed in the field, without trials. Those captured alive, about sixteen slaves and three free blacks, were condemned to hang. Turner, who hid in a cave he made under a pile of logs, avoided capture until October 30. After a short trial in the town of Jerusalem, on November 11, 1831, Turner was hanged.

The trial of Nat Turner wasn't really necessary, as he never denied his guilt. In fact, Turner gave a full confession to Thomas R. Gray, a white attorney who had defended several of the other rebels. Over a period of days, while chained in his jail cell, Turner dictated his story to Gray. Shortly after his trial and hanging, Gray published Turner's story as *The Confessions of Nat Turner*. In the aftermath, a wave of terror rolled over the entire slaveholding South. Thousands of blacks were killed as whites took their revenge on any slaves suspected of ever being involved in plotting to revolt.

Further Reading

Bisson, Terry. *Nat Turner: Slave Revolt Leader.* New York: Chelsea House Publishers, 1988.

The Confessions of Nat Turner as Told to Thomas R. Gray, reprinted in Herbert Aptheker, *Nat Turner's Slave Rebellion.* New York: Humanities Press, 1966.

Goldman, Martin, S. *Nat Turner and the Southampton Slave Revolt of 1831.* New York: Franklin Watts, 1992.

Logan, Rayford W., and Michael R. Winston, eds. *Dictionary of American Negro Biography.* New York: W. W. Norton & Co., 1982.

Tragle, Henry Irving. *The Southampton Slave Revolt of 1831: A Compilation of Source Material.* Amherst: The University of Massachusetts Press, 1971.

Denmark Vesey

Born c. 1767
Africa or St. Thomas, Danish West Indies
Died July 2, 1822
Charleston, South Carolina

Chattel slave, freedman, rebellion leader

A literate and worldly man, Denmark Vesey spent his life resisting the degrading forces of slavery and racism. He ultimately became the first slave revolt leader of note when in 1822 he organized thousands of slaves in Charleston, South Carolina, in a carefully planned uprising. Vesey's aim was to change the system by force, no matter what the cost.

Return to sender

Very little is known about Denmark Vesey's childhood years. Some historians claim he was born in the Danish colony of St. Thomas, an island in the Caribbean; others say he was born in Africa. The historical record begins in 1781, when Joseph Vesey, a sea captain and slave trader based in Bermuda, delivered 390 slaves from St. Thomas to St. Domingue (a French colony occupying the western third of the Caribbean island of Hispaniola). On the voyage, Captain Vesey and his officers took special notice of a fourteen-year-old male from the Danish slave market. They made a pet of him, gave him special clothes to wear, and, since he was acquired from a Danish colony, named him Denmark.

The leader of the most wide-reaching plan to strike back at the slave system in the United States.

Denmark and the rest of Captain Vesey's human cargo were sold in the slave market of Cap Francais, St. Domingue, to various planters for work on their sugarcane plantations. Three months later, when Captain Vesey was delivering another shipload of slaves to Cap Francais, Denmark's owner met him at the dock to return the slave and demand his money back. Denmark was examined by a physician and found "unsound and subject to epileptic fits," and according to slave-trading custom, Captain Vesey was forced to refund the buyer's money.

Witness to horror

Denmark, deemed "unsellable," became Captain Vesey's personal servant and assumed his master's surname, Vesey. From 1781 to 1783 Denmark sailed the seas on Vesey's vessel and witnessed all the horrors of the trans-Atlantic slave trade. It was a time when European colonists, especially in the West Indies, just couldn't seem to get enough African slaves for their sugarcane plantations. The French colonists of St. Domingue, for example, were importing slaves at the rate of twenty thousand per year.

Like most slave traders of the day, Captain Vesey traded for slaves with coastal West Africans, offering in return items from the colonies such as rum, gin, molasses, pistols, gunpowder, knives, tobacco, glass beads, salt, kettles, fishhooks, and needles. Typically, as many slaves as possible were crammed into a ship for the two-month journey to the West Indies known as the Middle Passage. Conditions on the slave ships were so bad that one-quarter to one-third of the slaves died before ever reaching the other side of the Atlantic. Spoiled food, stagnant water, diseases, and dark, damp, and dirty living conditions all took their toll.

Slave in the city

In 1783 Captain Vesey gave up slave trading on the high seas and settled in Charleston, South Carolina, one of many ports along America's coast where he had plied his trade. Denmark Vesey was now sixteen and had seen more of the world than most people. He picked up many languages along the way—English, French, Danish, and Spanish. And he knew firsthand of the brutal treatment of Africans and how they were whipped, branded, and tortured when they tried to resist or rebel.

Vesey quickly adapted to life in America's fourth largest city at the time. Life in an urban area provided more opportunities and freedoms for slaves, especially if they had marketable skills. While Captain Vesey retained a number of his slaves as household servants, there was little need on a daily basis for Vesey's services as a skilled carpenter. Vesey, like other slaves in the city, hired out his services and paid his master his weekly earnings. Captain Vesey then gave back to Vesey a portion of those wages as an allowance—an amount that was barely enough for food and clothing.

In the South, one out of eight slaves lived in urban areas. Vesey's arrangement with his master was fairly common for slaves in cities and towns. As a result, urban slaves had access to a whole different world than slaves isolated on plantations in rural areas. Vesey could move about freely in comparison and interact with a greater variety of people—whites, free blacks, and other slaves. He had access to newspapers and books, and was exposed to a broader range of ideas and news from near and far.

Free but not equal

In December 1799, Denmark Vesey won $1,500 in the East Bay Street lottery. Vesey bought his freedom from Captain Vesey in January for $600 and opened a carpentry shop. Vesey would no longer have to hand over his wages every week to his master. He was now one of about 1,000 free blacks in the city. Vesey had to carry his manumission (formal release from bondage) papers with him at all times to prove his free status. He also had to register with the state and pay taxes or risk re-enslavement.

Although Vesey was free, made a respectable living as a carpenter, and paid his taxes, he was still not entitled to the rights and privileges of white people. Free blacks could not vote, serve on a jury, or testify in court except in cases involving other blacks. If accused of a crime, free blacks were treated the same as slaves: they had no right to legal representation or a jury trial. In Charleston, both freed blacks and slaves were required to wear identification badges that indicated their status.

Spurred to revolution

Denmark Vesey was not a man who was easily intimidated by the rules of white society. He was known for arguing with whites about racial issues in public, sometimes just to show other blacks that it could be done. Vesey was literate and intelligent, aware of events in other parts of the world, especially the slave revolution that took place in the French colony of St. Domingue. Fed up with hundreds of years of abuse at the hands of their white masters, the colony's black slaves violently revolted in 1791. Through years of fighting and heavy losses, St. Domingue's slaves gained their emancipation in 1794, and in 1804 established Haiti—the first independent nation in the Western Hemisphere to be governed by blacks.

Through the years, Vesey came to believe that he had won the lottery and had been freed from slavery in order to help save his people from slavery and racism. He was a very religious man who was able to passionately quote scripture. He was especially familiar with the Old Testament stories of Moses leading the Israelites out of slavery in ancient Egypt. Vesey dreamed of becoming the Moses of his people.

Power through the church

Like many other blacks, Vesey found comfort and community in the black church. He also found an outlet for his radical view of the world, a view that held that slavery was against God's will and must be opposed by whatever means were necessary. In 1817 Vesey became an active and vocal member of Charleston's only independent black church, the African Methodist Episcopal (A.M.E.) Church. The church was located in the suburb of Hampstead. It had been formed after three-quarters of the city's six thousand black Methodists withdrew their membership from the white-controlled churches in a dispute over the custody of a burial ground for blacks.

White church officials quickly responded to the rebellion by having 469 black worshipers arrested one Sunday while at their Hampstead church. They were charged with disorderly conduct. The group was released after the arrests but the action served notice of more harassment to come. City officials again moved against the Hampstead A.M.E. Church on a Sunday in June 1818. They arrested 140 free blacks and slaves who belonged to the church and put them in jail. The church's bishop and four ministers were given a choice: leave the state or spend a month in jail. Eight other ministers were sentenced to ten lashes or a $10 fine. Still, the Hampstead A.M.E. Church continued to function through 1822.

For years Vesey had engaged many people, black and white, in conversations about slavery. His activities with the A.M.E. Church, which included giving sermons and leading some religious classes, enabled Vesey to preach his message to a much wider audience. Contrary to the opinion of white southern slaveholders, he argued with passion that God does *not* approve of slavery. Religious meetings offered Vesey the perfect opportunity to test his ideas on other blacks and to assess which people were sympathetic and might be trusted with his secret plan to free the slaves.

Betrayal and disaster

In December 1821 Vesey started to organize the area's slaves for an attack on Charleston. It would take place in the summer when many of the white residents would be away from the city on vacation. A slave army led by Vesey would kill as many whites as possible while seizing control of Charleston. His hope, based on what he knew of Haiti's slave revolution, was to spark a widespread rebellion among the slaves that would lead to the downfall of slavery in the United States.

Vesey was careful to select urban artisan slaves—mechanics, harness-makers, blacksmiths, and carpenters—as leaders for the revolt. He also chose as one of his lieutenants a man named Gullah Jack, a conjurer who some believed had magical powers. Vesey appealed to his followers to selectively recruit only slaves who could be trusted with the plans, but

Gullah Jack

Denmark Vesey recruited Gullah Jack to be one of his top lieutenants in the plot to violently seize the city of Charleston and incite a nationwide slave rebellion. Gullah Jack was also known as Cooter Jack, or Jack Pritchard. He was the slave of Paul Pritchard, a shipbuilder in Charleston. He joined Vesey's conspiracy sometime after Christmas of 1821. Vesey chose Gullah Jack because of his connections to the slaves of South Carolina's coastal islands known as the Gullah, or Kongo people of Angolan descent.

Gullah Jack was a member of Vesey's church and a well-respected man in the black community. He was known by his people to be a "conjurer," a person believed to have special, almost magical powers to manipulate the world. With Gullah Jack as a leader, many of the slave conspirators felt more confident of their success—some even believed that Gullah Jack himself was bulletproof. Gullah Jack provided charms to some of the rebels before the planned attack, saying they would prevent injury in battle.

The battle never happened. Instead the rebels were betrayed and arrested. Gullah Jack managed to avoid capture by the authorities until July 5, 1822, three days after Vesey had already been hanged. Gullah Jack was condemned to death for his part in the conspiracy and hanged on July 12, 1822.

the secret was eventually leaked to the wrong person, who informed on the rebels to the authorities.

Vesey had set the date for the attack on Charleston for the second Sunday of July 1822. When two of the leaders were arrested on May 30, Vesey moved the date ahead one month. Despite months of planning and the manufacture and stockpiling of bayonets and daggers, Vesey was unable to communicate the change of plans to the thousands of conspiring slaves, some of whom lived as far away as eighty miles from the city.

Aftermath

The planned attack, said by one witness to have involved as many as nine thousand slaves, never took place. In early June, authorities arrested 131 blacks in Charleston. Forty-nine rebels were condemned to die; twelve were eventually pardoned; and thirty-seven were hanged, including Vesey. Four white men were fined and imprisoned for helping the rebels.

In response to the conspiracy, the whites of Charleston tore down the Hampstead A.M.E. Church. The state of South Carolina reacted by passing even more restrictive laws in an effort to prevent future slave revolts. For example, slaves could no longer meet in a group for any purpose unless a white person was present; slaves were not allowed to hire out their time; and free blacks over fifteen years of age had to have a white guardian.

Further Reading

Aptheker, Herbert. *American Negro Slave Revolts,* New Edition. New York: International Publishers Co., Inc., 1974.

Edwards, Lillie, J. *Denmark Vesey: Slave Revolt Leader.* New York: Chelsea House Publishers, 1990.

Lofton, John. *Insurrection in South Carolina: The Turbulent World of Denmark Vesey.* Yellow Springs, Ohio: The Antioch Press, 1964.

Logan, Rayford W., and Michael R. Winston, eds. *Dictionary of American Negro Biography.* New York: W. W. Norton & Co., 1982.

Malone, Dumas, ed. *Dictionary of American Biography.* New York: Charles Scribner's Sons, 1936.

Index

A

A.M.E. Church. *See* African Methodist Episcopal (A.M.E.) Church.
Adams, John Quincy 29
Affonso. *See* Afonso I.
Afonso I 1–7
African Methodist Episcopal (A.M.E.) Church 12 (ill.), 13, 14, 232
"Ain't I a Woman?" 210
Albert I 128
Allen, Debbie 30
Allen, Richard 9–15, 9 (ill.)
American Anti-Slavery Society 69 (ill.), 70, 77
American Slavery As It Is: Testimony of a Thousand Witnesses 79
Amistad (motion picture) 28 (ill.), 30
Amistad (slave ship) 26, 27, 28
Anti-Slavery Sewing Society 37
Anti-Slavery Society of England 156
Appeal to the Christian Women of the South 77

Asia Peace National Fund for Women 109
August 1914 172

B

Babylonia 82
Bethel African Methodist Episcopal Church. *See* African Methodist Episcopal Church.
The Black Codes of the South 142, 199
Black Mutiny 30
Booth, John Wilkes 119
Brown, Henry "Box" 45
Brown, John 17–24, 17 (ill.), 23 (ill.), 55, 218

C

Cancer Ward 171
Charbonneau, Toussaint 160
Cinque, Joseph 25–31, 25 (ill.)

Bold type indicates main biographies and their page numbers. Illustrations are indicated by (ill).

Clark, William 160, 162 (ill.)
Code of Hammurabi 82, 83 (ill.), 84
Coffin, Levi 33–39, 33 (ill.)
Comfort station, operation of 106
Comfort women 105, 108 (ill.)
Confession (St. Patrick) 145
The Confessions of Nat Turner 222, 227
Congo Free State 122, 124
Congo Reform Association 127
Craft, Ellen 41–47, 44 (ill.)
Craft, William 41–47, 41 (ill.)

D

The Deeper Wrong; Or, Incidents in the Life of a Slave Girl 101
Democratic Republic of the Congo 1, 122
Diogo I 7
Douglass, Frederick 14, 19, **49–56**, 49 (ill.), 54 (ill.)
Dred Scott v. Sanford 210

E

Emancipation Proclamation 71, 115 (ill.), 116–118
Epistle to the Clergy of the Southern States 77
Equiano, Olaudah 57–64, 57 (ill.)

F

The First Circle 171
Ford's Theater 119
Free African Society 13
Free People of Color Congress 14
Fugitive Slave Laws 20, 38, 45, 100, 185, 216

G

Garrison, William Lloyd 45, **65–72**, 65 (ill.), 77, 183

Gettysburg Address 117
Gladiators 176, 177
Grant, Ulysses S. 118
Grimké, Angelina 73–80, 76 (ill.)
Grimké, Sarah 73–80, 73 (ill.)
The Gulag Archipelago 172
Gullah Jack 233, 234

H

Hammurabi 81–86, 81 (ill.), 83 (ill.)
Harpers Ferry, Virginia; raid on 21, 22
Harrison, William Henry 30
Hebrew slaves 129–133
Hemings, Madison 89, 91
Hemings, Sally 87–93
Henrique de Aviz (Henry the Navigator) 2
The History of Mary Prince, a West Indian Slave, Related by Herself 151, 156

I

Incidents in the Life of a Slave Girl: Written by Herself 95, 97 (ill.), 101
Indiana State Anti-Slavery Society 37
The Interesting Narrative of the Life of Olaudah Equiano 57, 63

J

Jacobs, Harriet Ann 95–101, 95 (ill.), 97 (ill.)
Japanese military 105, 106
Jefferson, Thomas 88, 89 (ill.), 90, 160
Jim Crow laws 211
John Brown: A Cry for Freedom: 22
John Brown: His Soul Goes Marching On 22
John II 2
John III 6
Jones, Absalom 13

K

Kansas-Nebraska Act of 1854 21, 113
Kim, Haksun 103–109, 103 (ill.), 108 (ill.)
Kongo Kingdom 1
Korean Council for Women Drafted for Military Sexual Slavery by Japan 109
Kruschev, Nikita S. 170
Ku Klux Klan 47
Kubrick, Stanley 180

L

Labor camps, Soviet 169
League of Gileadites 20
Lee, Robert E. 22, 118
Leopold II, King of Belgium 121–128, 123 (ill.)
Letter to the Soldiers of Coroticus 149, 150
Letters on the Equality of the Sexes 78
Lewis, Meriwether 160, 162 (ill.)
The Liberator 65, 68, 72, 77
The Life Experience and Gospel Labors of the Rt. Rev. Richard Allen 11, 15
Life and Times of Frederick Douglass 55
Lincoln, Abraham 55, 71, 111–119, 111 (ill.), 115 (ill.), 186, 211, 218
London Freedman's Aid Society 38

M

Manuel I 3
Manumission 155, 178, 231
Massachusetts Anti-Slavery Society 53
Mesopotamia 81
The Methodist Society 11
The Middle Passage 26, 59 (ill.), 60, 230
Missouri Compromise 113
Morel, Edmund Dene 121–128, 121 (ill.)

Moses 129–136, 129 (ill.), 134 (ill.), 218, 232
My Bondage and My Freedom 55

N

Napoleon Bonaparte 203
Narrative of Sojourner Truth: A Northern Slave 209
Narrative of the Life of Frederick Douglass, An American Slave 53, 55
National Negro Convention Movement 14
Native American women guides 161
New England Anti-Slavery Society 70
North Star 19, 54, 55
Northrup, Solomon 137–143
November 1916 172

O

One Day in the Life of Ivan Denisovich 171

P

Patrick, Saint 145–150, 145 (ill.)
Pedro I 7
Philadelphia Female Anti-Slavery Society 77
Prester John, the myth of 2
Prince, Mary 151–157

R

Raid on Harpers Ferry, Virginia 21, 22
Ramses II 131, 132, 132 (ill.)
Reconstruction 55
Reminiscences of Levi Coffin 33
Roosevelt, Theodore 127
Running a Thousand Miles to Freedom 46

S

Sacagawea 159–166, 159 (ill.), 162 (ill.), 164 (ill.)
Saint Domingue's slave revolution 200
Saint Patrick 145–150, 145 (ill.)
Saint Patrick, legends of 147
Scenes in the Life of Harriet Tubman 219
Scott, Dred 210
Sherman, William Tecumseh 118
Sierra Leone 26
Slave auction 140 (ill.)
Slave names, origins of 208
Slave revolts 200, 226
Slave shed 125 (ill.)
Slave ship 59 (ill.)
Slaves and ivory 193
Slaves in Roman society 177
Solzhenitsyn, Aleksandr Isayevich 167–173, 167 (ill.)
Spartacus 175–180, 175 (ill.)
Spartacus (motion picture) 179, 179 (ill.), 180
Spielberg, Steven 30
Stalin, Joseph 167, 169
Stowe, Harriet Beecher 181–188, 181 (ill.), 186 (ill.)

T

Temperance movement 37, 67
Ten Commandments 134, 134 (ill.)
Tippu Tib 189–195, 189 (ill.)
Toussaint L'Ouverture 197–204, 197 (ill.)
True Stories of the Korean Comfort Women 103
Truth, Sojourner 20, 205–212, 205 (ill.), 212 (ill.)
Tubman, Harriet 20, 213–220, 213 (ill.), 216 (ill.), 217 (ill.)

Turner, Nat 221–228, 221 (ill.), 227 (ill.)
Twelve Years a Slave 137, 143
Tyler, John 30

U

"Uncle Tom," stereotyping of 187
Uncle Tom's Cabin; or Life Among the Lowly 38, 79, 181, 185, 186, 186 (ill.)
Underground Railroad 35 (ill.), 36, 217 (ill.)
and Harriet Tubman 215–218, 216 (ill.)
and John Brown 18
and Levi Coffin 35–37
and the African Methodist Episcopal (A.M.E.) Church 14

V

Van Buren, Martin 28, 29
Vassa, Gustavus. *See* Olaudah Equiano.
Vesey, Denmark 229–235

W

West African Mail 126
Western Freedman's Aid Commission 38
World War I 128
World War II 107

Z

Zion African Methodist Episcopal Church 207, 220